THE
CHILEAN
POLITICAL PROCESS

THEMATIC STUDIES IN LATIN AMERICA

Series editor: Gilbert W. Merkx, Director, *Latin American Institute, University of New Mexico*

THE POLITICAL ECONOMY OF REVOLUTIONARY NICARAGUA
by Rose J. Spalding

WOMEN ON THE U.S.–MEXICO BORDER: RESPONSES TO CHANGE
edited by Vicki L. Ruiz and Susan Tiano

JEWISH PRESENCE IN LATIN AMERICA
edited by Judith Laikin Elkin and Gilbert W. Merkx

POLICYMAKING IN MEXICO: FROM BOOM TO CRISIS
by Judith A. Teichman

LAND, POWER, AND POVERTY: AGRARIAN TRANSFORMATION
AND POLITICAL CONFLICT IN CENTRAL AMERICA
by Charles D. Brockett

PINOCHET: THE POLITICS OF POWER
by Genaro Arriagada. Translated by Nancy Morris

THE CHILEAN POLITICAL PROCESS
by Manuel Antonio Garreton. Translated by Sharon Kellum

Additional titles in preparation

THE
CHILEAN
POLITICAL PROCESS

Manuel Antonio Garretón

translated by Sharon Kellum
in collaboration with
Gilbert W. Merkx

Boston
UNWIN HYMAN
London   Sydney   Wellington

WESTVIEW PRESS * BOULDER, COLORADO

WESTVIEW PRESS
Frederick A. Praeger, Publisher
5500 Central Avenue
Boulder, Colorado 80301

Unwin Hyman, Inc.
8 Winchester Place, Winchester, MA 01890, USA

Published by the Academic Division of
Unwin Hyman Ltd,
15/17 Broadwick Street, London W1V 1FP, UK

Allen & Unwin Australia Pty Ltd,
8 Napier Street, North Sydney, NSW 2060, Australia

Allen & Unwin (New Zealand) Ltd, in association with the Port
Nicholson Press Ltd, 60 Cambridge Terrace, Wellington, New Zealand

Library of Congress Cataloging-in Publication Data

Garretón Merino, Manuel A. (Manuel Antonio)
[Proceso politico chileno. English]
The Chilean political process / Manuel Antonio Garretón:
translated by Sharon Kellum.
p. cm. — (Thematic studies in Latin America)
Translation of: El proceso politico chileno.
Includes bibliographical references and index.
ISBN 0-04-497068-4. — ISBN 0-04-497069-2 (pbk.)
1. Civil-military relations—Chile. 2. Military government–
–Chile. 3. Chile—Politics and government—1973– I. Title.
II. Series.
JL3420.C58G3713 1989
322'.5'0983—dc19

British Library Cataloguing in Publication Data

Garretón, Manuel Antonio
The Chilean political process. – (Thematic
studies in Latin America).
1. Chile. Politics
I. Title II. Series
376.0014

Typeset in 10 on 12 point Garamond
and printed in Great Britain at
the University Press, Cambridge

ISBN 0-8133-1272-8 (Westview)

*To all those with whom we have shared
these times*

For my sons Antonio and Manuel

Contents

Acknowledgments

Over the years, many people and institutions have directly or indirectly facilitated the studies on which this book is based. As the author, however, I remain entirely responsible for its contents.

The chapter on the Chilean political system originated in a study supported by the Dag Hammarskjold Foundation in Uppsala, Sweden, and by the Instituto Latinoamericano de Estudios Transnacionales in Mexico City. That version was developed further during a stay at the Instituto de Investigaciones Sociales at the Universidad Nacional Autónoma de México, for which I thank Director Julio Labastida.

The chapter on the era of Popular Unity (Unidad Popular) originated as part of a project entitled "Ideología y procesos sociales en la sociedad chilena, 1970–1973," which was cosponsored by the Ford Foundation and the Joint Committee for Latin American Studies of the Social Science Research Council. Many of the ideas developed here were discussed with the project's research group, which included Enzo Faletto, Leopoldo Benavides, Cristián Cox, Eugenia Hola, Eduardo Morales, Diego Portales, and Tomás Moulián. A major portion of my contribution to the project was elaborated during my stay at St. Catherine's College, Oxford, and in the seminars given at St. Anthony's College, Oxford. This experience was made possible by an invitation from Robert Pring Mill and Alan Angell, to whom I would like to give special thanks.

The chapter on authoritarian regimes in Latin America originated in a FLACSO seminar sponsored by the Consejo Latinoamericano de Ciencias

Sociales (CLACSO). The chapter on national security ideology originated in a study on this theme completed jointly with Genaro Arriagada.

Key sections of the chapters on the Chilean military regime were elaborated during my participation in the Latin American Program at the Woodrow Wilson Center in Washington, D.C., and several of its projects. Important factors were the support of Abraham Lowenthal and Alex Wilde and the comments of Philippe Schmitter, Laurence Whitehead, Robert Kaufman, Alfred Stepan, Arturo Valenzuela, and especially Guillermo O'Donnell. Conversations with my generous friend Claudio Orrego also left an indelible imprint on these sections.

At various times in elaborating my thoughts, I have benefited from the comments of Anibal Pinto, Jorge Graciarena, Norbert Lechner, and Tomás Moulián, as well as from conversations and discussions with colleagues at academic meetings. Interchanges with assistants, students, and participants in the courses that I have given during these years have also provided welcome stimulation. In revising and ordering my manuscripts, I relied on the collaboration of Germán Bravo. I am also grateful for the assistance of the academic and administrative personnel at the institutions mentioned, especially those supporting FLACSO in Santiago, where I completed my main work during these years.

The original Spanish edition, entitled *El proceso político chileno*, contained a prologue by Alain Touraine, to whom I am very grateful for support and sponsorship through the Centre d'Analyses et d'Intervention Sociologiques (CADIS) of L'Ecole des Hautes Etudes en Sciences Sociales in Paris. That version was also sponsored by the Center for Research on Latin America and the Caribbean (CERLAC) at the University of York in Toronto, in collaboration with the Inter-American Foundation.

Note on the English Edition

The original Spanish edition was published by FLACSO in Santiago in 1983. It was translated into English by Sharon Kellum and Philip Oxhorn and was revised and updated by the author while a visiting professor at the Kellogg Institute and the Department of Sociology at the University of Notre Dame in the fall of 1987. In the English edition, Chapters 1 through 4 were maintained intact, with only minimal corrections. Chapter 5 was completely revised and brought up-to-date by incorporating sections from other chapters of the Spanish edition and other works, as indicated in the notes. Much of Chapter 6 of the Spanish edition was integrated into the new Chapter 5. Chapters 6 and 7 of the English version correspond to Chapters 7 and 8 in the original Spanish edition, without major modifications. Chapters 8 and 9 of the English edition correspond to Chapters 9 and 10 of the Spanish, with new sections added to bring each of them up-to-date. The last chapter of the Spanish edition was replaced in the English edition by a new chapter. Thus while the original Spanish edition analyzed the Chilean military regime through 1982, the English edition takes the analysis up through 1987.

INTRODUCTION

Recent Chilean politics, the processes that have shaped them, and their relation to Chilean society as a whole are the subjects of this book. It is not easy to study and interpret political processes during a military regime. The conditions under which my reflections have evolved are well known: destruction of the natural medium for such reflection—the universities; the disarticulation and slow reestablishment of a precarious intellectual community that has been subjected to isolation, threats, and fear; the lack of any institutional framework guaranteeing freedom of investigation, discussion, and public expression. As Lihn observed, "Happy were the times when debate was an art and not a police roundup."

In other contexts, I have shown how this general climate has affected those academic disciplines dedicated to political and social analysis, with sociology and political science in the universities being neutralized, barbarized, persecuted to the brink of disappearing, or, in some cases, pressed into the service of official truth.

But this problem applies not only to the "external" conditions needed to develop political analysis and reflection but to content as well. Politics itself has ceased to be what it always was and has largely disappeared from its natural public sphere. Secrecy and opacity now permeate politics. The players in the political game are new actors with unfamiliar rationales. Force and repression have become predominant, and the present reality requires reevaluating the past. Yet the past cannot be analyzed in the terms that were applied to events at the time they occurred. It thus becomes necessary to revise a theoretical and analytical tradition that seems to have vanished or been torn apart along with the social reality to which it pertained. To rediscover politics and its meaning, past and present, is also to rediscover a way of thinking and naming—that is to say, a language, which then assumes the weight and value of an identity threatened with extinction. To think and rethink politics is therefore an urgent part of rebuilding a society and a national destiny. It is also a challenge to those who decreed that politics had died.

The ten chapters of this book express the double *problématique* of the conditions and content of political reflection. Several tensions run through these pages. First is the inevitable tension between comprehending processes and condemning them. Academic language often divests itself of ethical content and cannot always recount the magnitude of the atrocity, perversion, or irrationality. Academic language is supposed to provide logic, to comprehend "not the combatant but the battle." Historical crimes are therefore supposed to be explained and not merely condemned. Chance or individual pathologies have little place in the analysis of historical phenomena. Moreover, there is a gap between the analyst's need to defend his or her identity and the need to comprehend historical processes. When analysts discuss developments they supported, the tone tends toward approval; when they discuss developments they opposed, the tone tends toward condemnation. This tension cannot be overcome once for all. It becomes part of our work, and we must live with it.

Another inevitable tension exists between the character of scientific or academic work and the need for language that, without losing rigor, attains greater cultural breadth, especially when talking about well-known phenomena about which almost everyone has an opinion. The chapters that make up this book have been written on an intermediate level that recognizes a dependence on academic disciplines but approximates essayistic form. This approach also represents an effort to transcend the stagnated and rigid language of political analysis and certain inadequacies of "modern" academic disciplines.

One last tension should be recognized between the analytic character and the normative aspect of these pages. In times like these, it is easy to become disillusioned with rather abstract reflections on political phenomena and to demand instead a plan of action that would provide the analysis with a political purpose. But neither a political proposal nor a detailed chronology of facts and figures will be found here: no detailed chronology because my main interest lies in developing an interpretive scheme of clues for comprehending and deciphering larger meanings rather than a painstaking reconstruction of events; and no political proposal because it would be pretentious to try to present a proposal that must necessarily be a collective undertaking. I cannot deny a personal commitment to a certain concept of politics, a normative judgment, and the latent presence in this book of broad political options or elements for constructing a political proposal. But in refusing to deny these elements, I am not claiming to have given the analysis a unilateral direction. On the contrary, my attempt is to convert the analysis into what Neruda describes as "signs of meeting places where roads cross." This effort manifests the tension between intellectual work and political responsibility that has marked my entire generation, a tension we have not always known how to resolve.

It is difficult to summarize a book, but if forced to, I would say that five basic ideas permeate this book. The first idea refers to the nature of the Chilean political system prior to its collapse in 1973, which I define as the "backbone" formed by the interlocking of base-level social organizations with the political party structure, both in tension with the state as the focal point for political action. This backbone was the mode of organizing political subjects and social actors of national scope. Its strength devolved from the capacity and relative efficiency for representation, which assured great stability. Its weakness lay in the fragility of the autonomous organization of civil society. The current crisis in Chilean society can be provisionally defined as the disarticulation of this backbone.

The second idea, which is dealt with explicitly in Chapter 2, refers to the inability of projects intended to transform Chilean society to take on a universalizing and national character that could transcend their political vehicles and bases of representation. This limitation is especially significant in the case of Popular Unity, whose valid principles of democratic socialism and egalitarian development failed to find formulations, symbols, and courses of action that could break out of a strictly class orientation, overcome its isolation, and confront the inevitable conservative conspiracy.

The third idea envisions the military regimes installed in the Southern Cone since the 1960s as ultimately unsuccessful attempts to not only deactivate a mobilized society in transformation but resolve the long-standing crisis of hegemony among the dominant sectors by restructuring Chilean capitalism and giving it a new role in the capitalist world system. This tension between "governments of reaction and constraint" and "revolutionary dictatorships of the Right," between what I call the reactive and foundational dimensions, appears to me to be the main distinction between these regimes and other authoritarian forms experienced in Latin America.

The fourth idea applies the preceding concepts to the Chilean military regime, defining it as an extreme case of exacerbation of the reactive-repressive and foundational dimensions. Although the intensity of the first dimension and the failure of the second have not brought down the military regime, they have nevertheless defined the current Chilean crisis in a particular way. If the project of capitalist restructuring had succeeded, the crisis provoked by the regime's authoritarian and exclusionary features would be defined in "modern" terms as a confrontation among sectors diversely affected by the new social order. Instead, the failure of the military regime's project laid bare the simple dismembering and destruction of a mode of organization and coexistence—the "backbone"—without any replacement being offered. Under these conditions, the crisis of Chilean society has taken on the characteristics of an overall crisis affecting national identity, threatening its destruction, and posing the problem of how to rebuild or reorganize the country as a historical entity.

Chile está lejano y es mentira.
No es cierto que alguna vez nos hayamos prometido
son espejismos los campos
y solo cenizas quedan de los sitios públicos.
Pero aunque casi todo es mentira,
sé que algún día Chile entero
se levantará sólo para verte
y aunque nada exista, mis ojos te verán.

Raúl Zurita

Chile is far away and an illusion.
It is not certain that we once told ourselves
that the fields are mirages
and only the ashes of public places remain.
But even if almost everything is an illusion,
I know that someday all Chileans
will rise up just to see you,
and even though nothing is there, my eyes will see you.

The last idea, which is related to the others, is that the nature of the disarticulated political system and the character of the national crisis in recent years have together defined the problems of the opposition and the prospects for democracy. The political opposition has been affected not only by the repression and the conditions in which opposition has developed but by a long process of restructuring and reestablishing its identity. The opposition inherited organizations from the past under historically new conditions and must therefore redefine its political leadership and its relations with society. Within a framework of partisan, consolidated structures, this process is necessarily a complex and lengthy one. Constructing a democratic political regime as an alternative to the military or authoritarian regime coincides with the larger undertaking of national reconstruction and redefines the classic problems of transition between political regimes, thus creating new challenges for the opposition.

The above ideas are developed in the three parts. The two chapters of Part I are devoted to the Chilean political system prevailing until 1973. Chapter 1 systematically describes how the political system functioned and its crisis points. Chapter 2 analyzes the period from 1970 to 1973 according to the historical project being attempted, its ideological formulation, and the political struggle that gave rise to it.

The three chapters of Part II address the authoritarian capitalist nature of the military regimes in the Southern Cone during the 1960s and 1970s. Chapter 3 discusses the nature of the historical project of these regimes and offers a perspective for analyzing them. Chapter 4 deals with the "national security" ideology invoked by military governments. Chapter 5 describes the evolution of these regimes, the process of transition to democracy, and the legacy of the dictatorships for future democracies.

Part III analyzes the Chilean military regime from 1973 until 1987 in five chapters. Chapters 6, 7, and 8 refer to the different phases or moments of the regime: its emergence, its institutionalization, and its crisis. Chapter 9 presents some general considerations about opposition movements to military or authoritarian regimes that are later applied to the Chilean case. The last chapter discusses the theme of political transitions from a military regime and the prospects for democracy in Chile.

Two problems become evident in the third part of the book, one of which I have already mentioned. The first concerns the focus adopted in this book, in which the search for hypotheses for understanding the Chilean military regime and the analysis of tendencies and processes seem to obscure the most sordid aspect of that history, whose events are more like a police chronicle or a sociopathology of crime and state violence than a sociopolitical study. Moreover, the analytical perspective stresses descriptions of structural characteristics and principles of intelligibility that may leave little room for psychological phenomena, chance, and the creative potential of political situations. The second problem derives from the proximity of the events analyzed and a concomitant lack of a distance that would allow full comprehension of them. Phenomena that can be interpreted in a certain manner while they are still unfolding may reveal an entirely different meaning in the future when they have run their course. I am conscious of these risks and assume them without any certainty that I will overcome them.

The chapters that make up this book originated in works that share a common perspective and intellectual preoccupation but were prepared in varying circumstances for different purposes. This fact has necessitated revising and adjusting the chapters in order to unify them into a book, even though all repetition could not be eliminated.

One might also point out the absence of a chapter, needed in a book like this, that would contain a systematic development of the theoretical perspective shaping analyses of social processes. In such a chapter, the concepts used most (state, political regime, power, political subject, social actor, hegemony, institutionalization, crisis, and so on) would be explained and the relations among them would be explicitly stated. The fact that this book's subject is political analysis of specific historical phenomena rather than political theory does not eliminate the need for a theoretical chapter. Its absence is due to the fact that, beyond the precise definitions provided here for the concepts used, political scientists still lack a fully structured theory that could be systematically set forth. Given the current state of thinking about political phenomena and the loss of faith in the monolithic nature of classical paradigms, what we have is a perspective under development or in a "practical state." From this perspective, it is possible to perceive an implicit critique of old categories and the search for new ones, but there seems to be a way to go before it can be considered elaborated. This book does have a theoretical perspective, one that draws on many streams of thought, but it is still under construction.

I have already attempted to explain why this book presents no "proposal‾" or political "alternative." While it was written on the level of political analysis and reflection, with a definite theoretical perspective under construction, this book makes no claim to draw directly from this perspective a specific political option that might be presented as the correct one. A political option demands analysis, reflection, and theory, but it does not emanate from any of these as the only real solution. A political option is both a drama and a gamble. Its categories are not exclusively those of logical and analytical coherence—the criteria of scientific truth—but justice, freedom, and equality. It would therefore be dishonest to claim that a political option is a truth inferred from a scientific discourse. My objective has been to conduct an analysis that would allow or prepare the ground for an alternative political option or a rational political proposal reflecting certain basic values, but without forcing that option or proposal in any given direction. In particular, the analysis has been shaped with reference to the needs of those who have lacked the material and institutional opportunities for political development and analysis that were enjoyed by my generation.

PART I

The Political System in Chile until 1973

Chapter 1

The Chilean Political System: An Overview[1]

A political system is not formed in a vacuum but out of complex and multicausal relations to economic processes, class structures, and cultural mechanisms. Just as a society can never be defined solely by its material base, neither can it be defined solely by its political relations or cultural manifestations. Its most important determinant, which constitutes it as a society is the manner in that social subjects are generated and interrelate within a society. In other words, the key definition derives from the way that identifiable classes and categories within a structural model become historical subjects and sociopolitical actors. The process of establishing a society always involves an economic model, a political model, and a cultural model. The economic model refers to the material bases for development. The political model refers to both the state and the system of mediations between the state and civil society—that is, the political regime. The cultural model refers to the world of representations and images that a society emanates. Among the economic, political, and cultural models, a system of multiple determinations arises that varies from one society to another, and from one era to another within the same society.[2]

In this sense, it is important to recall that until 1973, a historic relationship existed in Chile between phenomena that seemed unassociated in other Latin American countries. Three elements were uniquely interrelated in Chile: import-substituting industrialization with increasing state intervention in the economy; substantive democratization that was gradually incorporating diverse social sectors into the political system and improving their standards of living; and a democratic political regime. The combination of these elements explains some of the particular characteristics of the Chilean political model or system.

3

The Chilean Sociopolitical System

During the early decades of the twentieth century, the Chilean development model and political system suffered crises and were reformulated. The most significant turning points were the promulgation of the Constitution of 1925 and the economic crisis of 1929. The latter gave rise to what has been termed the "inward-looking" model of development, which was driven by the process of import-substituting industrialization. In the political sphere, the so-called compromise state emerged, which was oriented by an overall logic of dependent capitalist development. Because no single class could dominate the others, each class was obliged to adopt a strategy of accommodation and to permanently incorporate new groups into sociopolitical life in order to guarantee the stability of the political system. This approach necessarily led to a corollary instability in economic growth.[3]

The interesting highlight here is a double phenomenon. First, capitalist industrialization was accomplished in a "heterodox" fashion. It was not effected by an innovative and aggressive bourgeoisie creating an economic order to which the political sphere had to adjust. The state was the major actor in industrialization, and in order to benefit from the state's role, the bourgeoisie had to develop linkages with the state. This arrangement depended on the existence of a sociopolitical coalition in which the political Center, representing an aggregation of sectors that can be categorized as middle-class, could ensure stability through a shifting politics of alliances. As a result, the organized popular sectors were able to make room for asserting their short- and medium-term claims on society.

This phenomenon elucidates another that is more important: the relative correlation between industrialization directed by the state and a growing process of democratization, which is understood here as incorporating into the social system (and its benefits) new sectors that can exert pressure on the state. This process of substantive democratization was carried out within the framework of a democratic political system, that is to say, according to the rules of the game that provide representation for the various "incorporated" social sectors competing for satisfaction of their demands and interests. A relationship of mutual need thus existed between the process of democratization and the democratic political system, in which neither could be understood without the other. This relationship in Chile has differed from those in other Latin American countries, where the process of substantive democratization has been achieved by authoritarian means.

The correlation among import-substituting industrialization (or an "inward-looking" model of development), the democratization process, and the democratic political system is echoed today in two contradictory myths that tend to obscure the correlation by portraying it in black and white terms. The forces supporting the social model attempted since the military coup in 1973 view this triple process as the main cause of Chilean decline and consider its reversal absolutely necessary for rebuilding the country. This perspective emphasizes the unstable and unbalanced economic growth that occurred prior to 1973 and blames it on interference by redistributive and participatory elements that have utilized the state (dominated by a political leadership attuned to its own interests) in a demagogic manner to protect inefficient industry and grant privileges to various social groups. These elements are also charged with neglecting accumulation and obstructing the rules of the economic game based on free competition in all markets. According to this view, the demagogic, populist politics that were carried to their extreme between 1970 and 1973 ended up destroying not only the economy but the institutional bases of the Chilean state itself. The causes and consequences of these policies that are often cited as proof include the excessive growth of the state, the distortion of markets, the stifling of creative economic initiative, permanent inflation, and the instability of economic growth. Thus the interplay of the three processes (import-substituting industrialization, the democratization process, and the democratic political system) has been perceived as the original sin of Chilean society in the twentieth century, especially when compared with the grandeur of the nineteenth.[4]

A contradictory myth arising from the opposite perspective places the blame instead on the retrogression to dependent authoritarian capitalism brought about by the military regime and attempts to paint the rosy history of Chilean democracy. This myth stresses the progressive aspect of social inclusion and the stability of a political regime that, unlike others in Latin America, allowed solid political representation and a mechanism for articulating interests that assured the institutionalization of conflicts and their resolution through various formulas for legitimate arbitration. According to this view, the system's limited crises or bottlenecks in industrialization were dealt with by formulas for leaps forward through structural reforms. Thus the crisis of Chilean society did not result from the triple interplay of the processes described but from its interruption in the early 1970s, when equilibrium was destroyed to make way for a quest for absolute power in which the state attempted to direct all economic processes and control all political and social life by dismantling the entire economic structure.[5] One version of this nostalgic viewpoint perceives the government during 1970–1973 as having overcome all the contradictions of the development model of the previous decades. The Popular Unity government is also credited with having eliminated the imbalances and distortions that had prejudiced working-class interests by accentuating the role of the state, but this time using the power of the state to work against the "logic of capital." During these years, Chileans were supposedly witnessing the beginning of a process in which democracy was being transformed from "formal" to "real" democracy.

These conflicting ideological visions share one common assumption: the notion that history can be frozen. Whether Chile's history is said to have begun in 1973, to have been interrupted in 1970, or to have culminated between 1970 and 1973, all such representations distort the effects of continuity and discontinuity. Such conceptions would hold no further interest beyond the analysis of social constructs of reality were it not for their practical effects on formulating plans for the future by reproducing in "purified" form the era exalted by each perspective. Consider the desire to return to democracy as it was before 1970 by correcting its "excesses" but without questioning its development model, or the wish to fulfill the goals that could not be accomplished between 1970 and 1973 for lack of "power," or the attempt to remake Chile according to the authoritarian model imposed in 1973. Each of these views represents an outline of the future originating in a vision that appropriates history for the class or social actor that directed it. Such visions are based on stereotypes and caricatures, but they nevertheless live on in the consciousness of many social actors.

Setting mythical visions aside, it is worth recalling that the triple cor-relation among import-substituting industrialization (or "inward-looking" development), substantive democratization, and political democracy had its impact, but it was also contradictory, conflictive, and far from a rosy history. I refer not only to its dependent and unstable effects on economic growth and the tendency toward stagnation but to the price paid for compromise on development models and political systems: social exclusion that was basically structural in nature. Those excluded were the peasants and the urban poor, whose late incorporation during the 1960s has remained precarious as well as subordinate to and dependent on organization by the state.

Adding to structural exclusion has been yet another kind of exclusion affecting the political representation of popular sectors. It has consisted of excluding and repressing political parties during certain periods and of using state violence when popular pressures threaten the maintenance of the system.[6] In any case, the significant development of the long period culminating in 1970 was the set of mechanisms for consensual arbitration that involved large social sectors in the democratizing game but marginalized them as well.

As a result, the correlation among these three processes has been conflictive and ambivalent. Between "substantive democratization," or the process of social incorporation, and the democratic political process there evolved a relationship of mutual need and understanding. This tendency was positive in that the two processes legitimized one another. But the relationship was also subordinated to an industrializing development model that may have made the processes "compatible" in principle but set limits that were increasingly narrowed by the ultimate logic of capital. By the end of the 1960s, these limits had created an insurmountable obstacle. The period from 1964 until 1970 can be defined as the last effort to maintain this triple interplay, as an attempt to "leap forward" while maintaining the logic of the system by expanding internal and external markets and by eliminating structural exclusions through agrarian reform and the incorporation of rural and urban marginal sectors. But to achieve all these goals, it was necessary to accentuate the tendencies toward concentration and dependency in the development model in a climate of growing popular mobilization. I will return to this point later.

The triple correlation depended on the role assumed by the state and also on a particular social bloc. The state's role was strengthened by the exigencies of the dependent or enclave economy (the copper industry), the industrialization model, and the demands for social policies being made on the state. At that time, the state appeared to be the main sphere for alliances among groups and classes, and access to the state seemed a necessity for obtaining satisfaction of demands and claims. Yet this situation reinforced the need to establish an array of mechanisms and barriers at the state level to prevent any single sector or group from dominating the other partners in the compromise. Thus the state was simultaneously the field for alliances, the instrument for satisfying demands for incorporation, and a partial barrier to the development of an autonomous political project for transformation among the popular sectors. The state's logic of domination dictated neither unrestricted and exclusive domination by one class nor the state's remaining above classes as a neutral object of contention. The state's double logic was consequently contradictory: it sought to assure and sustain legitimacy by integrating new sectors while preserving the primacy of capitalist inter-ests—that is, the state sought to extend participation but keep it subordinate to the predominant interests.

Behind this process lay the interests of the capitalist class. In Chile these interests were the industrial sectors involved in commerce, finance, and agriculture. The agricultural sector's importance assured the ongoing pattern of excluding peasant sectors. But the larger process also expressed the interests of a broad range of "middle sectors" whose consolidation and survival were guaranteed by expansion of the state's economic power. These sectors' future depended on the capacity for political representation that they were acquiring through parties of the Center and on allying these parties with the dominant economic sectors and the popular sectors. Thus the political system apparently became the middle sectors' favorite object of identification and loyalty—not from any professed faith in democracy or deep-seated values (as certain myths regarding the "democratic middle class" have claimed) but because the political system appeared to be a fundamental instrument for their constitution, reproduction, and mobility as social actors.

It is also evident that the interests of organized popular sectors have been incorporated into this process, albeit in subordinate form.[7] The relationship of popular sectors to the state and the political system as a whole is necessarily ambivalent. These sectors have been seeking integration and incorporation that would allow them to consolidate their national identity and thus become citizens and political subjects capable of participating, making demands, and satisfying those demands. But to the extent that this incorporation is partial, segmented, and subordinate, it involves an increasingly autonomous effort to seek an alternative to the ultimate logic represented by the capitalist state.

These characteristics in turn significantly affect class structure and the process of incorporating classes, the institutional structure, the organizational system, the mechanisms for articulating and representing various social actors, and the political consciousness of these actors.

In terms of class structure,[8] several factors have combined to create an extremely complicated structure that cannot be reduced to the classic bourgeoisie-proletariat polarity: the unbalanced and contradictory development model, the burden of the state, the characteristics of preexisting structures, and the impact of relative modernization on them. As some analysts have stressed,[9] to take dependency analyses seriously, one must apply their consequences to class analysis in instances where the diversity in accumulation principles introduces a complex restructuring. The existence of the classical dimension is not denied, but other dimensions are added that complicate the situation. This complexity operates on different levels. For example, the mass called the "middle sectors" appears as an aggregation of extremely heterogeneous positions and interests whose only common denominators seem to be their relation with the state and a cultural-ideological element. In effect, these middle sectors include those who view themselves as clearly favored by the development scheme in that their interests coincide with the expansion of monopolistic groups (especially in certain professions and services) but also other sectors that perceive themselves as constrained and threatened by this expansion. Such diversity is also well-known among popular sectors, whose incorporation into the productive structure is far from stable and homogeneous. As a result, popular sectoral conflicts—whether they concern housing, health care, education, or all the complexities of access to urban services—are superimposed on the conflicts determined by the relationship of these sectors as participants in the industrial system. In the rural areas, the limited spread of modernization before 1965 and its being intensified and accelerated by subsequent agrarian reform have also caused substantial change and diversification. All this change, combined with its effects on political consciousness, has given a segmented and clientelistic character to incorporation into the social process and ties with the state. As a result, the capacity to organize and exert pressure has acquired increased importance, which has led in turn to greater diversity and fragmentation within major sectors.

Obviously, the institutional system responds to these characteristics and then presents itself as a series of mechanisms that keep newly incorporated sectors from acquiring excessive pull. The state's main response is to aggregate or superimpose regulations sanctioning the new incorporations and their costs but also ensuring that the system cannot be totally transformed. Social countermovements must therefore come to terms with the system, make concessions to it, and thus renounce the option of becoming alternatives to the entire system of domination.

The state's having to accede to various levels and benefits of social life and the type of incorporation described rewards political organization and mediation but also limits the development of autonomous social organizations with strength of their own. This weakness in the autonomous organizational structure—which oscillates between the narrowest corporatism and extreme politicization—does not result from any design by political leaders who would manipulate it as they wish. This debility is more accurately described as an effect of structural development accentuated by the perceptions and expectations that grow up around it. The problem in Chile has been illustrated in the organized labor movement and the student movement.[10]

All these factors create repercussions that limit mechanisms for articulating and representing interests about which the political party system itself seems ambivalent. On the one hand, the party system represents itself as being an effective vehicle for exerting demands on behalf of various social sectors. Political parties tend to express and represent social interests and aspirations effectively, a function that explains the transformations across the Chilean political party spectrum. On the other hand, the party system tends to mirror certain problems existing in society: the privileging of sectors with greater capacity to organize and exert pressure; clientelism at regional levels and in local representation; the dependency of local, functional, or corporatist organizations and the tendency for them to be replaced by a consolidated political leadership that is inclined to act independently of its base of representation; and the fetishizing of party interests and their identification with the general interest. Because of these factors, party apparatuses rigidified in the 1960s and hindered the development of social projects of national scope. This trend consolidated a tripolar political arrangement: the parties of the Right managed to unite and make inroads into the middle sectors;

the Center sacrificed its traditional capacity to forge alliances for the sake of an autonomous alternativistic undertaking; and popular parties found it difficult to break out of their isolation, which was partly the price of their recently won unity.[11]

From this rapid overview, two points stand out regarding the political consciousness and ideologies of the social actors involved. First, the spread of "middle-class" ideology to more incorporated popular sectors resulted in their political consciousness reflecting typically class elements combined with values of group and self-advancement. A second, related point is the mainly instrumental value attached to the political system, which came to be viewed as a competitive mechanism for satisfying particular interests. Herein lies the explanation of the latent vulnerability of a seemingly solid democratic system. This vulnerability becomes especially evident when analyzing the varying sociopolitical coalitions.

In the case of the Chilean Right, it did not exercise political hegemony directly during most of the time when the Constitution of 1925 was in force. But the existing system allowed the Right to thrive and grow via a defensive politics that was enhanced by this sector's great capacity to organize at the level of civil society. The Right exhibited not so much "democratic faith" as a desire to participate in the political game. It perceived itself as somehow obligated to participate but did so by means of an increasingly sharp critique of the "unsettling" effects of the divergent social sectors erupting on the political scene and their "negative" effect on development.[12]

The crisis of 1973 cast doubt on the widely held thesis of the democratic faith of the middle sectors. As noted, these sectors have been identified more closely with the political system in instances where there is a certain "inherent" common identification made between democratic loyalty and belonging to the middle class. It is also evident that the development of the political system throughout the period governed by the Constitution of 1925 cannot be dissociated from the actions and loyalty of the middle sectors, but only to the extent that these sectors perceived themselves as the privileged element in the political system and believed the political system to be their own—that is, only as long as the state apparatus seemed directly associated with granting them favors and satisfying their claims. But when the state structure was perceived as having been invaded by a cultural and political sphere appealing for legitimacy not to middle-class elements and values but to those originating in the popular sectors, especially the proletariat, the middle sectors' loyalty to the democratic system began to deteriorate. The value placed on order, security, hierarchy, and the possibility of upward social mobility prevailed over the value placed on liberty in the political system. This phenomenon also occurred among the political elites claiming to represent the middle sectors.

As for the Left and the popular sectors, their culture and political practices have manifested an ambivalent relationship with democracy.[13] Their participation has affirmed their strict adherence to the rules of the game. But successive electoral failures have been coupled with relative dissociation between a growing political participation and an uneven process of social democratization that has contradicted expectations. As a result, the discourse of the Left and the popular sectors began to emphasize the radicalism of a political project that would replace the capitalist system and the abstract formality of this project's political system. Thus the political democracy that the Left was participating in and legitimizing by its support was simultaneously being denounced in leftist discourse as a set of traps and obstacles impeding the overall realization of popular interests by allowing the dominant minorities to remain intact and social inequalities to continue.

All these factors underscore the unequal and ambivalent character of the democratization process in Chile and its correlation with the pattern of development and the political system. Nor is it surprising to see the overinstitutionalization and stability of the political structure accompanied by tendencies toward deinstitutionalization and vulnerability in the socio-economic structure.

As for the role of the armed forces in this political system,[14] it should be recalled that this system was developed and consolidated following a significant period of military intervention. This precedent, with its implied military distrust of political leadership, as well as the effective representation, exclusion, and conflict resolution provided by the political system combined to limit the Chilean military to professional development only. This "cloistering" of the military contained some counterbalancing elements, however. After World War II, the Chilean military became part of the hemispheric military system dominated by the United States and was consequently socialized in the prevailing U.S. doctrine of counterinsurgency or national security. This ideology, which derives from military socialization as well as political discourse, conceives of the role of the armed forces as the bastion of the nation and its institutions. All these elements contributed to a high level of hierarchy and discipline in the Chilean Armed Forces, where formal leadership became the only basis for internal legitimacy. The significance of this emphasis will be analyzed further on.

The "Backbone"

Reexamination of the arrangement of social subjects and actors in Chile reveals that it is enmeshed in a political system with six main features. The first is the relatively early establishment of a political party spectrum that was national in scope. The existence of such a spectrum implies a complete range of political options embodied in organizations as well as the nonexistence of parties or movements that would interfere with national politics because of regional or ethnic appeal.[15]

A second feature of this political structure was its interlocking pattern with social organizations as a whole. As a result, these organizations could become actors at the national level to whatever extent that they became part of the political party structure. This interlocking of political parties and social organizations favored the development of a diversified political leadership that could represent the varying options of the ideological spectrum.

Third, the political party system's significance in organizing relevant actors was associated with the relative weakness and dependency of autonomous organizations in civil society. This weakness resulted from social organizations having to go through the privileged political channel in order to reach the agent of approval and redistribution—the state. The dominant sectors, however, have been something of an exception in that they have their own mechanisms for succeeding in civil society, such as education, economic power, communications media, and business and professional organizations.

Fourth, and resulting from the preceding features, the dominant mode of political action consisted of organizing a social base in order to bind it to party structures and thus exert pressure on the state, at times demanding fulfillment of claims and at other times seeking to take control of the state itself. For the Left, this goal involved propounding socialism or obtaining power from the state in order to change society.

Fifth, it should be remembered that substantive democratization was not achieved suddenly through major upheavals but usually through the channels established by the formalized democratic system. It was a highly segmented process in which the extension of political participation did not necessarily correspond to the same degree of democracy at the level of society—social inequalities had their mechanisms of survival that political democracy could not eliminate or overcome. When combined with segmentations and exclusions, this type of substantive democratization generated a form of integration for popular sectors that lacked a parallel ideological co-optation. This outcome involved preserving political ideologies that advocated the radical nature of changes in and alternatives to the capitalist system. Thus from a sociological point of view, one can comprehend the significance and strong appeal of the Marxist Left in Chile, which displayed a vigor rarely seen in Latin America.

Finally, regarding the legitimacy of the system of relations between state and society, the generalized support for democracy was instrumental in kind, in my judgment. That is to say, Chileans were living under a political regime whose support depended more on its capacity to satisfy interests and sectoral claims than on its intrinsic value for the society. Crisis situations subsequently demonstrated the precariousness of this kind of support.

In sum, the backbone of Chilean society was formed by a system linking social subjects and actors to the state and a network of relationships between the organizations of civil society and political party structures. This backbone's strength derived from the increasing extension of political participation. Its weakness lay in the limited autonomy of civil society and the latent fragility of support for the political regime.

The Crisis of the Political System

By the mid-1960s, the main representative of the Chilean Center within the capitalist system, the Radical party (Partido Radical), had been replaced by the Christian Democratic party (Partido Demócrata Cristiano). The new party attempted to modernize and reformulate the basic compromises that had been sustaining the system.[16] This movement combined a technocratic elite with the socially expanded meaning of Christian thought to offer an alternative to both a Right that appeared too attached to its privileges and a Left still unable to break out of its class-based identity and its self-concept as a reflection of the Socialists' experiences. The Christian Democrats' project was capitalist modernization, but it introduced a particular rigidity into the political system because of the nature of the governing party. Unlike the former representative of the Center (the Radical party), the Christian Democratic party turned out to be incapable of establishing alliances with either end of the political spectrum. But its rigidity also derived from the kind of transformations introduced into Chilean society: the incorporation of peasants into social and political life, which attacked the *latifundista* relations central to preserving the oligarchic core; and the sociopolitical incorporation and organization of large sectors of the urban poor who had previously been excluded from genuine participation. Moreover, all this transformation was taking place in a climate of growing radicalization. The main criticisms from leftist currents and from within the governing party itself revolved around the lack of legitimacy of the capitalist system and the now-legitimized idea of making radical changes. Here one must not overlook the impact of the Cuban Revolution on Chilean leaders during that era. The sectors linked to or dominated by the capitalist class were voicing increasingly sharp criticism of the "chaotic" and "demagogic" nature of extended political participation and state intervention. They were also proclaiming the need for greater authoritarianism in the political system in order to guarantee the requirements of capitalist accumulation.

Thus capitalist sectors were critical of both the development and the political models followed until that time. Yet this embryonic movement to reorganize capitalist society by liberating it from participatory and redistributive interference emerged within the framework of a legitimate democracy. Indeed, when the reform process of the Christian Democratic government bogged down, or at least lost its initial vigor, criticisms from within the Christian Democratic party were reinforced and the basically anticapitalist critique by the Left was validated. This predicament was compounded by social mobilization and ideological radicalization that together assured the isolation of the Center as it attempted to manage the state.

Without delving into aspects deriving from changes under the Christian Democratic government in the 1960s, I would say that until 1970 Chilean society appeared to be confronting a complex crisis. On the one hand, the government was finding it increasingly difficult to satisfy the growing demands of the popular masses and organized social sectors who were exerting pressure through the political system. This pressure led to a crisis of confidence in the capitalist development model. On the other hand, a crisis developed in the "compromise state" due to the isolation and attrition suffered by the political actors who had been managing the state. These crises were compounded by two other factors: growing acceptance of ideologies of change and the socialist idea as well as the unifying of leftist organizations around the socialist possibility in the coalition known as Popular Unity (Unidad Popular, or UP), which emerged following the erosion of the Center. But the overall crisis was a limited one because the legitimacy of the democratic political regime was maintained.

From this perspective, the period between 1970 and 1973 can be viewed as a passage from this limited crisis to a generalized crisis in society due to increasing political polarization and deinstitutionalization of the forms of confrontation. Lost in the process was the factor that had kept the crises in the economic development model and state management under control in 1970—the legitimacy of the democratic regime. Legitimacy had been eroded by several factors, including the insurrectionary strategy followed by major right-wing organizations and the transformation strategy chosen by Popular Unity. Although the design of this strategy was subject to legal norms, the strategy itself questioned the principles of gradualism and negotiation on which the legitimacy of the Chilean political system had been based. Exacerbating the situation was the increasing rejection of democratic values by middle sectors and the Christian Democrats because of their opposition to the underlying goals of Popular Unity. All these factors facilitated the organized intervention of the armed forces, a recourse viewed by the military in 1973 as the only way out of a crisis that the political system seemed unable to resolve. But intervention presupposed an insurrectionary process that could endow the coup with legitimacy for the military hierarchy. From 1970 to 1973, the Chilean political system was suffering from the increasing inability of party structures to handle the claims, demands, and confrontations of various social sectors. Pressure from these sectors often obliged political parties to follow their agendas or risk losing all relevance.

Thus by 1973, Chilean society was manifesting crises on several levels. The first was an accelerated disintegration of capitalism without any coherent construction of an alternative system. Second, Chilean society was experiencing extreme levels of political polarization. The political mobilization and power achieved by popular sectors and the undeniable advance of substantive democratization were perceived negatively by the dominant economic sectors and by large sectors of the middle class. These two broad groups, formerly the pillars of the democratic system, had become increasingly fascistic. Third, the political system had lost its legitimacy. All these crises illuminate the double character assumed by the military intervention. In one sense, its reactionary element was expressed in massive levels of severe repression and the drastic measures used to eliminate the political system. In another sense, the military intervention provided capitalist sectors with the opportunity to reassert their domination by reorganizing society. In return, they provided the military with the mission it lacked when it burst onto the political scene. Consensus within the military, however, was limited to the purely reactionary element. This issue will be considered throughout the study.

Notes to Chapter 1

1. This chapter utilizes material from two other works of mine: "Democratización y otro desarrollo: el caso chileno," *Revista Mexicana de Sociología* 42, no. 1 (Jan.–Mar. 1980); and *Evolución política y problemas de la transición a la democracia en el régimen militar chileno*, FLACSO Documento de Trabajo (Santiago: FLACSO, 1982).

2. A conceptual discussion of this perspective can be found in Alain Touraine, *La voix et le regard* (Paris: Editions du Seuil, 1978); and also in two compilations by Norbert Lechner: *Estado y política en América Latina* (Mexico City: Siglo Veintiuno, 1982); and *?Qué significa hacer política?* (Lima: DESCO, 1982). Throughout this book, the term *state* will refer to the "public" institutions and organizations endowed with coercive power as well as the crystallization or "synthesis" of the relations of domination in the society that this institutional apparatus and organization politically express. The idea of a sociopolitical subject refers to those classes, categories, groups, agents, organizations, or sectors of society that are established as the vehicles of historical action by actively expressing historical contradictions or intervening in the determination of social

projects and counterprojects. A subject can be composed of or expressed by one or more individual actors or organizations. Other concepts will be defined as required.

3. In this regard, and to avoid citing a lengthy bibliography, see Aníbal Pinto's already classic work, "Desarrollo económico y relaciones sociales en Chile," in Aníbal Pinto, *Tres ensayos sobre Chile y América Latina* (Buenos Aires: Ediciones Solar, 1971). The ideas expounded in this section are further developed in Manuel Antonio Garretón and Tomás Moulián, "Procesos y bloques políticos en la crisis chilena, 1970–1973," *Revista Mexicana de Sociología* 41, no. 1 (Jan.–Mar. 1979). See also Tomás Moulián, "Desarrollo político y estado de compromiso: desajustes y crisis estatal en Chile," *Colección Estudios de CIEPLAN* 8 (1982). The "compromise state" is usually understood as the unstable pattern of political arrangements that follows the oligarchic state in Latin America. It can coexist with a democratic regime or occur without one. The compromise state is characterized by the strong influence of middle sectors and the incapacity of any single class or fraction to dominate. See J. Graciarena and R. Franco, "Social Formations and Power Structure in Latin America," *Current Sociology* 26, no. 1 (Spring 1978).

4. A synthesis of this vision is found in "Discurso de inauguración del añ⁻o académico en la Universidad de Chile," by Augusto Pinochet,[1] *El Mercurio*, 7 April 1979.

5. For an example of this type of analysis, see J. B. Luco, "Tendencias históricas de la sociedad chilena durante el período de vigencia de la Constitución Política de 1925," in *Mensaje* 25, no. 249 (June 1976), published in Santiago.

6. Recall, for example, the outlawing of the Communist party under the González Videla government.

7. On the role of lower-class sectors in industrialization, see Enzo Faletto, "Clases, crisis política y el problema del socialismo en Chile," FLACSO-ELAS mimeo, Santiago, 1973; Enzo Faletto and E. Ruíz, *Génesis histórica del proceso político chileno* (Santiago: Editorial Quimantú, 1971); and L. Castillo, *Capitalismo e industrialización: su incidencia en los grupos obreros en Chile* (Santiago: Cuadernos de la Realidad Nacional, June 1971).

8. On class structure in Chile, see Manuel Castells, *La estructura de clases en Chile,* CIDU Documento de Trabajo no. 55 (Santiago: CIDU, 1972); and Emilio de Ipola et al., *Teoría y método para el estudio de la estructura de clases sociales (con un análisis concreto: Chile),* FLACSO-CELADE Documento de Trabajo (Santiago: FLACSO-CELADE, 1976).

9. See Alain Touraine, *Les sociétés dependantes* (Paris: Gembloux, Ed. J. Duculot, 1976).

10. On the organized labor movement, see "Vicaría Pastoral Obrera: reflexiones acerca del sindicalismo actual," mimeo, Santiago, 1981; and A. Angell, *Partidos políticos y movimiento obrero en Chile* (Mexico City: ERA, 1974). On the university movement in recent decades, see Manuel Antonio Garretón, "Política y universidad en los procesos de transformación y reversión en Chile, 1967–1977," *Estudios Sociales* 26 (1981).

11. Here I am alluding to several party coalitions: on the Right, the fusion of the Liberal party and the Conservative party into the National party in the mid-1960s; the replacement of the Radical party by the Christian Democratic party as the main party of the political Center; and on the Left, the alliance of the Communist party with the Socialist party, which began in 1957 and was manifested in the Frente de Acción Popular (FRAP) until the 1960s. For a more detailed analysis of these political coalitions, see Garretón and Moulián, "Procesos y bloques políticos en la crisis chilena."

12. On authoritarianism in rightist thinking, see the works of G. Catalán and C. Ruíz in *Escritos de teoría* 3–4 (January 1979).

13. Garretón and Moulián, "Procesos y bloques políticos en la crisis chilena."

14. On this point, see A. Varas, *Chile, democracia, Fuerzas Armadas* (Santiago: FLACSO, 1980); and Genaro Arriagada and Manuel Antonio Garretón, "Doctrina de Seguridad

Nacional y régimen militar," *Estudios Sociales Centroamericanos*, no. 21 (Sept.–Dec. 1978) and no. 22 (Jan.–Apr 1979).

15. This point is developed in Arturo Valenzuela and Samuel Valenzuela, "Partidos de oposición bajo el régimen autoritario chileno," *Revista Mexicana de Sociología* 44, no. 2 (Apr.–June 1982).

16. On these subjects, and to avoid mentioning titles already cited, see Garretón and Moulián, "Procesos y bloques políticos en la crisis chilena"; and Varas, *Chile, democracia, Fuerzas Armadas*. See also Liliana de Riz, *Sociedad y política en Chile: de Portales a Pinochet* (Mexico City: UNAM, 1979); and Arturo Valenzuela, *The Breakdown of Democratic Regimes: Chile* (Baltimore, Md.: Johns Hopkins University Press, 1978). On the period from 1964 to 1970, see Sergio Molina, *El proceso de cambio en Chile: la experiencia 1965–1970* (Santiago: Editorial Universitaria, 1972); Ricardo Ffrench-Davis, *Políticas económicas en Chile, 1952–1970* (Santiago: Editorial Nueva Universidad, 1973); and from a more critical perspective, Barbara Stallings, *Class Conflict and Economic Development in Chile, 1958–1973* (Stanford, Calif.: Stanford University Press, 1978).

Chapter 2

A People's Project, 1970–1973: Its Meaning and Defeat

A Necessary Debate[1]

Unilateral views of a nation's history can have negative consequences on the life of a society. If particular historical moments are viewed as the victory of the "good guys" over the "bad guys," then the country's history will necessarily be built around stigmatizing certain social sectors and those historical moments when they achieved national significance. Something along this line appears to be true of certain perspectives on the period from 1970 to 1973 in Chile's history. One such perspective views this period as the "reign of chaos and anarchy" or the "struggle against Marxism that sought complete power in order to subject the country to the dictatorship of the proletariat and tyranny."

Such a perspective obscures the paradoxical reality that the "struggle for democracy" had already ended democracy in Chile and that the "struggle against Marxism" was actually the struggle against the social sector that had supported the defeated government. Moreover, when a unilateral viewpoint like this is the only one deemed legitimate, it reinforces an opposing unilateral viewpoint by the defeated faction. Thus the period from 1970 to 1973 tends to be perceived by the defeated faction as a time of pure self-affirmation whose absolute defense has become the defense of one's own identity. And because this experience cannot be transmitted beyond those who lived it as a moment of liberation, a ghetto mentality is reinforced and the defense of the participants' historical identity is transformed into an acritical affirmation of their past.

18

For large sectors in Chile, especially popular sectors, the period between 1970 and 1973 was an era of historical identity, a positive point of reference in their personal and collective experience. In dialectical terms, however, this identity was accompanied by a probing critical examination. The problem is that the need to defend against the total negation of this historical experience leads to presenting its positive features as absolute, thus obstructing the development of any self-critique and transforming the period from 1970 to 1973 into a paradise whose memory alleviates current tribulations and delimits the only path toward the future.

The prevailing climate has thus led some to deny the history of Chile between 1970 and 1973 and to limit themselves to viewing the years immediately preceding that period as the culmination of Chilean history. The same climate has led others to stigmatize the UP era as a means of legitimizing the present and still others to lose themselves in idealizing it as the only valid era in Chilean history. If some sectors want to legitimize the present by projecting it as the only possible future, they must totally deny the period between 1970 and 1973, but the cost of this disavowal is to deny the participation in Chilean history of sectors that identify positively with this period. If, on the contrary, the goal is to build a country on what is most valuable from its history and on the sectors that personified these times, it becomes necessary to conduct a rational debate on the period in question. Such a debate must assess the period as part of a long and conflictive process of democratization, criticize its errors, and welcome its contributions.

An Analytical Perspective

Analysis of the period between 1970 and 1973 has yielded an abundant bibliography oriented toward clarifying the facts and political situations, evaluating the government's policies, and attempting an overall interpretation of the process.[2] Various documents and studies have elucidated key points concerning the historical developments of this era, including the real nature of U.S. intervention, military antecedents to the coup, the development of the insurrectionary strategy, the reality of the economic situation, aid from socialist countries, evaluation of change made in the agricultural structure, and the consequences of nationalizing the copper industry.

In contrast, particularly at the party level, one finds many discussions of strategic and tactical problems whose conclusions and tone have varied over the years. Exhibiting a basically apologetic and self-justifying tone during the early years after the military coup, these works focused on factors "external" to the Popular Unity (UP) coalition that caused the government to fall, including the nature of the class struggle from the time when the opposition strategy began to evolve. This kind of analysis gradually began to stress the components of the crisis that were "internal" to Popular Unity and to develop some consensus in analyzing this aspect in terms of the problem of the political leadership. Thus inconsistencies in conduct, strategy, or tactics have been perceived and attributed to a variety of causes: the coexistence of two "contradictory strategic models"; the lack of a clearly defined line of strategy; the imposition of a mistaken line of strategy; tactical deviation from the main line of strategy adopted; or the particularistic logic of various parties in the alliance, each one wanting to dominate the political leadership.

But these problems have not been linked to a more general theoretical and ideological crisis of the Left. Rather, they end up confirming the diagnosis made and positions taken by Popular Unity in 1970, attributing subsequent problems and errors to the political decision-making process.[3] This distinction between a correct political ideological project and than errors made in its political implementation would appear to be at the root of a type of political analysis that could be called "functionalism of the Left." This mode of thinking questions functions and procedures and proposes solutions in terms of adjustments and readjustments rather than examine the tensions and contradictions that underlie or inhere in the historical and structural origins of a political project. The corollary of this type of analysis holds that if these problems in the political leadership had been resolved, the political process probably would have succeeded. The result is that such analyses do not penetrate below the organizational surface to the root of the problems of conducting politics.[4]

Eventually, political analyses written after the coup abandoned this emphasis, succumbing at times to a new unilateral vision of the class struggle that did not consider the two antagonistic positions. It is this analytical perspective that I am attempting to overcome because it hinders full comprehension of an extremely complex process and its possible consequences for the future.

My reflections are tentative because they attempt to elucidate aspects still obscured by the categories in use, for which we lack the required analytical tools. These reflections must therefore be hypothetical, broad lines of orientation that encompass the overall nature of the process but leave out analysis of many problems and levels in order to concentrate exclusively on the political "problématique." I will pose two central hypotheses as basic orientations for my analysis. The first sets forth the double character of continuity and discontinuity displayed by the Chilean political process during this period in relation to the development of the social system, tentatively describing this double character as a process of noncapitalist democratization.

My second hypothesis suggests the existence of a theoretical and ideological void in the Chilean Left that has impeded adequate theoretical and political definition of the social process triggered and directed by the Left. This perspective will be employed in characterizing the political struggle during the period from 1970 to 1973 and in evaluating the overall significance of the process and its reversal following the military coup in September 1973.

Popular Unity: Social Crisis and Historical Project

The period between 1970 and 1973 must be analyzed in the context of a double historical process: the general process of democratization in Chile in recent decades combined with the crisis building within this process that peaked around 1970, as the Christian Democratic government was ending. Let us recall three phenomena analyzed in the preceding chapter.

First, beginning with the reformulation of the development model after the great crisis of 1929, a relative compatibility seemed to emerge in Chile between industrialization and increasing incorporation of large social sectors into the socioeconomic and political life of the country. The state seemed to offer the potential for social inclusion that could be achieved through the popular sectors' social and political struggle, even when selective features benefiting middle and upper sectors were maintained and groups that were better organized and could exert greater pressure were favored. But over the long run, the state's economic base, or its dependent capitalist development model, created restrictions and barriers for increasing democratization once the initial degree of "compatibility" had been exhausted. This outcome left large popular sectors marginalized, and it generally consigned the popular movement to a subordinate role that hindered development of any autonomous political project.

Second, the 1960s marked an important turning point in this contradictory process of democratization along the capitalist path within a democratic political framework. In an international context favorable to measures for transformation and modernization within the prevailing economic structure, the party representing the Center was replaced by the Christian Democratic party. Its mission was to resolve the contradictions between the democratization process and the economic base by means of a set of policies that partially incorporated peasants and the urban poor. Midway through this period, however, the model seemed to break down. From 1967 on, all indicators of economic growth began to decline and the democratization process began to slow down. Toward the end of the 1960s, two contradictory processes reflecting a deep crisis in Chilean society were compounded. On one side, the reformist dynamic combined with the heightened political consciousness of popular sectors and radicalized middle-class and petit-bourgeoisie sectors to produce a high level of social mobilization. This activism expressed discontent and frustration and sought to overcome the impasse in democratization. Opposing it was a trend affirming a pattern of development that emphasized the economy's tendency toward concentration and dependence. This pattern's requirements of accumulation and stability left no room for redistribution and participation.

The third phenomenon, then, was a crisis of dependent capitalist development that could not guarantee a basis for continuing the democratization process. It also entailed a political crisis in the developmentalist state, where the reformist Center became isolated, lost legitimacy in the eyes of much of the organized popular movement, and lost the ability to represent capitalist interests as a whole. These interests then allied themselves with the Right, which was incapable of generating a national project, despite its attempts at modernization. The result was a crisis for the political actors who had been directing the state. All these crises took place in a regional climate of high social mobilization and growing legitimation of solutions requiring profound change. But although the national crisis ran deep in all respects, it was a limited crisis in that it did not threaten the democratic political regime. The government maintained its legitimacy, which was reinforced by a general perception of the viability of making profound changes.

Thus around 1970, Chilean society was facing an alternative whose schematic formulation did not belie its historical authenticity. On the one hand, the possibility existed of stabilizing or deepening of the capitalist development scheme by reinvolving it with international capitalist tendencies, thereby containing and reversing democratizing tendencies by excluding large sectors who had previously been incorporated. This possibility assumed making drastic changes in the prevailing political system and replacing democratic forms with an authoritarian model. This possibility had already been perceived in 1967 and enunciated by representatives of large capital and national business management, who viewed democratic forms as an obstacle to accumulation. On the international level, dominant sectors in the United States also seemed to support a solution of this kind because of their distrust of democracy in Latin America, their fear of dynamics that nationalistic popular governments could create within the U.S. sphere of influence, and their concern over possible threats to their investments and economic interests.[5] Jorge Alessandri's program, the so-called New Republic, was intended as a response at the programmatic level but could not be imposed because of the legitimacy of the political regime. Once the crisis culminated in 1973, Alessandri's program was adopted as the solution embodied by the military regime.

The second possibility was to take the opposite tack, to continue and deepen the democratization process in its double role as the democratic political regime and the tendency toward social equality by reversing and altering the bases of the dependent capitalist development model. This possibility was the one embodied by the political movement known as Popular Unity. Beyond the movement's ideological and programmatic formulations (or the oversimplified labels given them by opponents), the goal of noncapitalist democratization comprised the core of the movement's mission. It expressed the broad aspirations developed by the popular movement and other social sectors and also embodied the one possible solution to the social crisis in Chile. The universalistic dimension of this project was to be revealed when the ensuing military regime attempted to establish itself by radically reformulating the entire political system and dismantling not only Popular Unity but every political or functional expression or claim by popular sectors.

A frequent error prompted, in my opinion, by the ideological climate at the end of the 1960s was to confuse this alternative with the supposed dilemma of "fascism or socialism." Connotations were narrowed, and the term *socialism* was equated with the final outcome of a long-term trend rather than with the particular nature of a given historical moment, thus confusing the issue and obscuring analysis of that moment.

The sociopolitical project proposed by the popular movement in 1970, as expressed in the Popular Unity program, maintained continuity with the process of democratic expansion. Advances achieved by the popular masses during this expansion resulted from their being organized under the particular structural conditions of Chilean society, thus propelling this process toward a qualitative leap that could have altered its basically middle-class character. But this project also involved a somewhat radical break with the dependent capitalist development model. The continuity in democratization and the discontinuity or reversal of the development model together implied a change in the nature of prevailing power. Frequently, however, official political formulations by Popular Unity obscured this double aspect by making the aspect of discontinuity sound all-encompassing. Nevertheless, the Chilean process that began in 1970 can be characterized as noncapitalist democratization.[6]

Theoretical and Ideological Shortcomings of a Historical Project

Real history is made not only by projects that are feasible. Any given process is also partially defined by the way that the actors embodying the process perceive, formulate, and experience it, which has unavoidable consequences on the behavior of other actors in politics. In this sense, it can be said that the Chilean Left as a whole and Popular Unity were only partly capable of accounting for the programmatic formulations of the historical project that they embodied.

A brief review of the official formulations of Popular Unity's program yields this synthesis: the goal of the revolutionary process was "a democratic, pluralist, and free socialist society." The first phase in achieving this goal was to liquidate the bases of capitalist society: "the fundamental task that the Popular Government has before it is to end the domination of the imperialists, the monopolies, and the landowning oligarchies" in order "to initiate the construction of socialism." The guiding element in this process was to be the working class, which was to develop elements of its power as an alternative to the dominant classes, or the "fundamental enemies of the Chilean Revolution." But overcoming these "fundamental enemies" required seeking the broadest political support from all strata of the population, that is to say, an attempt to "gather forces." Within this process, measures promoting democratization, social welfare, and redistribution played a contributing role. Thus the program sought to fulfill a triple objective: first, to build a broad alliance of classes and groups around the parties within Popular Unity and the organizations of the proletariat, whose "historical interests" oriented the entire process; second, to break with "the power of national and foreign monopoly capital and the large landed estates"; and third, to initiate "the construction of socialism" through the creation of Social Property (Area de Propiedad Social), the Popular State (Estado Popular), and a New Culture (Nueva Cultura).[7]

These were the objectives formulated for Popular Unity when Salvador Allende assumed the presidency in 1970. But before attempting to discern the *problématique* and the real meaning of these formulations, I should point out that of the three elements proclaimed by the program—Social Property, the Popular State, and the New Culture—the only one based on a clear consensus and referent was Social Property. The so-called Popular State remained an ambiguous concept from the first formulations introducing this idea in the Popular Assembly (Asamblea Popular) to the last inflamed discussions of "Popular Power." The obscurity of the debate over the Popular State reflected two problems. The first was Popular Unity's great difficulty in managing the state apparatus and using it to further a mass movement that was expanding its political awareness, organization, and pressure for participation. The second problem was the recurring ambiguity in defining the political phase through which Popular Unity was passing. As for the New Culture, except for premature references to the "New Man" (Hombre Nuevo), it was never defined in specific and operational terms as an organized part of the political process. In general, the consensus regarding Social Property and the confusion and ambiguity concerning the other two concepts reveal a good deal about the political leadership within Popular Unity regarding the entire social movement that it was leading. I will return to this point later.

Such formulations seemed to lack any theorization about the particular nature of this phase of the Chilean Revolution. Instead, one finds constant recourse to a series of categories that obscured rather than clarified the nature of the phase while hindering comprehension and acceptance of these formulations by large sectors unsympathetic to Popular Unity. Thus there seems to have been a theoretical and ideological void, a relative inability to provide an account of the real nature of what the movement was doing. Looking at the other side of the coin, Popular Unity lacked a theoretical and ideological project of national scope that could transcend its own "labels" to express the exact meaning and larger implications of the process going on. Consequently, several elements that defined the Chilean situation were generally subsumed under a contradictory ideological formulation that sacrificed originality and specificity for the sake of abstract theoretical political schemes. These interconnected elements had resulted from the splintering of the political coalition in 1964, which facilitated a project of noncapitalist democratization within the prevailing social system. This process was directed from within the state by political parties and took place in a situation of shared political power that inverted the traditional sequence of the revolutionary process and gave each governmental act a double potential in the struggles for power and social construction.

The theoretical-ideological discourse of the Left displayed certain characteristics that seem to manifest this problem. Leftist discourse was dominated by "economistic" categories that mechanically projected the results of structural diagnoses of the Chilean economy onto the political dimension, without the necessary mediation of political and cultural ideological levels.[8] This tendency defined classes and social groups solely according to their positions in the economic structure and obscured analysis of the way they fit into the overall system of society. In contrast, political theory tended to conceive of politics almost exclusively as force and therefore to envision power as something that can be "physically possessed" rather than as a complex social relationship that materializes in various parts of society. This conception tended to confuse a social project with a political project for taking power and to subordinate the former to the latter.[9]

As a result, the predominant image of society in the theoretical and ideological project of the Left could not provide an adequate account of a set of important social phenomena. Some of the key difficulties concerned the "middle sectors," the armed forces, the diversified nature of the popular movement, and the exhaustion or inadequacy of the party system of political representation.

First, with respect to the middle sectors, the ongoing contradiction arose from proclaiming the necessity of allying with them and incorporating them into the revolutionary process when contrasted with the actual behavior of these sectors. This contradiction can be explained by the Left's inability to define and characterize the middle sectors on the ideological-political level, which led to its overlooking these sectors' identification with a system of political negotiation that they perceived as threatened by the "proletarian hegemony" of a process that proclaimed itself to be socialist.

Actually, the strategic role that Popular Unity assigned to the middle sectors should not be discounted. The very nature of the UP political undertaking defined a policy that was clearly antimonopoly, as expressed in the avowal that "the fundamental enemies of the Chilean Revolution are foreign imperialist capital, the monopolistic bourgeoisie, and the landed estates." The proletariat and its political organizations were envisioned as confronting these "fundamental enemies," and between the two was a large mass of the population, the "middle strata," which the proletariat had to unify around itself in order "to be the majority," isolate the "fundamental enemies," and defeat them. This analysis is admittedly somewhat economistic and schematic and does not take into account the way that the classes fit together at the political and ideological levels. But in any case, the goal of "winning the middle sectors" acquired strategic importance from the beginning. Yet when Popular Unity won the election in 1970, the quantitative support of these sectors was insignificant. Election analyses show that the impressive electoral gains made by Popular Unity in the April 1971 elections came not from the middle sectors but from marginal rural and urban groups.[10] This finding proves that the middle sectors never joined in the process led by Popular Unity. On the contrary, to the extent that political polarization intensified, these sectors became a key factor in the struggle against the UP government. The instances of the associations (*gremios*) of storekeepers, truck drivers, and professionals, all potential allies in the initial scheme, speak eloquently to this point.

Although such a phenomenon is extremely complex and requires more exhaustive analysis, I want to explore only two levels of explanation. First, it should be pointed out that talking about "the middle sectors" applies a single name to an extremely diversified reality. Professionals, shopkeepers, industrialists from small and medium-sized firms, and public employees all belong to these "sectors." The interests of each group or category that composes the "middle sectors" are not only distinct but at times antagonistic. Some of these sectors were favored enough by the monopolistic structure of the Chilean economy that some economic surplus was transferred to them through various mechanisms, as happened with professional groups. But others were adversely affected by the monopolistic structure to the point of being strangled by it. Thus the "middle sectors" cannot be spoken of as a homogeneous class with common interests of its own. The only element that gives these sectors a certain homogeneity is ideological or cultural in nature, being transmitted as much through the educational system as through the sociopolitical system and its media. Perhaps the only common denominators capable of binding the diverse groups that make up the "middle sectors" are the search for personal security and stability, the ideology of individual social mobility and its horror of downward mobility, and the ideology of social "stability and order." Thus when trying to win the loyalty of these sectors to a political process, manipulating economic factors alone is not enough.

Herein lies the main flaw in the UP's relationship with the "middle sectors," in my judgment. UP leaders believed that "allying" with these sectors and incorporating them into the process was purely a matter of redistributing and increasing their incomes. In other words, an economistic and mechanical conception of class alliances placed all responsibility on economic policy by assuming that a sector's political support depends exclusively on the degree or magnitude of its economic benefit. By not considering the cultural elements of a social project emphasizing socialist ideology and the historical role of the proletariat, UP strategists failed to grant the middle sectors a visible space or role that was acceptable to them. This conceptual failure was illustrated dramatically by groups like shopkeepers. At no other time in Chilean history did they achieve such gains in income yet organize themselves against the government with such frenzy.

Related to the ideological shortsightedness about the middle sectors was the need to assess the political level on which middle sectors articulate their overall interests. To obtain the support of these sectors, some kind of arrangement or agreement had to be reached with the political organizations representing or somehow articulating their interests—in this case, the Christian Democrats. But in this regard, although the Left was imperceptive, heavy responsibility fell on the Christian Democratic party. From the outset, factions of its political leadership and technocracy imposed a line of tenacious opposition to the new government. There were moments when the political clientele of the Christian Democrats, largely made up of the middle sectors, might have been inclined toward the UP government. Later on, however, political radicalization led the clientele of the Christian Democrats to stake out positions of extreme opposition that often outflanked their own leadership, making any accord with Popular Unity impossible. Even so, the ground had already been prepared for this development during the first months of UP government and even before it took power.

It has been said that if Popular Unity could not count on the middle sectors, the alternative was not so much to try to neutralize them as to confront them directly with greater radicalization of the process, as expressed in the slogan "Hit all the bosses at once." This alternative seems to me a false one, inasmuch as such a decision would have left the popular movement clearly isolated, and considering the makeup of most of the armed forces and its close ties with the middle sectors, would have meant military intervention from the beginning of the process.

Second, a serious void existed vis-à-vis the "problem of the Armed Forces." Perhaps the explanation is that the Chilean Left fell into the military's "ideological trap." The military's constitutionalist and professionalizing ideology, developed out of the role assigned to them in recent years, concealed the true nature of the armed forces as a potential arbiter favoring the interests of the established system. Popular Unity mistook this ideology for a fact in assuming that it defined the true role of the armed forces. In actuality, the nature and bent of the armed forces were not widely understood in Chile, the military being perhaps the only sphere, institution, or social group that had not been studied in serious intellectual or political analyses. This ignorance and confusion existed in every political sector of the country. Whatever the reason, the truth is that because of the ideological trap, Popular Unity never developed a coherent policy toward the military. President Allende's personal preoccupation with politically neutralizing the military high command sufficed for the first phase, but it became sterile and inadequate once political polarization enveloped the armed forces and the constitutionalist ideology began to lose ground in key sectors of the military.

The options of creating an armed popular force as an alternative to the armed forces or infiltrating or dividing the Army in case of a confrontation were never viable UP alternatives. As has been observed, the armed popular force was not feasible because it assumed resolution of the fundamental problem of arming the population in front of those who had a monopoly on arms without the military intervening. The searches for arms conducted by the armed forces months before the coup demonstrated the fallaciousness of this "alternative." The second and the third options failed to recognize the strictly hierarchical and disciplined character of the armed forces, which are steeped in an ideology that is deeply zealous of its unity and integrity. Any potential for infiltration or division was immediately repressed, often brutally. The possibility of the Army dividing against itself in a confrontation appeared at first sight to be the most probable, but it was doomed by the reality that the Army's institutional structure reflected the makeup of its key strata, most of whom opposed the UP government. These factions, which had been radicalized by the political process, gradually excluded those who were loyal to the constitutional government.

A third important factor derived from errors in handling the incorporation, participation, and mobilization of popular sectors. These sectors, together with a core of radicalized petty bourgeoisie, composed the "social base" of Popular Unity. But the social makeup of this base was fairly heterogeneous, and the social diversity of the working class and the popular masses yielded specific short-term interests that were also divergent, a reality that is often forgotten. The existence of diverse popular parties, especially the two main currents within the UP alliance that produced Allende (the Socialist party and the Communist party), manifested this social diversity in some way. The selection of Social Property as a key element in the UP program led to a particular political direction that satisfied immediate interests but reflected the interests of only limited fractions of the proletariat—those in certain productive sectors with some level of organization and a history of activism.

Existing alongside these groups were large sectors of the proletariat and the urban and rural masses whose political awareness and organization had mushroomed out of the polarizing and radicalizing of Chilean society set in motion in 1970. These sectors had no adequate channels for participation, nor were their interests being expressed in the policies concerning Social Property. These sectors had less experience in traditional class organizations, and their degree of support for the government and increased awareness of being free human beings with the right to influence the course of history far exceeded the direct benefits that they had received. These sectors were one of the most typical expressions of "Popular Chile." But their roots in the modern productive system were rather weak, and their immediate demands emphasized the problems of daily life not so much as producers but as neighborhood residents or consumers. In any case, the awakening of their political and organizational awareness, their yearning for participation, and their urge to mobilize were all expressed in immediate demands made in terms of "power" or "popular power" and in creating, sometimes spontaneously, organizations with various functions. Some organizations were created to defend their purchasing power (the *juntas de abastecimientos y precios*), which was being threatened by speculation and the black market, others to integrate their aspirations and struggles at the territorial level (the *comandos comunales*), and still others to express their demands and interests in the productive sector (the *cordones industriales*). All these organizations symbolized for the popular sectors their "power" and their capacity to exert pressure.

The dominant political strategy of Popular Unity, which was shaped by the central element of the construct of Social Property, did not always integrate these sectors' interests or create channels for expressing them. When the UP leadership did respond, it was always belatedly and without real comprehension. And because some sectors were very heterogeneous, their political role (in those parties where it existed) was often dysfunctional and disjointed. This limitation, combined with ideological autonomy and the peculiar characteristics of socialist ideology, gave rise to slogans, stances, and ideological formulations that paid no heed to the real possibilities allowed by the political process. The situation also encouraged debates that obscured genuine problems, damaged prospects for progress, and hindered viable solutions to the problem of mobilizing and incorporating these sectors into the decision-making process. This problem derived from the inadequately perceived crisis in the network of relations between the political parties and the social movement, a system of relations that was eventually circumvented by the opposition coalition via the collective action of interest groups (the *gremios*) and on the Left by the dynamic of the mass movement and new leftist organizations.

These deficiencies within Popular Unity, which reflected difficulty in thinking specifically about Chile and its possible historical mission, tended to be compounded by various mechanisms, some of which made adequate formulation of a theoretical-ideological project even more difficult. On the theoretical level, two tendencies will be discussed. The first was constant recourse to doctrine inherited from socialist theory and ideology, which made the theory or concept into a "fetish" and viewed social theory as something fixed and elaborated, like a series of universal laws that particular situations merely illustrate. Although Popular Unity certainly would not have come into being without this socialist ideological heritage (the field of convergence that made the movement viable), it often obscured clarification of the particular characteristics of the process.[11] Second, the socialist heritage explains the almost mythical role assigned to Social Property. As seemingly yet another economistic feature of the image of society prevailing in the Chilean Left, Social Property appeared to be the element enjoying the greatest programmatic consensus among the sectors comprising Popular Unity, even when the motivations of various sectors for such consensus might differ totally. For some, Social Property was the element that ensured the political dominance of certain sectors of the working class; for others, it guaranteed the socialist character of the process—even though this consensus might later dissolve regarding the extension of Social Property and methods for organizing it. In any case, the lack of clarity about the nature of this phase, its political transformations, and the other central elements of Popular Unity's basic program (like the Popular State and New Culture) gave top priority to Social Property, even though its real impact in terms of political transformations and popular mobilization fell far below the expectations created for it.

On a practical level, some UP decision makers sought to overcome theoretical and ideological shortcomings by emphasizing the fundamental role of President Allende as guarantor of a political unity not always founded on ideology. This emphasis necessarily created conflict between his two roles as head of state and arbiter of the contradictions within his political coalition. Yet when Popular Unity sought to fulfill programmatic undertakings, party affiliation was stressed as a guarantee of ideological identity.[12]

The roots of this theoretical and ideological void can be explored on two levels.[13] The first level is the Latin American ideological-political climate during the 1960s as reflected in the Chilean Left. This era witnessed the crisis in expectations for development provoked by the failure of so-called reformist projects and the rise of models of authoritarian capitalism in the more developed countries, that is to say, by the breakdown of the "compromise state." But this era also experienced the internal crisis of revolutionary movements, failed attempts to follow the "Cuban path," and a crisis in the relationship between "political vanguards" and "popular masses." Hence was confirmed the idea of the "inviability of capitalist development," with its corollary that the only alternatives were "socialism or fascism."

These two tendencies were manifested in Chile in the political failure of the Christian Democratic experiment, which led to a legitimacy crisis for capitalism and a generalized acceptance of the imminent socialist character of the revolution. This ideological-political climate favored a programmatic alliance between the two major leftist popular parties in Chile and allowed them to unite with other radicalized groups during the "reformist" era. But the situation also tended to obscure the real nature of the process at work, and this loss of perception seemed to be the price paid by the Left for its alliance. This point leads to the second level of this problem, the ideological situation of the Chilean Left.

The political alliance between the Socialist and Communist parties consolidated in the Popular Action Front (Frente de Acción Popular, or FRAP) did not put forth a socialistic program in the 1964 elections. The Chilean Communist party had been developing a political line emphasizing the "anti-feudal," "anti-oligarchic," and "anti-imperialist" character of the Chilean revolution but had not developed a theory of Chilean society, an ideological mission for national revolution. The Communist party's ideological discourse mainly seemed to follow the line of the international Communist movement. Although the party's political behavior had shown great flexibility and keen sensitivity to the mass movement, it demonstrated much theoretical dogmatism and difficulty in researching specific issues. All these problems diminished the Communist party's chances for elaborating a theoretical and ideological project attuned to the phase being faced by the popular movement. As for the Socialist party, its extreme diffuseness precluded its elaborating any theoretical or ideological alternative to the Communist position. In the 1960s, when the theme of the lack of viability of capitalist development was being elaborated in certain university circles and the possibility of the "armed road" was being broached in the Latin American debate, the Socialist party managed to establish an ideological identity separate from the Communist party, despite its lack of internal ideological unity. This self-definition led the party to advocate socialism and to oppose the politics of broad coalitions and their electoral manifestation.

Around 1970 this political alliance made an ideological accommodation in accepting some political parties that represented middle sectors (the Radical party, for example) but positing the socialist character of the revolution. This general direction or tendency thus obscured the real character of the phase and prevented the needed theorizing about the dimensions of continuity and discontinuity. As a result, the socialist ideological heritage played a double role as the doctrinal sphere that allowed for a political alliance and made it viable but also as the factor that impeded clarification of the particular historical circumstances.

Responsibility for this outcome was shared, however. In one sense, some responsibility belongs to political groups like the Movement for Unified Popular Action (Movimiento de Acción Popular Unitaria, or MAPU) and the Christian Left (Izquierda Cristiana) that emerged from the Christian Democratic experience. These groups apparently sacrificed their potential for intellectually renewing the popular movement for the sake of legitimizing themselves as the "vanguards" of the masses within the same theoretical and ideological scheme of the traditional Left. In another sense, some responsibility falls on those intellectuals who did not always manage to escape the parties' purely functional requirements and the theoretical legitimation sought by the parties. When these intellectuals did evade such roles, they frequently distanced their work from what they knew of the national reality out of loyalty to an intellectual heritage typical of a certain academicism of the international Left.[14]

One important exception was the effort made to conceptualize the "Chilean road to socialism" (Vía Chilena al Socialismo).[15] Use of this expression risks falling into the errors just described, given that a sufficiently coherent theoretical body has not yet been elaborated, but this effort at least represented some grasp of the necessity of constructing an original ideological project. Its late appearance, however, paid the price exacted by the political debate going on in those days in that much effort was diverted to trying to distinguish the Chilean process from other revolutionary processes in history, demonstrating the feasibility of a noninsurrectionary revolution, and legitimizing such a revolution in terms of the political theory of classic or contemporary models of socialist revolution. This apologetic effort centered on institutional aspects of society and strategic problems of viability. In any case, the "Chilean road to socialism" was never considered by the leftist parties as an concept worthy of theoretical and ideological elaboration. They could accept it as a political slogan, albeit reluctantly in some cases, but not as an indicator of a problem of greater significance. The result was that this concept could not take on the luster of a mission of national scope.

It is evident that many of these problems (which are pointed out here as schematic illustrations) were perceived during the course of the UP era. But the factors mentioned and the radicalization of the opposition and the political debate made it impossible to overcome the original inadequacies. All these problems were reflected in the Left's difficulty in coming forward and presenting an ideological project that might explain the nature of the revolutionary process, characterize a complex of social sectors being dominated ideologically by the ruling groups, and take more precise account of the interests of certain mobilized sectors.

What has been said thus far could shed new light on the subject of the political leadership. The problem did not develop from the coexistence or contradiction within the Chilean Left of two coherent strategic models and alternatives, one more "reformist" and the other more "revolutionary." The problem arose instead from a theoretical and ideological void produced by a double inconsistency: one tendency stressing the "transitional" nature of the phase while another stressed its "socialist" character. Attempts at formulations in either sense suffered from the same inadequacy, which was reflected in the difficulty of expressing clear strategic alternatives when the process required them, as in joint endeavors needed to resolve tensions.

The Meaning of the Political Struggle[16]

Up to this point, I have been emphasizing the tension between a process of "noncapitalist democratization" and an ideological project incapable of defining the nature of this process by affirming its character and national scope. Although this emphasis highlights the problems of the Chilean Left, it seems to obscure analysis of the overall nature of the process and the unilateral character assumed by the class struggle. This kind of approach would seem to imply that success depended exclusively on Popular Unity and its capacity to resolve the contradiction. But the hypothesis about the double character of continuity and discontinuity and the real meaning of the UP program seems to me capable of accounting for the overall nature of the process and the behavior of various social actors and classes during its course. Beyond the issue of the adequacy or inadequacy of the ideological project of the Left, the possibility of a national project of "noncapitalist democratization" met from the outset with radical opposition by those sectors whose interests were tied to monopolistic national and foreign capital, to large agricultural estates (even if they were subsistence estates), and to the political expressions of these interests. A project of noncapitalist democratization, directed by parties representing broad popular sectors, was incompatible with the interests of the other sectors and with their consolidation and success as dominant social groups. This incompatibility was grasped from the beginning by certain sectors of the Chilean Right and also by influential groups in the United States, as demonstrated by the premature attempts between September and November of 1970 to prevent Allende from taking office and by formulation of a U.S. strategy for "destabilization."[17] These attempts initially failed due to the Allende regime's double legitimacy and the necessity of deepening the democratization process. This reinforced legitimacy operated both in the political Center and the sectors it represented and in the armed forces, where the military's relative isolation and dependence on state power combined to prevent effective formation of an autonomous project and favored constitutionalist tendencies instead. As a result, the actions of sectors initially opposed to Popular Unity focused during the entire period on finding ways to destroy the legitimacy that had impeded their schemes in 1970.

Thus a strategy for eliminating or overthrowing the Allende government was established from its earliest days in office. But to prevail over the strategy of negotiated neutralization attempted by the political Center (the Christian Democrats), the overthrow strategy had to rebuild the unity of the 1964 political coalition that had been split in 1970 and to achieve dominance over the middle sectors. In this way, the Christian Democrats would be dragged along and the legitimacy of the political system would be destroyed in the eyes of the military. Following the logic of its class interests, the Right sacrificed all its short-term political interests to these objectives, which pointed toward deinstitutionalizing the political struggle, polarizing it, and discrediting the government. To achieve these ends, the Right developed initial tactics that were adaptive and seemed to represent a pulling back: compromising on the leadership of the opposition coalition, massive demonstrations by political organizations, ideological use of communications media and state institutions, economic boycotts and sabotage, infiltration of the armed forces, acceptance and advocacy of terrorist activities, and in the end, self-dissolution after the regime was overthrown.

The scenario for the political struggle was thus organized around the confrontation between the governing coalition's logic of tenaciously carrying out a historical project defined as socialism (or the transition to socialism) that could overcome the crisis in Chilean society versus the logic of the coalition of interests affected by this project, which sought to nullify it and eliminate the governing coalition. This confrontation took place within the framework of democratic legitimacy, initially with the factions of a possible opposition coalition divided and in a context where individual and civil liberties were operating without restrictions. The political logic of both coalitions was tied to defending class interests. One side was evading efforts to build a new kind of society that would destroy the identity and privileges of dominant groups, meanwhile laying the groundwork for an authoritarian capitalist project. The other side was carrying out a program that would satisfy the expectations of an increasingly radicalized popular base, broaden political support, and quickly facilitate managing the economic process according to a new model of accumulation and redistribution. This polarized scenario explains why the political struggle set off the economic crisis and why both factors became involved in an ongoing interaction.

The hypothesis that the evolution of the strategy for overthrowing the UP government and responses by the government and the popular movement determined the character of the political struggle allows the process to be analyzed over three main phases. This approach is helpful even though certain elements characteristic of one phase may also appear in another.

The first phase was defined by the emergence of the strategy for overthrowing Popular Unity (between September and November 1970) and included attempts to prevent Allende from taking office that culminated in the assassination of General René Schneider, the commander in chief of the Army. The second phase (from November 1970 through August 1972) was characterized by the internal struggle within the opposition coalition between strategies advocating overthrow versus those advocating neutralization, with the latter prevailing. This phase also witnessed the initial retreat of the opposition and progressive utilization of all institutions not controlled by Popular Unity to block fulfillment of its program. The third phase (from September 1972 to September 1973) saw the growing predominance of the overthrow strategy, which had several phases: making opposition a mass undertaking through organizations that could break away from the political parties (October 1972); searching for a means of constitutionally overthrowing the government (March 1973); attempting to divide the armed forces (June 1973); and finally, triggering the coup d'état by the military as a whole (September 1973). The passage from the second phase to the third was marked by an upper-middle-class strike in October 1972. This event also represented the first overt and widespread escalation of the overthrow strategy, the height of lower-class mobilization in support of the government, and the decisive entrance of the armed forces into the political scene. In my judgment, incorporating the armed forces into the Allende government as a result of the "October strike" was, despite its ultimate consequences, the only alternative possible at the time, given that the military's behavior during the strike had been favorable to the government and that constitutionalist elements loyal to the legitimate government still dominated the military leadership. If the price paid was the explicit political participation of the armed forces, it was an inevitable price paid under the best of conditions for the government. Only after this episode did Popular Unity's treatment of the armed forces demonstrate serious lapses and shortcomings. One of them was not assuming that the consequences of this political eruption would progressively undermine the "constitutionalist" ideology at various levels of the armed forces.

But this bipolar aspect of the political struggle alone cannot explain the process of political polarization and the triggering of the regime crisis. At least three social sectors played a fundamental role in the development of these two opposing logics: the political Center represented by the Christian Democrats, the so-called middle sectors, and the armed forces. Each group played a collaborating role in the problems described in the final outcome.

The logic of the Christian Democrats' behavior during this period was dictated by the desire to preserve its organizational identity and to protect its long-term political interests as an independent power alternative. The Christian Democrats' attempt to capture the leadership of the opposition between September and November 1970 contributed to the rise of Allende. Yet the Christian Democrats did not commit themselves fully to an alliance with Popular Unity at the beginning of the Allende government because of their obsession with party identity and the internal pull of capitalist factions.[18] Ensnared in a centrist position amid growing polarization, the Christian Democrats' ideological alternativism and sensitivity to popular sectors combined with internal divisions to prevent the party from assuming leadership of the opposition to Popular Unity. By the time internal polarization eased, the Christian Democrats' political role had become irrelevant because the military had already assumed power. Thus the Christian Democratic party was caught between its own rhetoric of defending democracy and the authoritarian radicalization of its bases combined with its failure to perceive that the popular character of the UP government would inevitably lead to an antipopular and nondemocratic solution if it was overthrown. Consequently, the behavior of the Christian Democrats contributed decisively to the collapse of the political regime.

During the polarizing of the middle sectors, the only component uniting these sectors (which are heterogeneous to the point of being contradictory), and perhaps the only common denominator, was the ideological-cultural dimension. By manipulating this element, the rightist opposition pulled the middle sectors into adopting radical stances favoring authoritarianism and thus loosened their loyalty to a political system that these sectors had associated with possible satisfaction of claims and interests. But here too the theoretical and ideological deficiencies of the Left can be readily perceived. As noted, the UP project made no room for these sectors to recognize their own interests within it and thus consider themselves "tactical allies" or "subordinate partners" in the coalition. Formulations emphasizing the role of the proletariat jarred the sensibilities of those who preferred to keep their distance from the popular element and had an irrational fear of pauperization and its representatives in society. Thus merely to provide economic benefits for the middle sectors without acknowledging any ideological or political space for them bespoke an inability to recognize the true nature of the Chilean social formation. Another factor was the impact of the economic crisis. Triggered both by the economic strategy of national and foreign sectors seeking to overthrow the government and by the government's relative contempt for financial mechanisms and its difficulties in managing the economy, the economic crisis created the perception of a crisis in daily living that was difficult to bear.

Another contributing factor in polarizing all these sectors and discrediting the political regime was the UP strategy of economic transformations—the nationalizations, interventions, and requisitionings. Although this strategy was responding to the dire need to accelerate state capacity to manage the economy and although it followed existing laws, its implementation brought into question the principle of the balance of powers that had been built into the mechanism for gradualist defense of the system against profound change. This questioning made the middle sectors more susceptible to the opposition slogan claiming that Popular Unity was seeking "the conquest of complete power." Although this strategy could not count on majority support, it fueled the fires of those who sought to struggle outside political institutions and to discredit the political regime.

Finally, the Right's strategies for polarizing politics and deinstitutionalizing and discrediting the political system were aimed at precipitating military intervention. Popular Unity had no coherent project for the armed forces that did not rely on their constitutional support. Thus the triggering of the military crisis cannot be attributed to any unilateral action by Popular Unity within the armed forces or to any plan or project in this regard. Military personnel were guided mainly by the wish to preserve their institutional interests and unity, and as a result, premature attempts at overthrowing the government were countered by the legitimacy of the political regime and the absence of any autonomous joint mission among the armed forces. No mission was evident until October 1972, when the military emerged from its cloistering, which until then had been interrupted only by the external tie that had socialized the military in the new versions of national security doctrine.[19] Only when the military began to share political functions and the political crisis began to permeate the ranks did the unfolding of this autonomous project manifest itself in displacing "constitutionalist" loyalties and those who expressed them. In a situation of open politicization, those factions within the armed forces favoring a coup can consolidate and eliminate, whether institutionally or via brutal repression, the progressive elements opposing a military coup. This possibility, the partial abrogation of state arbitration mechanisms, the internal unity fomented by military ideology, and its hierarchical structure all combined to allow the armed forces to fulfill their role as potential arbitrators favoring the established system and its dominant classes in the coup of 11 September 1973.

At this point, it should be noted that the military coup by the armed forces as a whole was the alternative for overthrowing the UP government that was most favorable to the upper bourgeoisie and to foreign interests. The reasons were that a military coup avoided the danger of a civil war with its concomitant risks for the bourgeoisie and created the best political and institutional conditions for starting immediately to rebuild a capitalist society.

Popular Chile and Capitalism in Disarray[20]

Turning now to the historical project of Popular Unity as it had crystallized by the end of this era, two aspects can be distinguished. First, in terms of democratization, Chile was experiencing an explosion of popular presence in every dimension. Not only had the repressive mechanisms against the popular movement disappeared for the first time in Chilean history, but significant sectors of the movement were experiencing this era as far more than the objective benefits received—rather, as a moment of liberation, participation, and free expression when the hallmarks of social privilege were being discredited and abolished. This experience of self-affirmation as masters of their personal and collective destiny was the basis of the strong support for the UP government among these sectors. But Popular Unity was not capable of extending this experience to many other important sectors of society and thus contributed to the isolation of popular sectors and a parallel radicalization of those who were not sharing this experience. Severe tension again developed between the poles of "class" and "nation" because of the ideological and practical appropriation of the universalistic nature of Popular Unity's historical project by a single social sector.

Second, in terms of a noncapitalist project, Chileans were witnessing the comprehensive dismantling of an unjust economic system that had been threatening the potential of the democratizing process. But because no minimal system was organized to replace the unjust system—due to the crisis provoked by the economic Right, the so-called invisible blockade imposed by the United States, and the technical shortcomings of Popular Unity—this dismantling took the form of capitalism in disarray, with all the aftermath of black markets, speculation, hoarding, and so on.

This dual reality explains the tasks facing the project set up as an alternative to Popular Unity, which began to unfold from the moment that Popular Unity was overthrown. Rebuilding the disarticulated capitalist system required reversing the popular process and nullifying its political and organizational manifestation. These interrelated goals could not be undertaken except in an authoritarian framework, and the initial bases for such a regime were provided by the way in which the constitutionally legitimate government was overthrown.

Conclusions: Rescuing a Historical Project and Its Political-Ideological Reformulation

I will end my reflections on the period from 1970 to 1973 with a double affirmation about the future. The goal of deepening a democratic system by reversing tendencies toward concentration, exclusion, and dependency on the capitalist development scheme—with the aid of the growing popular movement and a perspective reconciling socialism with a democratic regime—continues to be a valid project for Chile. But assuming the correctness of the analysis presented here and the reversal of the mission carried out by the military regime, then this assertion must be complemented by a second statement: the validity or force of this democratic mission requires thorough reformulation of the ideological-political project by whoever might attempt to revive the historical alternative. This reformulation assumes two major accomplishments: first, adequately combining the dimensions of class and nation so that all interests and values that can be subsumed within this project are integrated effectively—not by means of any pretext or spurious alliance—which is to say that the popular project can be nothing less than a national project; and second, adequately combining the social and substantive popular interests that an egalitarian economic order should preserve with the rules of the political game, whose value must derive from criteria that are not merely instrumental but ethical and political. In this sense, the history of Chile demonstrates that purely instrumental support of democracy as a space allowing for satisfaction of competing interests inevitably undermines a political regime. It is evident that both aspects involve a reformulation of political actors and their complete theoretical and ideological renewal, which will require sacrificing predetermined schemes that obscure understanding of national uniqueness.

NOTES TO CHAPTER 2

1. In this chapter, I have used materials from the following works of mine: "Elementos para el análisis del proceso político chileno, 1970–1973," *Revista Latinoamericana de Sociología*, n.s., 2 (Feb. 1975); "Continuidad y ruptura y vacío teórico-ideológico: dos hipótesis sobre el proceso político chileno, 1970–1973," *Revista Mexicana de Sociología* 39, no. 4 (Oct.–Dec. 1977); and "1970–1973: sentido y derrota de un proyecto popular," *Mensaje* 28, no. 266 (Jan.–Feb.1978), published in Santiago.

2. In addition to the works cited in the first chapter, other important works analyzing this period are: Sergio Bitar, *Transición, socialismo y democracia: la experiencia chilena* (Mexico City: Siglo Veintiuno, 1979); and J. Garcés, *Allende y la experiencia chilena* (Barcelona: Ariel, 1976). For a complete bibliography, see Manuel Antonio Garretón and E. Hola, *Bibliografía del proceso chileno, 1970–1973* (Santiago: FLACSO, 1978).

3. Evidently, this position is not the one taken by the MIR (Movimiento de Izquierda Revolucionaria). But in this case, it must be said that although the MIR represented a strategy that was radically opposed to the UP strategy before 1970, from that time on, the MIR was incapable of elaborating a coherent overall strategy for the popular movement as an alternative to the positions won by Popular Unity. Thus the MIR's strength and merit were based entirely on exploiting the errors of Popular Unity in regard to the mass movement.

4. Here and throughout this work, when I refer to the shortcomings and voids within the Left or Popular Unity, I am treating the movement as a whole, without evaluating individual groups or behaviors that might be exceptions to my general assertions.

5. See Genaro Arriagada and Manuel Antonio Garretón, "Doctrina de Seguridad Nacional y régimen militar," *Estudios Sociales Centroamericanos*, no. 21 (Sept.–Dec. 1978) and no. 22 (Jan.–Mar 1979).

6. This historical project was most directly expounded by Allende. For example, his First Message to Congress (Primer Mensaje al Congreso Nacional) in May 1971 defined Popular Unity's historical project thus: "The sustained fight to open the path to economic democracy and achieve social liberties is our greatest contribution to developing the democratic regime. To fulfill this struggle while defending civil and individual liberties . . . is the historical challenge that all Chileans are facing." This passage partially illustrates the nature of a process "of noncapitalist democratization." I am aware of the extreme fluidity of this concept and the difficulties that it poses. They relate to the absence of an analytical tool in the theoretical-ideological tradition of the Chilean Left that would allow the concept to be formulated and specified more exactly. This characterization is latent in leftist formulations, but it lacks the coherence, clarity, and projection necessary to account for the richness of the process begun in 1970. I therefore view this characterization as indicating a void left by political elaboration as well as a path that avoids discussing the process in terms of alternatives like revolution versus legality, peaceful road versus armed road, and socialism versus institutionality—alternatives that seem in this case to lead to an analytical dead end.

7. The quotations are taken from the *Programa básico de la Unidad Popular* (Santiago: PLA, 1970); and from Allende's speech of 5 Nov. 1970., "Discurso en el Estadio Nacional," in Hernán Godoy U., *Estructura Social de Chile* (Santiago: Ed. Universitaria, 1971). It must be remembered that the broad outlines of Popular Unity's economic project included the following goals: nationalizing basic wealth, eliminating monopolies and the *latifundio*, and establishing a major state sector of the economy that would generate and transfer a surplus and reorient the development strategy toward satisfying popular needs. In the short term, Popular Unity's two main goals were economic reactivation and income redistribution for the benefit of low-income sectors. For more on this subject, see Stefan de Vylder, *Chile, 1970–1973: The Political Economy of the Rise and Fall of Popular Unity* (Stockholm: Unga Filosofers Fölai, 1974).

8. This point is illustrated by the shift from analyses of concentration and economic dependency to political formulas characterizing the "fundamental enemies of the Chilean revolution."

9. Expressions based on slogans like "Conquer all power" and "Create popular power" seem typical of this "institutionalist" vision of political power. In contrast, the lack of conceptions and vagueness in facing problems like those of the universities illustrate the generalized attitude of subordinating the definition of certain spheres of social life to the "resolution of the problem of power."

10. See Urs Müller-Planteberg, "La voz de las cifras: un análisis de las elecciones en Chile entre 1957 y 1971," *Cuadernos de la Realidad Nacional* 14 (Oct. 1972).

11. Three specific illustrations of this conclusion can be cited. The first is the discussion concerning the concept of the "dictatorship of the proletariat" following Allende's first presidential message to Congress in May 1971. The second is the debate regarding "popular power" and its relationship to the "bourgeois state," which obscured analysis of the real problem of channeling the mass movement, which was not being represented in the political leadership. The third illustration is provided by the Project for National School Unification (Proyecto de la Escuela Nacional Unificada), a technical scheme for democratizing and modernizing education with an ideological formulation that impeded its general comprehension and acceptance. All three instances were seized upon by the opposition coalition as major weapons in its ideological campaign.

12. This phenomenon was known as *cuoteo*—the distribution of government positions and jobs among parties.

13. This discussion seeks not to condemn the proliferation of ideological discourse and debate during the period, which achieved high degrees of autonomy with respect to real phenomena, but to point out the roots and character of this proliferation and autonomy.

14. This statement must be understood as a general one that recognizes the existence of important exceptions. Nevertheless, the contribution of intellectuals to elaborating the structural diagnosis of Chilean society as a basis for the Popular Unity program must not be ignored. The void here occurred in the area of clarifying the general meaning of a process.

15. The main statements in this regard are found in Allende's presidential messages to the Congress (21 May 1971, 21 May 1972, and 21 May 1973); and in "Allende habla con Debray," *Puntó Final* 126 (Mar. 1971). They can also be found in anthologies of Allende's speeches: *Nuestro camino al socialismo: la vía chilena* (Buenos Aires: Ediciones Papiro, 1971); and *Allende: su pensamiento político* (Santiago: Quimantú, 1972). This topic is also discussed in some works by Allende's political and economic advisors. See Joan Garcés, *El Estado y los problemas tácticos en el Gobierno de Allende* (Madrid: Siglo Veintiuno, 1974); and Garcés, "Estado burgués y gobierno popular," *Cuadernos de la Realidad Nacional* 15 (Dec. 1972):132–52, published in Santiago. On the legal problems involved, see Eduardo Novoa, "Vías legales para avanzar al socialismo," *Revista de Derecho Económico* 33–34 (Oct. 1972); and Novoa, "El difícil camino de la legalidad," *Revista de la Universidad Técnica del Estado* 7 (Apr. 1972). On the economic sphere, see Sergio Ramos, *Chile: ?una economía de transición?* (Havana: Casa de las Américas, 1972); and *El pensamiento económico del Gobierno de Allende*, edited by Gonzalo Martner (Santiago: Editorial Universitaria, 1971). Systematization of the concept of the Chilean road to socialism and an evaluation of the problems in its formulation can be found in my article coauthored with Felipe Agüero, "Vía chilena al socialismo," in the Spanish version of the *Diccionario de Ciencias Sociales de UNESCO* (Paris: UNESCO, 1976).

16. Here I am drawing on ideas developed in Garretón and Moulián, "Procesos y bloques políticos en la crisis chilena, 1970–1973," *Revista Mexicana de Sociología* 44, no. 1 (Jan.–Mar. 1979); and in Garretón and Moulián, *Análisis coyuntural y proceso político: las fases del conflicto en Chile, 1970–1973* (San José, Costa Rica: EDUCA, 1978).

17. U.S. intervention throughout this period in an effort to overthrow Allende has been sufficiently admitted and proven by now. On this subject, see *Covert Action in Chile, 1963–1973: Staff Report of the Select Committee to Study Governmental Operations with Respect to Intelligence Activities* (Washington, D.C.: Government Printing Office, 1975); and *Documentos secretos de la ITT* (Santiago: Quimantú, 1972). For a general overview, see Richard Fagen, "The United States in Chile: Roots and Branches," *Foreign Affairs* 53, no. 2 (Jan. 1975).

18. Also adding to the situation was the dominant position of Popular Unity at this time. The Christian Democrats contributed to the rise of Allende by voting for him in Congress after the presidential election in which he obtained the first relative majority. This vote followed Chilean tradition, and the Christian Democrats did not want to lose legitimacy by voting against Allende.

19. On this theme, see the second part of this book.

20. The expression "Popular Chile" was taken from A. Touraine, *Vida y muerte del Chile Popular* (Mexico City: Siglo Veintiuno, 1974).

PART II

Military Regimes and Authoritarian Capitalism in the Southern Cone

CHAPTER 3

The Historical Project of the New Military Regimes in Latin America

Analytical Problems[1]

The emergence of a "new style" of military regime in several Latin American countries during the last two decades has engendered abundant literature in the social sciences.[2] In this chapter, I will employ a general perspective that avoids detailed consideration of particular cases and emphasizes the sociological dimension instead in order to highlight relevant problems, formulate questions, and suggest several directions for analysis.

The term *political regime* is understood here to mean a system of mediations between the state and civil society. Thus when speaking of authoritarian regimes, I am referring to a specific model of this system of mediations.[3] Consequently, the term *authoritarianism* is not used here in the sense of describing a feature of class society as a whole, that is, as a general element of capitalist society. Rather, it is used in reference to a given historical occurrence. Nor do I identify the set of elements that define these regimes with a particular historical form of authoritarianism like fascism, even when they might be comparable or have similar features or when this concept is expanded by adding "neo" or "dependent." The historical form of the phase of world and local capitalism, with its implications for class structure, as well as the type of political regime without mass organization or mobilization all make it preferable to leave this designation aside.[4]

Whether these regimes are referred to as examples of "fascism," "neofascism," "dependent fascism," "authoritarian states," "bureaucratic-authoritarian states," "defensive authoritarianism," "technocratic military regimes," "authoritarian capitalism," or "national security states," certain common features differentiate these new regimes from other Latin American political-military systems. First, the "new style" regimes emerge in countries with a certain level of development or industrialization and, in some cases, a political regime with a history of stability. Second, they follow periods of broad and relatively intense popular mobilization and political presence that assumed populist or revolutionary forms. Third, within the coalition that takes over running the state, the armed forces assume a dominant role by rupturing the political system and becoming functionally involved in conducting state governance through their institutional hierarchy. Fourth, a coalition is structured around the military representing the classes that predominate economically and exercise control over the state apparatus through technocratic teams. Fifth, this dominant coalition then sets up a project for restructuring society by establishing new patterns and mechanisms of accumulation and distribution and by reordering politics. Sixth, the new political order, which is characterized by its authoritarian and exclusionary pattern, requires the use of repressive force to eliminate, dismantle, or control the political and class organizations of popular sectors as well as the political organizations surviving from the preceding period.

These features, which are purely descriptive, have stimulated diverse explanatory and interpretive analyses attempting to deal with new problems in the sociological dimension. In considering processes involving high social mobilization, strong social forces and actors on the political scene, and an elevated level of ideological discourse, analysis risks becoming caught up in the representations of the actors confronting each other and becoming a mere systematization of their discourse. But in situations where political power seems to assert itself in pure form without mediations and where social forces and actors are manifested clearly, analysis risks being confined to an apocalyptic description of a dominating force that imposes itself unhindered, as if obeying some natural logic. In the first instance, the temptation is to view the actors as being endowed with totally independent will, to detach them from the "situation" and ask the simple "meaning" of each action, identifying it with each actor's discourse. In the second case, the question of "meaning" seems to lose significance because of the temptation to subsume it under the description of the "situation." At one extreme, the social forces interact as if part of a drama without a script. At the other, the "objective forces" exercise their power as if acting out a tragedy with no cast of characters.

Analysis of authoritarian regimes, at least in their initial phases, seems to confront problems typical of the second situation. Domination tends to be envisioned as a phenomenon having an irreversible logic, as the product of objective forces. Its evolution is described in terms of "tensions" or "splits" in the great mantle that covers society. Here the logic of world capitalism and the international division of labor or the logic of the unfettered power of the state fills the role of the god that rules over history: human beings, whether collective actors or social forces, are mere carriers of this logic that is imposing itself on them. Analysis is then reduced to describing the development of this logic and its internal tensions or to condemning it from the outset. Description and condemnation consequently become confused with explanation and interpretation. Structural data assume the governing role, while the discourse of the actors appears to be pure ideology.

Partly in response to this emphasis, some analyses of authoritarian regimes focus more closely on political aspects: the actors and social forces are viewed as more than manifestations of a situation or the embodiment of a logic. While closer to a sociological approach, such analyses run the risk of normativism or voluntarism. Another problem with this focus, one that is inherent in analyzing this type of political regime, is finding out what is actually happening in the society when "structural" data and the actors' discourse are not sufficiently revealing. The opacity of such regimes hinders comprehension of their behavior, adequate reconstruction of social activity, and interpretation of its meaning. Lacking the necessary antecedents, analysts may be tempted to replace analysis of facts with an imputation of rationality by constructing schemes that give coherence or intelligibility to opaque social phenomena. Here the risk arises that the interpretations will be arbitrary and removed from actual events.

Both analytic approaches, one emphasizing determinative structures of authoritarian regimes and the other the relative autonomy of dynamic and sociopolitical factors, tend to appear when studying various dimensions of these regimes—their gestation, trajectory, durability, crises, and so on.

The Crisis of Origin

The emergence of an authoritarian regime seems to represent both a response to the political crisis in society and an attempt to make a historical social project materialize. These two dimensions are distinct yet interrelated.

Reference to the political crisis alludes to more than the widely recognized hegemonic crisis that characterized Latin American countries following the collapse of the oligarchic state. This crisis gave rise to the "compromise state" as defined during the following decades in a succession of unstable arrangements that did not preclude occasional resolutions by force.[5] The immediate political crisis giving rise to the authoritarian regime was thus a specific, historically conditioned manifestation, a particular moment in this larger hegemonic crisis, but one that cannot be reduced to its pure generic traits. The specifics of the crisis related to a choice between continuing and deepening a partial process of political and social democratization (which demanded a drastic change in the pattern of "dependent capitalist" development) or intensifying the dependent capitalist development model by abruptly reversing the democratization process (which presupposed eliminating and replacing the prevailing political regime).[6] The genuine political manifestation of this crisis was the mobilizing of popular forces and pressure, which varied in strength from country to country. Thus a growing political polarization was initiated in which significant middle and upper social strata perceived a threat to the social order with which they identified. At this point, a broad (although relatively heterogeneous) popular movement—at the height of its influence vis-à-vis the state—confronted the social sectors that perceived the situation as a threatening crisis. But this confrontation occurred before other social sectors had been thoroughly incorporated into the popular movement.

The element of political crisis underscores one of the basic dimensions of these regimes: they are regimes of reaction and containment that are in some cases counterrevolutionary. When faced with a threat to the established order from popular mobilization (accompanied by growing radicalization, polarization, and sometimes crisis in the functioning of society), what these tendencies seek is to impose order, to demobilize, to "normalize," and to "pacify." This response requires rupturing the political regime, which in turn requires the presence of the one actor with the force and (for some) the legitimacy to do the job—the armed forces. But beyond the reactive component, military intervention must be explained in terms of the second dimension associated with these regimes, the foundational dimension, which will be discussed later.

The crisis of origin and the way it is conceptualized by the major actors thus help determine the defensive or reactive dimension,[7] which becomes the dominant logic during the installation or reinstallation of these regimes. Although some authors have asserted the necessity of analyzing the regime without considering the originating crisis, others incorporate it when describing the nature of the phenomenon. I would argue that the nature of the crisis of origin determines not only the moment of reaction but also what I call the "foundational logic."

The type, magnitude, duration, and scope of the reactive dimension seem to be determined by two factors: first, by the degree of articulation of the popular forces, their level of ideological mobilization, and their relative power in society; and second, by the degree to which the popular phenomenon and the crisis are perceived by various sectors (those objectively threatened as the dominant class and the broader or narrower middle sectors) as a definitive attack on the system. The first factor conditions the range and depth of the repression. The second legitimizes the repression, even in its most brutal and irrational forms.

Although the political crisis is mainly expressed in the reactive, defensive, or counterrevolutionary logic of these regimes, it also leaves its imprint on the foundational logic or the "revolutionary moment." This logic becomes the historical project of the regime, which will be discussed in more detail later. This relationship is determined above all by the degree of crisis in the functioning of society, as evidenced in the dual aspect of discontinuities in the economy and disjointedness in daily life. The need to reestablish or normalize the economy will set the course for the foundational project in terms of the economy and sociopolitical organization. This necessity will also provide new ideological resources for legitimation.

But this relationship is not a mechanical one. The political crisis is characterized by a confrontation between classes and social sectors. Its resolution therefore implies that one social class that felt threatened will become victorious over the other. This element of "revenge," which is typical of a counterrevolution, helps to explain many features of the reactive or defensive period. The "structural" requirements of economic normalization or stabilization alone cannot explain certain aspects of the repression, and social control will therefore seem to be exceeding economic requirements at times. But this "excessiveness" is neither an accident nor a "deviation" susceptible to being "corrected." The dynamic of class confrontation and its subjectivization are objective elements that have a logic of their own, at times independent of the material base's requirements for development. In other words, the crisis produces three kinds of requirements for the new regime: requirements deriving from the economic project that demand political-organizational constraints; separate requirements originating out of the necessity for political control by those sectors assuming direction of the state and society; and other requirements relating to the collective subjectivization of the previous confrontation.

It should be noted nonetheless that associating the rise of these authoritarian or military regimes with a political crisis in no case postulates a necessary causal relationship between the two. Despite the persuasions of the ideology of legitimation, the rupture that gave rise to these regimes was not the only possible solution. But that is another story.

The Historical Project

The character of vehicles or carriers of a historical project defines what can be called the foundational or (in some cases) "revolutionary" logic or dynamic of these authoritarian regimes. Here I am no longer referring only to the defensive or reactive aspect but also to an attempt at transforming the society as a whole in a chosen direction. This project seems to have two determinants: a crisis of national capitalism, or the passage from one distinct phase in its process of accumulation and development to another; and a contrasting process of capitalist restructuring at the world level that redefines the role of peripheral capitalist countries.[8]

Two distinct problems arise in analyzing this subject. The first has to do with the specifics of the historical project when diverse national cases are considered. Description of this process in the specific sense of "capitalist deepening" can no longer be accepted as the only possibility.[9] Various authors have pointed out that capitalist deepening was not the main orientation adopted by these regimes, even in those cases that have been used to test the "deepening" hypothesis. Some analysts have pointed out various other "economic connections," warning nonetheless that no single one is sufficient to explain these regimes. They also warn that an excess of economic determinism is implied in characterizing these regimes according to their project for material development,[10] a point I will return to later.

It is thus appropriate to question whether in characterizing these regimes, one must take into account the diversity of their historical projects (despite their similar economic policies)[11] and abandon the idea of a historical social project with a material base of development, which would involve reducing their common elements to features of political organization and decision-making styles. If this were the case, one could find similar formal features but still would not be able to establish how and through what historical social substrate they are explained. Although in speaking of these regimes, we are referring to phenomena of a political nature, they clearly do not arise as products of interaction among actors without settings or scripts. The script is not written entirely beforehand, nor is the stage a setting that "produces" actors. Thus it does not seem possible to conceive of such regimes without reference to a dominant historical social project. Yet neither does it seem possible, when trying to describe the common features of various historical situations, to go beyond characterizing the project in terms of a process of internal capitalist recomposition or restructuring and reinsertion in the capitalist world system.[12]

The matter is one of constructing a coherent sociopolitical organization with accelerated development following a crisis envisioned by the economy's dominant sectors as a dissolution of the system. Obviously, this interpretation does not ignore the dominant character assumed up to this point by the capitalist development scheme. But it is a "distorted capitalism" full of inefficiencies typical of its late structuring, subject to a consistently erratic quality arising from participatory and redistributive tendencies, and incapable of conferring homogeneity on an entire society with diverse dimensions. The necessity of restructuring obeys the defining goals of the phase of capitalist development and the perception of these goals by sectors dominating or beginning to dominate the economy. But above all, this necessity follows the demand for a response to the political-social crisis, which functions as its catalyst.

If this is the broad historical project, then historical national characteristics will determine which of various "directions" will be taken by this process of capitalist restructuring and reinsertion. Determining national characteristics include the stage of development when the break is made with the previous political regime as well as particular structural features like population, actual size and potential of the market, and quantity, quality, and diversity of national resources.

The second problem in analyzing the historical project of such regimes is the question of to what extent the requirements of restructuring and reinsertion account for the set of transformations experienced by the society. In other words, is there a complete correspondence between "objective" or "structural" requirements and the transformations in society? If not, is this outcome explained only by distortions produced by social resistance to policies expressing these requirements or imperatives?

From one perspective, the answer to the second question would appear to be affirmative: a very tight structural relationship does exist between the economic model for capitalist restructuring and reinsertion and the authoritarian political model. As already pointed out, processes of capitalist accumulation seem to become contradictory at a certain point, catalyzed by the political-social crisis, with too many demands for democratization and redistribution and multiple social actors attacking the stability required by the new forms of accumulation. All these factors threaten to break down the system. Thus, establishing new forms of accumulation requires certain political arrangements that involve dismantling the mechanisms and organizations that are vehicles for demands pressuring the system's redistributive capacity. The result is that establishing new forms requires restrictive policies promoting stabilization that seriously harm the achievements, expectations, and demands of not only the popular sectors defeated during the political crisis but also the middle sectors exacerbated by the polarization preceding the break. Thus the need to "normalize" the economy in a specific sense and exclude large groups of the population from its immediate benefits means confronting politically active sectors. Demobilizing these sectors requires repressing their organizations by eliminating or dismantling them and encouraging their passivity with the promise of better times. As discussed, this approach requires wiping out the preceding political system, which makes repression and political control imperatives of the project of restructuring and reinsertion, even when its purely economic aspects are not sufficient to explain these measures.

But this relationship is not strictly structural in origin. The authoritarian model seems to be demanded by both the need for long-term stability and the exclusionary consequences of the economic model. Many social sectors are affected, and many demands are blocked because their intrusion through an open organizational and institutional system would exert pressure on the weak inclusionary capacity of the system and wreck the delicate mechanisms put in place to achieve the equilibrium that will guarantee "internal stability" and "external confidence." The latter turns out to be truly indispensable for attracting the foreign capital needed for the economy to function.

As a consequence of adopting certain political "constraints," economic "revitalization" seems to require establishing an ongoing authoritarian order whose dynamic of constrictions and openings (*aperturas*) can be controlled according to progress of this economic scheme. Moreover, in certain cases, these "constraints" extend beyond the political system, requiring that other spheres of social life be reordered to make them functional for the model of accumulation, distribution, and reproduction. The educational system seems to be one of these spheres.

But certain errors must be avoided in this approach, in which the model of sociopolitical organization seems to be purely an adaptation to structural imperatives of the economic base. This perspective would imply a correspondence between the two structures, in which one determines all the characteristics of the other. But as several analysts have pointed out, this interpretation does not consider the evidence indicating that many elements in economic models of restructuring and reinsertion have been applied in political systems that differ greatly from authoritarian regimes.[13] It is thus appropriate to turn to the issue of the mediation of class structure and class relations. Discussing a project of capitalist restructuring cannot ignore the classes or fractions of classes and social actors that formulate (more or less explicitly) the project and attempt to implement it by confronting other classes, fractions, and actors.

The set of changes that these regimes attempt to introduce amount to social transformations of a "revolutionary" kind. In content and method, these changes can be thought of as an attempt at late capitalist revolution "from above" by a military-dominated state seeking less to restore some lost order than to reorder an entire society along different lines.[14] This undertaking is an attempt at late capitalist revolution, not an attack on a feudal or precapitalist order or on an old, oligarchic dominant class. It is a situation in which the evolution and expansion of social and popular forces appear to be the main obstacle to reestablishing the capitalist order. Antipopular sentiment is consequently a hallmark of this kind of process.

In referring to an attempt at transformation from the level of the state, I am alluding to the inability of the dominant classes and sectors to establish hegemony in civil society by creating an "incorporating" order, which would be expressed in a political system with a base that is relatively consensual, although not exempt from contradictions and conflicts. The contrasting recourse to force is another component of experiences of this kind. Thus a dissociation occurs between the "democratic" and "bourgeois" elements in classic capitalist transformations. If democratic aspirations and undertakings have been attained to varying degrees in some Latin American countries or a democratic political order has been established in some cases, it was not a hegemonic construct by a strong and triumphant bourgeoisie that beckoned other classes to participate in a political order. Rather, such accomplishments have resulted from complex processes in which middle and popular sectors played a fundamental role through manifestations that were populist, developmentalist, reformist, or more revolutionary. And if attempts have been made at "bourgeois revolution," they have been aimed against the democratic regime, in some cases following its collapse, and have made their goal the destruction of the bases of development that provided a logic for diverse forms of populism or popular incorporation.

But an attempt of a revolutionary kind—regardless of its ultimate success or failure—is accomplished by classes or class fractions and social groups and actors. Its project results from relations established among these groups and with the whole of society as the new dominant coalition. The basic dynamic that evolves in society is the search for dominance within this coalition, which can then be imposed on the society as a whole and thus counter the resistance of the sectors that the coalition seeks to subordinate. This search for hegemony, whose crux is capitalistic restructuring and reinsertion, still cannot be reduced to economic exigencies. Thus it is possible to interpret social transformations as expressing a process in which the dominant coalition seeks to resolve its internal and external problems of hegemony by constructing and directing a coherent social structure in all its dimensions. The economic model undoubtedly has its "exigencies." But there are also unresolved problems of hegemony: social visions that are sometimes complementary, sometimes contradictory, seeking form in structural policies; interests, demands, and sectoral aspirations that seek fulfillment and must be internalized within the dominant coalition; significant groups that must be won over, even if only ideologically; corporatist claims, and so on. These factors give content and historical significance to a project that cannot be defined metasocially. They also explain why many "government" measures contradict economic logic (as do military expenditures) or operate independently of it.

Thus it is appropriate to speak of structural exigencies and requirements or imperatives. But these demands pertain to an attempt at social refounding, not to an order that is purely economic. They go through the mediation of a social coalition that comprises more than economic agents, and they are enacted through actors, classes, and class relations. These demands express the whole range of challenges and undertakings that a given coalition must face in order to reorder an entire society from the top down. This process—in which a class coalition attempts to establish and extend its domination, direct society, and confront "internal" and "external" contradictions—effectively determines the rhythm and dynamics of political openings and constrictions.

Some Analytical Consequences

The preceding emphasis on the double dimension of crisis and project has consequences on analysis of these regimes. First, it directs attention beyond the sociopolitical crisis toward the "state of society" at the moment when the process of capitalist restructuring is initiated via the authoritarian route. This focus involves considering the historical development of the state, the political regime, and civil society, which obviously vary from one country to another. Many of the policies of structural reform undertaken by these regimes obey not only the requirements of the economic model but the necessity of "adjusting" this state of society to a process of overall domination. In this sense, a number of factors become crucial: the degree, extension, and phase of capitalist industrial development; the level of social intervention attained by the state; the structure of the system of political representation; the mechanisms linking state and society; and finally, the breadth and depth of democratization during the preceding cycle and the stage at which it was interrupted. Although one orientation of this attempt at "capitalist revolution" is to destroy the bases that made populism and its various forms of agitation possible, the level of democratization attained by these processes sometimes allows sectoral policies of partial extension or democratization that are not incompatible with the general scheme of domination. At the same time, the possibilities for state intervention are related to the nature and degree of the state's involvement and its role in social and political activation during the previous phase. Finally, the possibilities for political reordering and for tolerating political actors will bear some relationship to the previous level of structuring of political actors and their role in the articulation of classes and social groups during the preceding period.

Second, the proposed emphasis for characterizing the project of these regimes points to the particular historical features of the sectors that make up the dominant coalition. Such characteristics, which cannot be subsumed under the formal features of one situation or another, require analyzing the dominant coalition's mechanisms of internal dominance, systems for making decisions and compromises, ideological expression, and so on.[15] Configuration of a dominant coalition is undoubtedly not a random occurrence. As has been emphasized, the goals set for a project of capitalist restructuring and reinsertion take shape within in particular classes, fractions, and social organizations as dominant actors. But the specific nature of these actors, as well as the state in which they emerge from the crisis, will largely determine not only the internal dynamic of the dominant coalition but the dynamic imparted to society as a whole.

This argument should be made for each component of the dominant coalition, but the historical role played by the specific nature of the armed forces and its particular place in society are especially worth highlighting.

The standardizing of Latin American armed forces has been well established in various studies in terms of their modernization, professionalization, and ideological indoctrination during the postwar era following their incorporation into the U.S. military sphere of influence.[16] Also well known are the role assigned to the armed forces by counterinsurgency doctrine as the ultimate guarantors of the nation and its destiny and the consequent social definition and self-definition of military's political role (a subject to be examined in a subsequent chapter). When this legacy is compounded by a long hegemonic crisis and another crisis perceived as threatening to dissolve society via heightened popular mobilization, polarization, and political confrontation, it is easy to understand why the role of armed institutions becomes crucial in all cases in making the political rupture and launching the project of restructuring.

But here we are dealing with a generic antecedent that alone cannot illuminate historical specifics. Isolated data on the military's formal organizational character, social composition, and level of technical development explain less about the particularities of diverse authoritarian models or projects than about the kind of historical relation that the armed forces have had with the political sphere and with society as a whole. At one extreme are armed forces that have been permeated by politics and had their historical options refracted or reelaborated. Paradoxically, the "institutional proposal" or project that the armed forces sets forth tends to be more autonomous or original in relation to the projects of civilian groups, while military decision-making mechanisms tend to be more collectively institutional, with the stability of the military regime less associated with individual leaders. At the other extreme, there are armed forces that have not intervened in the legitimate arbitration mechanisms of political society, that have remained subordinate to political power, confined to fulfilling professional duties and developing a suitable ideology. In such a case, the military's messianic self-perception would find no counterpart in a political project that is autonomous and original with regard to social forces and not simply a "consensus for termination"[17] at the moment of the rupture. The point is that once political intervention has occurred, the "formal" direction belongs to the military power, which becomes merely a vehicle for a project of "content" provided by those social forces capable of dominating the ruling coalition. If no consensual project results from an "internal reelaboration," the consequence within the armed forces will be increasing personalization of hierarchical institutional leadership and probably a close relationship between this personalized leadership and maintenance of the regime.[18] This tendency undoubtedly entails significant uncertainty about mechanisms for succession and, more generally, about the dynamics of these regimes, a subject discussed further on.

Third, these characteristics affect comparative analysis of the diverse "authoritarian models" or the variations among these regimes. Rather than base analysis on a single factor or element, one must examine the specifics of the historical combinations of sets of factors indicated by the reactive and foundational dimensions. It is probable that the weight of each dimension varies greatly in different situations, as in the instance where a reactive or defensive logic predominates and foundational logic is feeble or cannot materialize. In any case, both dimensions must be considered in attempting to make the entire process intelligible. Conversely, comparative analysis of authoritarian variants that considers common denominators is enriched when similarities and differences are established not only in overall terms but for one factor or another in each dimension.

The Dominant Ideology

Reference to a foundational project and the social actors and forces that embody it brings up the question of the nature of the dominant ideology of these regimes. Here too it might be said that analysis oscillates between two extremes. On the one hand, the predominance of force, coercion, or repression makes recourse to ideology expendable, thereby explaining the "theoretical-cultural" void in these regimes and their extreme ideological weakness. On the other hand, the same substrate yields a polar vision that assigns great ideological rationality and coherence to these regimes. Whether in a kind of "conspiratorial" or "idealistic" vision linked to political phenomena or in a more deterministic vision linked to economic phenomena, this coherence or rationality is commensurate with the one ideology that can best account for and justify the repressive character of these regimes—the ideology of "national security."

This ideology will be discussed at length in another chapter. Here I will say merely that its initial importance arises from the preeminence of military power and the imperative of undertaking various tasks favoring the opportunity for coercion and finding ample justification in this ideology. But it also supplies the elements that fit best with the growing hegemony of certain fractions of the dominant coalition. From an opposite perspective, the goal of surmounting the most repressive phases (once these regimes are consolidated) and initiating "foundational" tasks in various social spheres (which have little to do with concepts of national security) would explain this ideology's being eclipsed within the ruling coalition by other conceptions like economic neoliberalism and the technocratic vision.

Emphasis on the coherence of national security ideology and its affinity for new forms of domination by certain sectors of national and foreign capital cannot fully explain its lack of appeal to society as a whole, however, and such emphasis can obscure other aspects at the ideological level. Some of these aspects are related to the problems of legitimacy facing these regimes. During the first phase of installation, a kind of counterrevolutionary legitimacy exists in which the situation of force or direct confrontation can be manipulated into a systematic unfolding of this ideology, given the practical ascendence of purely military aspects. But this rationale would be insufficient if it could not rely on certain common sentiments like fear, insecurity, and a desire for order, which are routinely incorporated into conceptions of "national security." This mingling of elements common to society, especially among middle-class sectors, can explain the ideological prominence during the period of counterrevolutionary legitimacy of a conceptual value system so otherwise "foreign" to the society.

In a second phase, when counterrevolutionary legitimacy is nearly used up, the new ruling coalition needs to come up with a mission for society that goes beyond the tasks of reaction and normalization, even if some of them are still viable. The ideological dimension of this phase has three components. First, a vision of national society emerges that emphasizes a radical critique of the former type of development and its political history, accusing it of having caused the crisis that led to the advent of "good new days." Typically, the core of the new ideology consists of historical elements and the redemption of certain moments, values, and public figures that made the nation "great," in contrast with those who dragged it to the brink of destruction. The second and complementary component in the search for a new ideology is made up of elements coming from programmatic lines. Here certain features of economic neoliberalism and technocratic thinking become prominent.[19] These ideological elements, which act as the normative values for the policies being implemented, are accompanied by a third component—a vision of the future and a new society that facilitates accepting the necessary difficulties of the present. This vision must be called democracy, but it is a democracy "purified of the defects of the past." Freedom and economic growth thus found a "new democracy."

By this stage, the ideology of national security has ceased to be the nucleus of the dominant ideology and remains as only the ideological reserve of the hard-line sectors that are most nostalgic about the early days of the regime. Nevertheless, many of the elements of this ideology have been thoroughly incorporated and assimilated.

It is appropriate here to discuss the need for an ideology in these regimes, but it is difficult to consider ideology as merely a doctrinal body, an organized and systematic whole. This ideology is formed by elements derived from diverse sources that make it seem disjointed and heterogeneous. But these "partial coherences" are far more important in the search for hegemony than the totalizing vision.

The ideological mechanisms of hegemony differ according to whether the problem is located within the dominant coalition or in relation to the entire society. In the first case, the principles, values, norms, and concepts deriving from the programmatic dimension are most important, a priority implying that ideological dominance is determined by the capacity to impose a program of action and make it viable. But in relation to society as a whole, the dominant ideology favors those aspects found in the culture of everyday life, both in reference to the historical vision of the society and in terms of values and norms. Nevertheless, because many of these common aspects contradict elements of the dominant ideology, it acquires an incomplete quality that is full of gaps.

As a result, one dominant ideology reflects that of the coalition in power, into which are integrated elements of various organized or systematic ideologies. Another ideology partially dominates the society, by means of those few elements capable of expressing the common sense shared by relatively broad social sectors. This is the area that seeks to expand by controlling and manipulating communications media and mechanisms of socialization.

This partially dominant ideology and culture reflect the great difficulties experienced by the coalition in power in establishing hegemony over society as a whole. The structural problems of economic, social, and political exclusion stemming from the attempt to radically reverse popular participation cannot be easily resolved at the ideological level. Yet one effect of this partial penetration is the relative incongruence of the ideologies expressed in popular movements (except in the most established instances), those elaborated in reference to a history, a development scheme, and a political system that tend to disappear and be subsumed into a new reality. Hence the recourse by opposition organizations invoking popular representation to certain more permanent elements of popular culture outside their systematic ideological expressions. That is to say, paralleling this process of partial penetration and relative disarticulation is another process that redeems popular identity and expression, which leads to ideological renewal and reformulation.

The role that institutions like the Catholic Church play in some of these regimes can be analyzed on this ideological and cultural level. These institutions provide categories and language of general connotation that permit universalizing elements of the oppressed culture that can no longer be expressed in their old ideologies but cannot yet be integrated into a new ideological system capable of coherently opposing the dominant cultural model.

Dynamic and Evolution

The internal dynamic of these regimes is associated with the particular genetic and structural form of the elements discussed above, meaning that each particular "authoritarian model" has its own dynamic or form of evolution. To generalize, this dynamic or tendency toward change has been identified with the *problématique* of establishing the dominant core.[20] Subsequently, this analysis has been complemented by the theme of the "tensions" experienced by these regimes: on the one hand, the eroding of their initial base of support and the contradictions among the components of the dominant core; and on the other, the regime's distance from the excluded masses, with whom it must somehow reestablish mediation. This point brings up the subject of conditional openings and recourse to "transformed" or "renovated" democracy as the point of reference for such openings. The concomitant fear that these openings might lead to unforeseen outcomes that could threaten regime survival would explain the tendencies toward regrouping and returning to the hard line of the first phase.

In alluding earlier to the attempt by the state to revolutionize society according to a project of capitalist restructuring, I pointed out not its successful accession to power but rather the meaning or comprehensibility of a triumphant military coup. In the end, the success of a project of this kind is determined by effective creation of a sociopolitical organization consistent with development or by a coalition's capacity to incorporate society as a whole into its hegemonic project. The enormous difficulties involved in fulfilling the entire mission do not prevent the regime from achieving partial successes, at least in dismantling the preceding society.

The evolution or dynamic of an authoritarian political regime expresses the original or basic contradiction activated by opposition forces between the exclusionary and unbalancing character of a project for capitalist restructuring and dependent reinsertion in an established world system. This dynamic also expresses the need to broaden the bases of regime legitimacy when the principles of counterrevolutionary legitimacy have deteriorated.

But beyond this original contradiction (and leaving aside the dynamics created by the vicissitudes of the world economy or by external pressures), these regimes face two different kinds of problems that condition their political evolution. On one side are the difficulties stemming from resistance to implanting the new historical project, which are inherent in asynchronous changes in various spheres of society. On the other side are the new contradictions arising from structural changes already operating and new struggles not attributable to the transition to a new order but to its partial and sectoral beginnings. This kind of contradiction produces profound changes in social actors that lead to the restructuring of their political expressions and organizations. The difficulties in adaptation (which are subordinate to survival under repressive conditions) are manifested in problems of conducting politics and as peripheral struggles, such as the very slow maturing of visible alternatives to the authoritarian project of domination.

The project of capitalist restructuring and reinsertion faces enormous obstacles due to the particular circumstances of these countries: the difficulties of standardizing structures and actors according to the project and the inability to "incorporate," which gives rise to the need for force and control by the state. But as noted, spheres of society that are deeply penetrated and transformed can coexist alongside spaces and spheres from the "old regime." There can be no thoroughly new society in the sense of complete fulfillment of the historical project, but a new society is possible in the sense that the radical transformation of the political regime is accompanied by partial structural changes modifying society as a whole and restructuring classes and social actors.

It is thus possible to distinguish between a diachronic analysis of the transition from a democratic or populist regime to an authoritarian regime, which emphasizes the problems or contradictions derived from the difficulties of establishing dominance, and a synchronic analysis, which centers on the new contradictions emerging from the partial or sectoral advent of the new order. This distinction is related on the political level to the passage from counterrevolutionary legitimacy to the search for new legitimizing principles. This aspect in turn relates to the two major phases of these regimes—their implantation and their institutionalization. Thus the two great challenges for the dominant coalition are the creation of power and the creation of society.[21] No predetermined chronological order exists for these dimensions, however. Given the heterogeneity of society and the lack of synchronization, they are two facets of a single historical action and can coexist in various spheres of society.

Viability and Crisis

All these factors must be considered when discussing such topics as the viability of these regimes and their crises . The theme of viability sometimes leads to dimensions being confused in a perspective that is excessively all-encompassing. Without attempting to respond to varying national cases, one distinction is worth making. The first dimension is the viability of dependent capitalism, which goes back to the polemics of the 1960s, now somewhat overtaken by the course of history.[22] A second dimension is the capacity of a project of capitalist restructuring and reinsertion to fuse the goals of a developmentalist utopia: the capitalist model, national development, and growing substantive and political democratization. The unfeasibility of this objective is not difficult to argue. A third dimension refers to the viability of the political regime, or its capacity to maintain the authoritarian pattern. The attempt at capitalist revolution can fail or the totality of the undertaking can be renounced, yet domination can be maintained for a long time with the use of force, partial successes, or some combination of the two (assuming the absence of an acute economic crisis or catastrophe). Thus success or failure in one dimension does not necessarily mean success or failure in another.[23]

The viability of the regime must be distinguished from the viability of social domination, that is, from the capacity of the dominant bloc to sustain its power beyond the openings and the erosion of the authoritarian path. Partial overcoming of the crisis of origin or partial creation of a new order could permit variations or adaptations by the bloc in the power of the state. In such a situation (which is not immune to contradictions and conflicts), the general crisis and political crisis would tend to dissociate from one other. This outcome would nevertheless assume overcoming heterogeneity, standardizing society, and regulating the multiplicity of actors who exert pressure on the state, or at least the expanding expectations for incorporation. In this case, overcoming authoritarian domination would not necessarily be associated with a full-scale crisis or crisis of dissolution. The political regime could approach democratic forms through successive approximations, even as it continued to express the hegemony of the capitalist class.

There is an understandable tendency to associate a crisis in political forms of domination with the larger crisis within the capitalist order that is being imposed.[24] Both aspects appear closely tied to the origin of these regimes, but under what circumstances can a dissociation between these two crises take place? The dominant coalition is betting on this dissociation and on the creation of a social order that will allow a new political regime. Thus the call is for "goals," not for "time limits." But the problem always comes down to having enough time for restructuring class relations and developing new forms of political expression. This factor, however, would require a case-by-case analysis.

It is thus possible to make analytical distinctions among the crisis within the military regime, the crisis within the authoritarian regime, and the crisis of the historical project. But whether this distinction is a real one depends on the particular case. The specific potential of the historical project, which is partly related to economic resources and structures, plays a crucial role in the possible dissociation of these crises.[25] But this potential is always expressed through class structure and actors. Whether or not an association occurs between the overall crisis (the collapse of a historical project of domination) and the political crisis (a change in regime or political form of domination) depends as much on the incorporating capacity of the historical project of restructuring as on the struggle exerted by the dominated masses and classes.

Just as the concept of "progress" from the dominant point of view can be discussed according to various aspects, such as maintaining the type of domination or partially creating a new order, so the success of opposition forces is measured not only by the collapse of a regime or the wholesale replacement of its project but in terms of partial accomplishments, such as creating new political conditions, making headway (including inroads into the authoritarian regime), and organizing collective actions. Here, however, one must deal with the double dimension of opposition and negation on one side and consolidation and legitimation on the other.[26] It is possible that the confusion between the societal crisis and the political crisis, and the undertakings involved in each, lies at the root of the difficulties encountered by alliances and the sometimes immobilizing perplexity of the dominant forces.

Finally, is it possible to go beyond a relationship of one-to-one correspondence between the type of capitalism and the political form of domination? This issue seems to me a problem that has not been resolved theoretically, and I am not sure whether dissociation is possible in developing dependent capitalist societies today. But in any case, this relationship is not a mechanical transposition of the structural requirements of the material base to the political system. It again goes through the mediation of class structure, social actors, and their historical relations, which are ideological and political in nature. The relations between capitalism and political regime, the compatibility or incompatibility between a type of capitalism and an authoritarian or democratic regime, are neither essential nor abstract in nature. They are historical, meaning that they are mediated by specific class and group relations, forms of social organization, values, and social demands. This topic, however, would require an empirical, case-by-case analysis. Otherwise, one is left facing two extremes: determinism, which basically associates social crisis with political crisis and generically postulates the dilemma of socialism or fascism; and its inverse, utopian voluntarism, which postulates the reestablishment or recovery of democracy without analyzing the sociohistorical conditions that make it possible. Both extremes have major political consequences.

Exits

This line of reasoning brings us at last to the subject of "exits" from authoritarian regimes. In choosing this word, I am alluding not to just any political crisis or change at the top levels of government but to those crises that lead to a substantive transformation of the authoritarian regime—that is, its replacement—which involves analysis of the transition.[27] Whether dealing with a "programmed" exit (the product of internal transformations including pressures and demands of social and political opposition forces) or with an exit imposed by some or all of these forces, reference is made in either case to the "democratic" exit.

The openings that go with a programmed exit always allude to a renovated democratic order, purified of its earlier defects and somehow restricted or protected. What brings the dominant coalition or fractions within it to create openings that could lead to an exit? It appears that this phenomenon is related to an attempt to recreate the bases of a legitimacy undermined by the regime's inability to make the historical project materialize, or it may arise out of a situation of immobility or political isolation that may or may not be related to the first factor. The basic contradiction deriving from the exclusionary nature of the project of restructuring and reinsertion would lead to an enlargement of the political game. But this phenomenon can also arise from a situation of relative success, where the historical project has been partially achieved. This instance involves the political co-optation of sectors that have not received the benefits expected from the economic model. An opening can also be created before the crisis of legitimacy arises as a means of avoiding a forced opening later that would allow only negotiation to salvage a few prerogatives. Thus an opening cannot always be equated with a situation of vulnerability. Whichever is the case, if "openings" obey the need for relegitimation within the dominant coalition and in society as a whole, "programmed exits" are essential for preserving the social changes achieved. Therefore, programmed exits from above are generally directed at a political order with a regulated system for excluding social-political actors, even when change in the bases of legitimacy requires invoking popular sovereignty and where recourse to military power is always a possibility.[28]

If we now examine the alternative exits that oppose the dynamics of relegitimizing the dominant bloc, it is possible to distinguish broadly between two kinds: first, those arising from a violent collapse of the regime (due to internal or external causes), in which the newly installed order does not necessarily maintain continuity with the political alternative being established; and second, those exits expressing the creation of an alternative coalition through the rearticulation and restructuring of the forces defeated by the military regime and, to a lesser degree, the forces that have broken away from the dominant bloc.

In both cases, the alternative always refers to a democratic political order. But this issue is a problematic one. Reference to democracy follows a double logic: the principle of opposing the authoritarian order but also the principle of reappropriating a history that, although experienced as exploitation and domination, is identified with a possible form of struggle, a basic principle denied by authoritarian domination. According to different national cases, this principle clashes either with the reference to a reality more ideal than historical (taking the form of a utopia that never actually existed) or with an actual historical referent, but one in which the social conditions that made it possible have radically changed. In both cases, democracy as an alternative order has an ambiguous referent and dissimilar content and meaning for various forces making up the opposition coalition. Thus democracy necessarily becomes a search. This search claims all the forms of mediation denied by the authoritarian order, but to the extent that the authoritarian order is linked to a historical project, context, or development model, the search also demands that its alternative somehow contain this reference. Merely invoking a political order or a system of rules of the game tends to conceal the problems of hegemony and the social conditions that foster a stable institutional system. Yet it is not possible for the opposition to trigger a change in the military or authoritarian regime without promoting political democracy over other dimensions of social change.

The need exists for a historical project that can counter the attempt at capitalist restructuring and can express the rejoining of interests of classes and heterogeneous groups in order to sustain and give content to a democratic political order. Also needed is a strategy that can combine the daily demand for democracy with the steps that will trigger the exit from authoritarian rule. This two-part political problem has its counterpart in the analysis needed: reelaboration of the relationship between the development model and the political order and study of the real demand for democracy by going outside the bounds of organized discussion and rediscovering social practice and its meaning. In other words, the authoritarian regime has redefined the political space, which requires the political proposals of established actors to conform to real social demands.

NOTES TO CHAPTER 3

1. This chapter is a revised and corrected version of *En torno a la discusión de los nuevos regímenes autoritarios en América Latina*, copublished by the Latin American Program of the Wilson Center, Washington, D.C., and FLACSO, Santiago, in 1980.

2. I am referring generally to the Brazilian, Argentine, Chilean, and Uruguayan military regimes since the mid-1960s, although some characteristics also apply to other cases. At this point, I will cite only those texts that I used frequently: *The New Authoritarianism in Latin America*, edited by David Collier (Princeton, N.J.: Princeton University Press, 1979); Fernando Henrique Cardoso, *Autoritarianismo e democratização* (Rio de Janeiro: Paz e Terra, 1975); and Guillermo O'Donnell, *Reflexiones sobre las tendencias de cambio en el Estado burocrático autoritario*, CEDES Documento de Trabajo (Buenos Aires: CEDES, 1976).

3. For more on this subject, see the discussion in Collier, *New Authoritarianism in Latin America*. The term *authoritarian* is used here in a descriptive sense, without any theoretical

connotation. Later, I will introduce the distinction between military regime and authoritarian regime, but for the moment, I am using both terms interchangeably in reference to the military regimes of the Southern Cone.

4. These regimes have been defined as fascist in A. Briones, *Economía y política del fascismo dependiente* (Mexico City: Siglo Veintiuno, 1978); and in Theotônio dos Santos, "Socialismo y fascismo en América Latina hoy," *Revista Mexicana de Sociología* 39, no. 1 (Jan.–Mar. 1977). For a critique of this designation, see A. Borón, "El fascismo como categoría histórica: en torno al problema de las dictaduras en América Latina," *Revista Mexicana de Sociología* 39, no. 2 (Apr.–June 1977).

5. On the hegemonic crisis and the crisis of the compromise state, see Instituto de Investigaciones Sociales (UNAM), *Clases sociales y crisis política en América Latina* (Mexico City: Siglo Veintiuno, 1977); J. Graciarena and R. Franco, "Social Formations and Power Structure in Latin America," *Current Sociology* 26, no. 1 (Spring 1975); S. Zermeño, "Estado y sociedad en el capitalismo tardío," *Revista Mexicana de Sociología* 39, no. 1 (Jan.–Mar. 1977); and Norbert Lechner, *La crisis del Estado en América Latina* (Buenos Aires: El Cid Editor, 1977).

6. I am using the term *deepening* here in a general sense and not in the sense of a particular type of industrialization with vertical integration, as used by O'Donnell in *Reflexiones sobre las tendencias de cambio*.

7. I am using the terms *defensive* and *reactive* interchangeably here.

8. See CIDE, "La Comisión Trilateral y la coordinación de políticas del mundo capitalista," *Latin American Perspectives* 2–3 (1977–78).

9. This concept is the same one developed by O'Donnell in *Reflexiones sobre las tendencias de cambio*. He has reformulated this thesis in "Tensions of the Bureaucratic-Authoritarian State and the Question of Democracy," in Collier, *New Authoritarianism in Latin America*.

10. See the following contributions to Collier, *New Authoritarianism in Latin America*: José Serra, "Three Mistaken Theses regarding the Connection between Industrialization and Authoritarian Regimes"; Fernando Henrique Cardoso, "On the Characterization of Authoritarian Regimes in Latin America"; and Albert O. Hirschman, "The Turn to Authoritarianism in Latin America and the Search for Its Economic Determinants."

11. Alejandro Foxley, "Experimentos neo-liberales en América Latina," *Colección Estudios CIEPLAN* 7 (March 1982). English version: *Latin American Experiments in Neoconservative Economics* (Berkeley: University of California Press, 1983).

12. I am using the terms *restructuring* and *recomposition* interchangeably.

13. See the essays in Collier, *New Authoritarianism in Latin America*.

14. For discussions of these concepts, see Cardoso, *Autoritarianismo e democratização*; Instituto de Investigaciones Sociales, *Clases sociales y crisis política en América Latina*; Zermeño, "Estado y sociedad en el capitalismo tardío"; and the classic work by Barrington Moore, Jr., *Social Origins of Dictatorship and Democracy* (Boston: Beacon Press, 1966).

15. Here the theme of the "hegemonic nucleus" of the dominant coalition is posed, which I will refer to in the third part of this book.

16. See Arriagada and Garretón, "Doctrina de Seguridad Nacional y régimen militar," *Estudios Sociales Centroamericanos*, no. 21 (Sept.–Dec. 1978) and no. 22 (Jan.–Apr. 1979); and Chapter 4 of this book. See also A. Varas and F. Agüero, *Acumulación financiera, gobiernos militares y seguridad nacional en América Latina* (Santiago: FLACSO, 1978).

17. Guillermo O'Donnell, "Modernización y golpes militares," *Desarrollo Económico* 47 no. 12 (Oct.–Dec. 1972).

18. I will examine this phenomenon in the third part of this book.

19. For example, the values of efficiency, the primacy of the market and competition, and the role of private property became fundamental elements of the new ideology and culture of the dominant coalition.

20. O'Donnell, *Reflexiones sobre las tendencias de cambio.*

21. The theme of institutionalization will be treated extensively in subsequent chapters.

22. See Cardoso, *Autoritarianismo e democratização*; also his contribution to the work of the Instituto de Investigaciones Sociales (UNAM), *Clases sociales y crisis política en América Latina.*

23. See Chapter 5 on the parameters of advance of these regimes.

24. The debate of the Spanish Communist party in this regard is illustrative. See the material presented by F. Claudín in *Documentos de una divergencia comunista* Madrid: El Viejo Topo, 1978).

25. On the potential of the historical project in various cases, see Zermeño, "Estado y sociedad en el capitalismo tardío."

26. The opposition will be discussed in detail in Chapters 5 and 9.

27. The crisis of authoritarian regimes and transitions will be discussed in subsequent chapters.

28. A distinction can be made here between a military regime as such and an authoritarian regime. This distinction will be discussed in Part III.

Chapter 4

National Security Ideology and Military Regimes[1]

The point of departure for this chapter is the assumption that the ideological aspects of the new military regimes can not only provide a more complete picture of this type of domination but shed light on the specific behavior of major social actors. Consideration of the "ideological" level of the new military regimes in Latin America has tended toward one of two extremes: it is either relegated by structural analyses to second-rank importance or acquires an all-encompassing explanatory character when it becomes the particular object of study. Thus what in one case appears to be a reflection or a secondary element is converted in the other into a world that is self-sufficient and capable of arbitrarily imposing itself on a society that cannot explain how or whence it emerged. In the first instance, a specific debate on the ideological level is not possible. In the second, the debate remains encased in the self-sufficient world of discourse and concept, without outlining the specific history and the forms of domination and counterdomination expressed in these discourses and concepts.

Although this chapter focuses on the level of ideological discourse, it aspires to bring in the social mediations that make this discourse fully intelligible and to locate it within the overall process of implanting the new system of domination. I will examine only one aspect of the ideology of these military regimes, not their ideology as a whole.

The Components of National Security Ideology

"National security" is the principle invoked by military regimes at the moment of the rupture with the prevailing political system.[2] What is the meaning of this principle? The term *national security* defines the problems of survival and maintenance of sovereignty that every national state must confront. This core cannot be confused with conceptualizations built around these problems. But when these conceptualizations are transformed into systematic bodies of a normative kind, sanctioned by some part of officialdom, and converted into an object of socialization, we find ourselves in the presence of national security doctrines.

Although national security doctrines must not be confused with just any military thought or an exclusively military matter, the conception of national security invoked by military regimes is often confused with these aspects and is referred to as a particular conceptualization named "the" national security doctrine or the "modern" concept of national security. What does this particular national security doctrine involve?[3]

Three major components of national security doctrine can be distinguished. They come from various levels of thought and intellectual origins but have somehow become connected and mingled. The first level or component of national security doctrine consists of a series of abstract concepts that usually belong to social or political philosophy but in this case come from systematizations of geopolitics. The basic concepts are the nation and the state, along with the related concepts of national unity and national power.

The concepts of nation and state in this version of national security doctrine present several features worth considering. First, both the nation and the state are envisioned as living organisms that complete a "vital cycle" in which national security functions as a natural instinct. Second, nation and state are discussed as interchangeable concepts. Thus, whether dealing with the biological analogy or with approaches related to systems analysis, state and nation appear as entities larger than individuals, as totalities in which individuals are only members or subordinate parts. This relationship of whole to part is reflected in the identification of the nation with the state, which views citizens as subordinate subjects.

At the same time, this assimilation or mutual reduction of state and nation is ambivalently complex. At given moments, military interventions are justified in the name of the nation against a state that "has turned away from the lofty destinies of the Nation," thus compromising the nation's survival. But once a military regime has established itself, the state becomes identified with the nation and is charged with realizing this destiny, which may be invoked as the "common good" or by some other name. The state is viewed not as the arena for expressing and resolving diverse interests and conflicts but as the embodiment of the nation itself and the national spirit, rising above particular interests and possible conflicts. The result is that dissent is interpreted as questioning the essence of the nation.

The equated state and nation are in turn identified with the established political regime, which produces a triple identification among nation, state, and armed forces or military government. The armed forces are envisioned as the bulwark of the nation, the guarantor of its historical continuity.[4]

In this process of identification and reduction, the concept of national unity plays a key role. National unity is viewed not as the historical product of social consensus but as a fact that is "natural" and metasocial, one derived from an "essence," a "national soul," or a tradition.[5] But the tradition will not be the one imagined by the citizens, however. It will consist of freezing certain historical facts or universalizing particular features that are defined outside the freely expressed collective will. Consequently, when the collective will strays from the "essence" of the nation or from "tradition," it falls to the armed forces, the depository of that tradition, to restore order and take into its hands directly the destiny of the nation and reestablish national unity. The security of the nation therefore consists in preserving this national unity, with the armed forces being its most solid guarantee.

This concept of national unity rejects the existence of conflicts that are not the work of enemies of the fatherland or their infiltrators. There is no room here for structural conflicts. Conflicts among groups, positions, interests, and institutions are all denied or discredited as prejudicial to unity. There is no place for dissent regarding the destiny and lofty objectives of the nation; and because these goals are always defined abstractly and the nation is identified with the state and the armed forces (that is, with the government), any dissent regarding government policies is viewed as prejudicial to national unity—something that must be prevented and punished. This conception of national unity inevitably perceives a danger in democratic forms because it views them as mechanisms by which particular groups and interests can obtain and express power.

Power is the attribute that allows a nation to survive over time and hold its own with other nations. Without a substantive development in national power, a nation would disintegrate and succumb to other nations. Because each nation seeks to maximize its power, nations always confront each other as potential enemies. National power is envisioned as all the resources that a nation possesses, develops, and can mobilize to achieve "national objectives."[6] Thus development is a process destined to make national power grow. National power is composed of political power, economic power, psycho-social power, and military power, which are in turn composed of various elements also conceptualized in terms of power. Here the concept of power is abstracted from its content of domination and elevated to the rank of the nation's basic tool for realizing its objectives, without reference to the distribution of power or access to it within the nation.

The second level of national security doctrine is provided by a set of geopolitical options that can be relatively autonomous of the first conceptual component or connected with it. The second level makes explicit the historic definition of national security and constitutes the core of national security doctrine.

The place of the nation in the contemporary world, beyond its relations with neighboring nations, determines two kinds of antagonism that appear relevant to its security. The first is the antagonism between the two world powers who create blocs of nations—the opposition between East and West, the socialist world and the Western world. The second antagonism evolves between developed and underdeveloped nations—the tension between North and South or development and underdevelopment. Although both tensions are considered in national security doctrine, the emphasis and priority assigned to each are determined by sociohistorical factors that have defined national variants of this doctrine in recent years. In most of these military regimes, the East-West opposition occupies the central role. In the Chilean variant of national security doctrine, the fundamental definition of the modern world centers around the problem of confronting Marxism or Communism.

This confrontation does not take the form of a conventional external war, however. It battles against an enemy whose originality consists precisely in a subversive presence in the bosom of the nation. This struggle against subversion, against an enemy that has infiltrated society, defines the basic imperative of national security. With such an enemy, there is no room for dialogue or compromise, only the search to eliminate or totally eradicate this foe. Total war includes confronting not only the enemy per se but all those weaklings who allow the enemy to expand its influence in society. Now that democracy has proved incapable of resolving the problem, having allowed most of the nation's institutions to be infiltrated, only one alternative can again close the circle: "in the face of Marxism converted into a permanent aggression, it becomes imperative that power be invested in the Armed Forces of Order because only they possess the organization and the means for standing up to it. That is the profound truth of what is taking place in most of our continent, although some refuse to recognize it publicly."[7] Once again, the nation and its security are identified with the armed forces and with military governments.

Within a conception that defines national security in terms of subversion, the internal enemy, and the struggle against Marxism, the *problématique* of underdevelopment and development is relegated to a strictly subordinate role. This priority seems to be one of the characteristics of the Chilean version of national security doctrine.

The third level or component of national security doctrine comprises various elements of a political mechanism that shapes or implements the destiny of the nation and the state's role in it. Certain "principles" are equated with the essence of national tradition and shape the regime's official doctrine.

These principles include concepts belonging to the previously described levels of national security doctrine as well as some derived from other doctrinal bodies, a mixture occasioning appreciable contradiction. From these principles flow the national objectives, the great aspirations and interests of the nation, some "permanent" and others "current" with the degree of national power attained. These objectives are defined in abstract terms, and their attainment relates to "national strategy," which embraces the "external front" and the "internal front." As a whole, these elements create what is called the national project, to which the entire nation must be committed.[8] The national project is made known through various documents elaborated by the authority of the state, such as the *Declaration of Principles* (*Declaración de principios*) or the *Declaration of National Objectives* (*Declaración de objetivos nacionales*). Their origin gives these documents an official character that is also binding.

Beyond the variations assumed by this political mechanism on the formal level, some of its characteristic features are worth pointing out. First, principles and objectives are proclaimed by the government but are viewed as emanating from the "essence" of the nation. They are therefore viewed as the only ones possible, and they define the nation. Consequently, any disagreement with them must be the work of those who want to destroy national unity and therefore constitutes an attack on the nation itself. Once again, this time via political mechanisms, nation, state, and government are presented as one and the same. Conflict over the interests and aspirations of the nation is illegal because it violates the principle of national unity. Second, principles and objectives that are actually imposed from above are assumed to be accepted by everyone. But there is no room for citizens to participate in their elaboration. Instead, the authorities interpret national sentiment and "national interest" and impute a consensus to them. Citizens may participate only by comprehending and solving the problems entailed in attaining the "national objectives." This capacity to interpret national sentiment and express national consensus, in the absence of any mechanisms for establishing consensus, assumes the existence of certain clear-sighted groups or minorities who are better endowed by their abilities and qualities to define the "national interest." The national project thus expresses the perceptiveness of these elites, basically those oriented toward the military regime.

Historical Features

Three inherent features of national security doctrine seem relevant in analyzing its social consequences. First, national security doctrine did not originate in Latin America, even though it has acquired its full force there. It was actually elaborated in the United States from various European currents of thought and then transmitted to Latin American armies through officer-training institutions set up by the United States. The doctrine is thus maintained by the set of institutions linking Latin American armies with the U.S. Armed Forces.

This is not the place for elaborating a lengthy historical outline of the various phases of counterinsurgency doctrine and its links with U.S. policy toward Latin America.[9] It will suffice to point out that this elaboration began when Latin American countries were incorporated into the system of hemispheric defense, a process originating in the economic and geopolitical relations that developed before and during World War II and then evolved according to the division of the world into blocs. Latin America's being incorporated into one bloc inevitably caused its political-military subordination to the power dominating this bloc. But because such subordination originates in specific historical situations, it must be maintained over time, a goal that cannot be achieved without internationalizing the subordinated military force. This effort involves three basic elements in the relationship between the dominant power and the Latin American armed forces: the military supply system; the institutional system of relations through pacts, treaties, and organizational structures; and the officer-training system created especially for this purpose. The goals of this training are systematic indoctrination, standardization of perspectives, and conscious acceptance of the geopolitical and strategic options of the dominant power, that is to say, its legitimation. Such goals cannot be achieved without recourse to a systematic, homogeneous body of thought that provides a vehicle for these options and builds a sense of identity around a historical mission. This body of thought is national security doctrine. One need only consider the similarities in form and content in the versions of national security doctrine guiding various Latin American armed forces to confirm that they are the result of a systematic, internalized indoctrination.

I would nevertheless caution here against adopting a simplistic vision that would mechanically convert these assertions into a reality and view this political-military dependency as the driving force of history. The emergence of the ideology described would not have been possible if internal factors had not been present, a topic to be discussed later.

The second inherent feature of national security doctrine is its purely military development. A normative theoretical conception of the problems of the survival and sovereignty of nation-states does not have to be the exclusive domain of the military. Yet national security appears to be the particular private objective of the armed forces. The military may say that this doctrine must be understood by civilian leaders and that citizens must be involved in national security as necessary supporters. Even so, the content of national security doctrine has already been fixed, and the last bastion of the "correct national security doctrine" is the armed forces.

The exclusively military origin of national security doctrine yields certain important traits. Within it are mingled elements and categories from the distinct sources of military thought already described, but the theoretical elements and values furnished by the sociopolitical projects of civil society are not incorporated. Thus when projected in a given historical moment onto society as a whole, national security doctrine cannot avoid being a militarization of sociopolitical thought. Consequently, the categories that will absorb the contents of national security doctrine are those typical of military thinking and socialization.

This particularized and privatized aspect of national security doctrine has complex historical roots in its U.S. origins. In the Chilean case, the matter is related to the cloistering of the military, its lengthy isolation from the civilian world, and its confinement to a cultural, intellectual, and social universe reduced to technical functions and knowledge and values that are typically military. As noted, following the "military unrest" between 1925 and 1932, a system was created that made the Chilean Armed Forces dependent on civilian political power in many ways, and civilian political elites developed a general distrust of direct military intervention. The counterpart of this isolation or cloistering was the inevitable reinforcement of an identity viewed as superior to other groups, who were subject to the contingencies of civilian political life—that is to say, the development of a consciousness of being the "last bastion" of nationality and of playing the supreme role of defending the nation and its higher destiny.

Thus the purely military origin of national security doctrine reinforces two of its key features. First, it endows the military with a very limited body of knowledge that remains untouched by the findings of secularized systems of research and learning. Second, this origin gives the armed forces a conception of self and a role that allow them to assign themselves a supreme mission, especially when the dangers of conventional war have been greatly reduced.

There is also a close relationship between the foreign and the purely military origins of national security doctrine. The counterpart of the military's relative isolation from national society is its entrée into the world of international relations, although almost exclusively in the orbit of the dominant bloc to which it subscribes. Hence the military's paradoxical situation of existing in impermeable isolation within national society but having ties and dependent relations with the international dominant power. This paradox reinforces military subordination to the values and experiences transmitted through the formative and socializing institutions created by the United States.

The third inherent feature of national security doctrine is the way it unfolds within the new military regimes. National security doctrine elaborated and developed in foreign and national military institutions remains latent in relation to the larger society or, at most, provides only partial elements that can be aggregated into the political projects of civil society. But with the advent of military regimes, national security doctrine becomes an official doctrine or ideology and thus reaches its peak force. Nevertheless, these regimes should not be explained in terms of national security doctrine but in terms of other phenomena or social processes, as discussed in the preceding chapter. It is appropriate, however, to ask why this doctrine acquires such importance in military regimes.

In my judgment, the connection is rooted in the two elements that become fully activated when the society confronts a major crisis. First, national security doctrine provides the armed forces with a perception of themselves as the ultimate trustees of the destiny of the nation, the supreme guarantors of the threatened national unity, and the bastion that stands above divisions among groups in civil society. The doctrine also assigns them a messianic but practical role for saving the nation when faced with a crisis that "threatens its destruction." This first element is central to legitimizing the "rupture" of the prevailing order and for intervening in the political scene. But it is also a key element in legitimizing the military's staying in power as long as the "dangers" threatening the nation persist. Second, national security doctrine provides the military with the only body of knowledge with which the military can begin to govern—that is, it gives them the illusion of a political project. This illusion is what eventually leads critics to talk about "national security states."[10]

Thus the centrality of national security doctrine for the armed forces leads them to constantly refer to its concepts and to make them known. These elements are the only ones employed by the military for socializing the population and the only intellectual arsenal at hand for justifying the measures demanded by the system of domination. As a result, all regime measures will make references to national security, even if their connection with it is remote or their contents contradict it.[11]

Ideological Convergences and the Role of National Security Doctrine

A project for governing a society defined as being in a crisis situation cannot be based exclusively on a concept elaborated from categories of foreign socialization or developed only within the cultural and professional universe of the armed forces. Military training does not contemplate the more extensive theoretical elements needed to comprehend and act on behalf of the entire society. Consequently, military regimes attempt to fill this void with an undigested mixture of elements from other bodies of doctrine. National security doctrine alludes to a particular social actor who is the carrier of this doctrine, the armed forces. Similarly, when talking about elements originating from other bodies of doctrine, I am indicating other social actors who are their carriers. I am thus talking about a combination of elites at the apex of government, subordinated to the military, whose influence is manifested in the somewhat contradictory formation of the regime's official ideology. National security doctrine's role as the key element in this ideology reflects the armed forces' dominance in the government and the particularized and privatized aspect of national security doctrine. Which other bodies of doctrine may mix with national security doctrine will depend on the nature of the elites offering immediate civilian support for military power. The range of possibilities is finite because of the limited number of possible combinations of elites at the moment of a military coup, which yields a narrow range of "compatibilities" with the elements dominating the military cultural universe. In other words, the inadequacy of national security doctrine as an overall ideology of legitimation and as a political project or specific program make it necessary to resort to elements compatible with the military worldview from bodies of thought belonging to those civilian groups who most strongly support military power.

The result is that military regime ideology is never a "chemically pure" national security doctrine but is mixed with other conceptions.[12] All of them go back to the specific historical character of the project of domination that makes up its basis, without which the project is unintelligible. More on this subject will be said later, but for now, let it be said that what appear as alliances among classes, fractions, or groups at the sociopolitical level turn up as "convergences" between given "ideological dimensions" at the ideological level. These dimensions of convergence consist of five main concepts: the idea of national unity as the expression of an "essence," "soul," or "tradition"; a vision of national grandeur ruined by demagogy and threatened by aggression; a view of social inequalities as a natural order; an authoritarian concept of government and a critical view of democratic forms; and a definition of Marxism in theory and practice as the main enemy of society.

In Chile at least three large ideological spheres have converged with national security ideology. The first sphere consists of various nationalistic manifestations, some more traditional, others more authoritarian, each with distinct emphases. These currents have long existed in Chile, but their carriers (various civilian groups on the political Right) have garnered a prominent role in the military regime. These factions bring with them a perspective expressed in such recurring themes as "great national destiny," the sacred character of the nation, and so on. The nation is viewed as constituting a higher principle of organization to whose greatness private interests must be sacrificed. The contrasting idea of "national decadence" or the "threatened nation" is also omnipresent in the nationalist perspective, which views it as resulting from foreign activity in which opponents or dissidents are always, consciously or unconsciously, internal agents of the enemies of the nation.

What is said to sustain a nation is its unity, and the unifying principle of the nation is tradition. But the tradition stressed does not necessarily identify with the historical experience of the majority of the citizens, rather, it invokes the notion of "Christian Western civilization." This idea nevertheless allows for localizing some "peak" moments from the past to be used as the historical paradigm for nourishing national tradition. In another sense, this Christian Western tradition permits targeting Marxism as the nation's main enemy. Thus as the unifying principle of the nation, tradition creates the nation's "soul."

This idea of a national soul as an essence rising above history and the particular society (which is typical of Spanish traditionalists) is realized in the notion of national security. Once national security doctrine is conceived of as the defense of the soul of the nation, it can assume the key role in the political project: "National security thus understood emerges as a concept destined not only to protect territorial integrity but very especially to defend the national values that shape the soul or tradition, since without them national identity itself would be destroyed."[13]

Along with the traditionalist perspective, the currents of Chilean nationalism have also contributed the authoritarian perspective and the critique of liberal democracy. This critique has mixed roots that should not be confused. In some instances, it becomes a critique of the previous forms of Chilean democracy in which mechanisms favored the interests of groups and parties over the general interests of the nation, or in which executive authority was weakened or impotent vis-à-vis other powers of the state. In other instances, criticism becomes a radical critique of democracy for one of several reasons: because democracy is incapable of defending the nation against enemies who infiltrate through the democratic system; because democracy divides the nation and undermines its unity; or because democracy subordinates tradition, the immutable truth, or the wisdom of the most capable citizens to the law of numbers, fleeting majorities, or the will of incompetent masses. In all cases, the critique of democracy is associated with descriptions like "national decadence," "corruption," "demagogy and low politics," and "the destruction of national unity." From this perspective, there seems to be no solution other than authoritarian government, whether justified in purely historical terms or in more essentialist terms that approximate versions of "the divine right of kings." Depending on the current of thought, the authoritarian solution will lead to a temporary or permanent justification of dictatorship or to variations on the theme of a "new democracy."

The second ideological sphere found in military regime ideology is Catholic social thought in its most traditional forms, which lack any reference to modern developments and contradict the progressive role adopted by the Church under some of these regimes. This stream of thought becomes incorporated for two reasons. First, it is difficult to legitimize a sociohistorical project in Latin America and in Chile without referring to the world of Christian values and representations, which are reinforced by the kind of education received by a key sector of the military. Second, some small civilian groups supporting the regime from the outset are identified with certain social conceptions of Catholicism, those closest to its integrist and traditional forms. This branch of social philosophy is usually called the "Christian social conception of man and society" or the "Christian humanist conception of man and society," even though it may contradict the current teachings of the contemporary Church in Latin America. Its basic concepts are those of the person, the family, the common good, the natural right to private property, the principle of subsidiarity, intermediate bodies, and the "intrinsically perverse" character of Communism. All these concepts are incorporated into the official language and documents that become the doctrinal sources for the military regime. The principle opposing this "Christian conception of man and society" is Marxism in particular and all conceptions that "foment social antagonisms" and "misunderstood pluralism."[14]

This conceptual sphere within the official ideology has several features. First, it is juxtaposed with concepts derived from other ideologies, especially national security doctrine, to which it is subordinated. When contradictions exist between traditional Catholic social thought and the other concepts, the latter always prevail. This hierarchy becomes obvious, for example, when contrasting the concept of the person (central to the "Christian humanist" conception) as a being endowed with "natural rights before the State"[15] with a concept of the state derived from geopolitical concepts, in which individuals are subordinated to the ends of the state as parts of a whole. This contradiction is resolved rhetorically in the concept of the "common good," but the meaning gives primacy to the state over the person. Moreover, in theory as well as in practice, elements derived from national security doctrine predominate, thus reducing the concepts of "Christian humanism" to a purely formal expression.

Second and related is the legitimating role played by the introduction of this conceptual universe into official ideology. This end is well illustrated by adoption of the concepts of subsidiarity and the natural right to private property. Used profusely in official discourse, both concepts serve to endorse an economic model that diverges from the traditional canons of state intervention in the Chilean economy and hands over economic decision making to free private initiative regulated by the market. Yet the principle of subsidiarity is not applied to the sociopolitical order, where the all-embracing power of the state reigns unchecked.

Third, it must be remembered that we are dealing here with a particular variant of Christian social thought that is usually characterized as Catholic traditionalism, which favors a particular orientation toward the central concepts mentioned above. This approach is especially evident in the idea of the "common good," which is featured prominently in all official documents of the Chilean military regime. The "common good" is framed as a truth that is external to history and the nation as a historical community. Certain men or social institutions are depositories of this truth. A corollary asserts that "the end of the State is the Common Good,"[16] which means that the state possesses a truth that allows it to impose demands on a community, even if they go against the perceptions and will of the community. Thus the particular notion of the "common good" that is posed justifies and reinforces authoritarianism, an additional point of convergence with national security doctrine. This doctrine also permeates perspectives on democracy and participation. The critique of democracy assumes democratic decadence while reducing participation to its most corporatist forms. These perspectives are confusingly expressed in the ill-defined idea of a "new democracy" and in the concept of participation as limited to "knowledge of the great national problems,"[17] with the key element of decision-making having been eliminated.

One last sphere should be noted within the ideology of military regimes, one that seems less systematized precisely because it refuses to consider itself a doctrine. This sphere is technocratic thought, which was contributed mainly by elites in the state bureaucracy involved in developing and directing the military regime's economic model. According to technocratic thought, society exists in a natural equilibrium, without structural conflicts or real antagonisms. The basic principle for resolving the problems confronting a society is efficiency—that is to say, the correct allocation of resources. According to economic neoliberalism (the best-known version of techno-cratic thought), the mechanism that regulates this allocation of resources is the market. Efficiency derives from correctly applying knowledge to the solu-tion of problems. This knowledge is provided by science and technology, and such solutions do not admit the existence of conflicts of orientation beyond scientific and technological options. Technocratic thought also assigns a key role in society to those who possess this desideratum of science and technology. It is evident that this approach obscures the existence of conflicts deriving from the different positions occupied by individuals, groups, and social classes in society and in the market as well as conflicts over competing social projects arising from these positions. In this sense, technocratic thought is realized in and reinforces authoritarianism at the same time that it provides the material content lacked by national security doctrine, clothed in images of order and natural equilibriums and wrapped in the universal and unassailable mantle of science. The affinities of technological thought with the other ideologies cohering around national security doctrine in the official ideology are obvious, particularly its affinity with the principle of subsidiarity and the concept of private property as a natural right.

The convergence of diverse ideological spheres as the expression of various social alliances (whether real or desired) highlights two salient features of the ideology of these regimes. The first is the contradictory character of many of its concepts and the rhetorical resolution of these contradictions. Mentioning only some of the basic ideological contradictions yields a long list: the contradictions between the "Christian humanist" conception of the person versus the definition of the state and the nation prevalent in national security doctrine; the principle of subsidiarity versus the concentration of political power; authoritarian conceptions versus the social Christian ideal of participation; the nationalist conception versus the principles of the free market, in which foreign firms have the same rights as nationals (between political nationalism and economic transnationalism); economic privatization versus political statism; the concept of tradition versus the concept of national history; the messianic role assigned to the armed forces versus the participation of the collectivity in the national project, and so on. These contradictions emanate from one basic source: the initial lack of a theory, model, and political project capable of establishing an efficient relationship between the state and civil society that is not merely the reflection of direct power being exercised without mediations. This void is eventually filled by the appeal to "limited democracy," as will be shown in the following chapters.

Second, the contradictory character of the regime's ideological discourse is resolved by the predominance of national security ideology. Thus in the name of national security, other principles and concepts within the ideological universe are subordinated. National security, and what I call its central core, is also the locus of the effort to legitimize the regime. This theoretical primacy in one sense represents the expression of military dominance of the ruling political alliance and in another sense has its counterpart in a practical primacy. The implication is that national security doctrine becomes a kind of substitute for a political model or project. But to the degree that this doctrine is not and cannot be a political model (a design for efficient relations between state and civil society) in order to fill this function and the ideological void, the doctrine can only validate as the prevailing political project with universal appeal the context and type of domination already existing in society. That is to say, national security doctrine validates the act and effects of the military rupture of the preceding political order. What has been expressed as the product of an "emergency" (the military takeover) during the initial lack of a political model is later sanctioned by national security ideology as a permanent principle, or at least one of indefinite duration. Thus the initial "abnormality" becomes "normal."

Ideology in the Phases of Installation and Institutionalization

Until now, I have been analyzing ideology, but always establishing the necessary connections that allow it to be viewed not as a self-sufficient world but as one directly connected with the world of social processes in which it operates. This chapter is not intended to describe and analyze these processes in relation to the new military regimes of Latin America. Let us now consider only some features in the context of ideas discussed in the previous chapter.

The attempt to overcome the crisis of the compromise state and resolve the contradiction of democratization and social mobilization versus concentration and economic dependency by reversing democratization and imposing a model of capitalist restructuring confronts a set of structural requirements. These requirements consist of guaranteeing order and the necessary conditions for capitalist restructuring without the interference of social demands as well as structuring a dominant core that can make a socioeconomic project viable. This goal can only be achieved by excluding the large economic, social, and political working-class masses who were previously mobilized (assuming the passive acceptance of the middle sectors). This scenario also assumes a rupture with the prevailing political system because the new social ordering requires a long period of authoritarian domination in all spheres where emerging social demands could challenge it. The requirements are the lack of social organizations, political silence, and manipulation and control of the mechanisms of expression, socialization, and communication.

This exclusionary tendency creates severe difficulties in formulating a coherent and stable political model of relations between the state and civil society. Hence the continuing ambiguity of political power: the need to broaden the circle of support and legitimacy and the inability to do so because of the threat of an outburst of social demands. This ambiguity perpetuates itself, occasioning efforts to make the initial characteristics of the "rupture" appear normal.

It is the combination of these requirements and their effects that find their elements of legitimation in national security ideology. The difficulty in achieving a stable relation between the state and civil society, which leads to justifying and prolonging the situation of emergency, also finds its ideological legitimation and justification in national security doctrine.

But the primarily military character of this ideology becomes insufficient when the authoritarian regime seeks to institutionalize, and the regime therefore must appeal to new legitimizing principles in dealing with the passage of time, the erosion of its bases of support, and the swelling the chorus of opposition. Mere references to the "chaos and anarchy of the past" and internal subversion cannot justify indefinite continuation of a regime that proclaimed itself the indispensable recourse for overcoming a crisis and "returning to normality." Also found wanting is the heterogeneous mixture of abstract ideological ideas clustered around the core of national security. Consequently, the dominant coalition must come up with a project for society that cannot be reduced to simple "normalization."

During this phase, in which the foundational dimension becomes relevant without the reactive dimension disappearing, the dominant ideology directing the state has the three components noted: a historical critique of the development scheme and the political model of society prevailing prior to the military rupture, which are blamed for "national decadence"; a series of typically programmatic elements characterized by extreme economic neoliberalism and technocratic concepts; and finally, a vision of the future of society that attempts to resolve the Achilles' heel of these regimes—the political model—by invoking democracy, but a version "purified of the defects of the past" and thus "protected," "restricted," or "limited." These three components now shape the dominant coalition's ideological core. Within this group, ideological primacy rests on principles, values, and concepts of a programmatic kind—the ones capable of imposing a program of action. In relation to the society as a whole, the dominant ideology tends to favor elements found in the historical vision, values, and norms common to certain social strata. But all these tendencies give the dominant ideology a rather incoherent and contradictory quality, even when "partial coherences" seek to expand in society by manipulating the media.

By the arrival of the phase of institutionalizing and seeking relegitimation, the doctrine of national security has lost its systematic and coherent character as the core of the dominant coalition's ideology because it cannot account for the foundational project of capitalist restructuring and reinsertion. The emerging ideological core is tied much more closely to the necessities of legitimizing this project of late capitalist revolution. What then happens to national security doctrine? It maintains its integrity as the ideological reserve of the hard-line sectors of the regime, those anxious to return to the first phase or to establish a permanent authoritarian regime. The doctrine also serves as an ideological resource for legitimizing new waves of repression. Finally and most important, many fragmented elements of national security doctrine have nevertheless become part of the new ideological formulations of the dominant coalition in a metamorphosed form. This transformation is especially applicable in the attempt to implant a political model through various exclusionary and restrictive formulas that still invoke the name of democracy.

Conclusion

Rather than analyze the content of national security doctrine, I have attempted to explain its role as the legitimizing ideology in various phases of the new authoritarian regimes in Latin America. My intent has been to guard against an idealistic bias that turns national security doctrine into the "main enemy" by centering more on its conceptual content than on the sociohistorical project that it obscures and thus to rediscover its monolithic coherence rather than its ideological metamorphoses and functions in society.

But the ideological character of national security doctrine does not prevent it from revealing certain substantive problems that have not been resolved in this discourse and appear to be a drawback in discussing an alternative project to the actual system of domination. At least two problems brought up by this ideology should be mentioned here. The first is the national problem that was subsumed under the problem of classes in the political mission expressed by the popular movement, which impeded adequate conceptualization of the theme of the nation and its security. The second problem is the place and role of the armed forces in society, which must be conceptualized in an alternative social project as the democratic control of the armed forces by society.

NOTES TO CHAPTER 4

1. This chapter utilizes materials from two articles of mine: "De la seguridad nacional a la nueva institucionalidad: notas sobre la trayectoria ideológica del nuevo Estado autoritario," *Foro Internacional*, 19, no. 1 (July–Sept. 1978); and "Auge y decadencia de una ideología: la seguridad nacional en los regímenes autoritarios," *Revista SIC* no. 425 (May 1980), Caracas.

2. Compare the first proclamations of the military junta in Chile in September 1973 with the Decreto Ley número 1 of 11 September 1973 that corresponds to the *Acta de constitución de la Junta.*

3. Many works have been written on this subject, including José Alfredo Amaral Gurgel, *Segurança e Democracia* (Rio de Janeiro: Livraria José Olympo Editora, 1975); and Joseph Comblin, *La doctrina de Seguridad Nacional* (Santiago: Vicaría de la Solidaridad, 1977). A version that has common roots but makes original and divergent deductions can be found in Edgardo Mercado Jarrín, *Seguridad, política y estrategia* (Lima: Ministerio de Guerra, 1974). For general information, see *Estudio bibliográfico sobre Seguridad Nacional* (Santiago: Vicaría de la Solidaridad, 1977). See also A. Varas and F. Agüero, *Acumulación financiera, gobiernos militares y seguridad nacional en América Latina* (FLACSO: Santiago, 1978); and Genaro Arriagada and Manuel Antonio Garretón, "Doctrina de Seguridad Nacional y régimen militar," *Estudios Sociales Centroamericanos,* nos. 21 (Sept.–Dec. 1978) and 22 (Jan.–Apr. 1979).

In analyzing this ideology in the Chilean case, I will avoid continuous citations by listing the main texts consulted here: *Declaración de principios de la Junta de Gobierno de Chile* (11 Mar. 1974); *Objetivo nacional de Gobierno de Chile* (Dec. 1975); *Mensaje del General Pinochet del 11 de septiembre de 1976;* and *Actas constitucionales* nos. 2, 3, and 4 (Sept. 1976). I also drew on the following analyses: Alejandro Medina, "Seguridad Nacional," *Economía e Inversiones,* no. 1 (July 1975); "Seguridad Nacional: ?doctrina bélica?" in *El Mercurio,* 18 May 1976; "Teoría de la Seguridad Nacional," *Seguridad Nacional,* no. 2 (Sept.–Oct. 1976), a publication of the Academia Superior de Seguridad Nacional; Agustín Toro Dávila, *La Seguridad Nacional* (Santiago: University of Chile, Dept. of Economics, 1976); and Gerardo Cortés, "Introducción a la Seguridad Nacional," *Cuadernos del Instituto de Ciencias Políticas, Universidad Católica,* no. 2 (Feb. 1976).

It is evident that this ideology is not always set forth as a formal doctrine and that not all discussions include every component that I consider. Although these components tend to be present, the degree of coherence and expression varies. What I am presenting here is a "reconstruction" of the literature on this topic.

4. See, for example, the first paragraph and article of *Actas constitucionales,* no. 2; article 11 of *Actas constitucionales,* no. 3; and *Objetivo nacional.*

5. Compare *Declaración de principios, Objetivo nacional,* and "Considerandos" of the *Actas constitucionales,* no. 1. For a critical perspective on this subject, see Tomás Moulián, "Seguridad Nacional e institucionalidad política," mimeo, Santiago, Nov. 1976.

6. See Augusto Pinochet, *Geopolítica* (Santiago: Editorial Andrés Bello, 1974); and Medina, "Seguridad Nacional."

7. Augusto Pinochet, "Discurso del 11 de septiembre de 1976," *El Mercurio,* 12 Sept. 1976.

8. See *Objetivo nacional del Gobierno de Chile.*

9. See Arriagada and Garretón, *Doctrina de Seguridad Nacional;* Comblin, *La doctrina de Seguridad Nacional;* and Varas and Agüero, *Acumulación financiera.*

10. See Comblin, *La doctrina de Seguridad Nacional.*

11. Extensive attempts were made to publicize these concepts through the newly created National Security Academy (Academia Superior de Seguridad Nacional), required university courses, media education, and newspapers and journals.

12. On this point, I have drawn from Moulián, "Seguridad Nacional e institucionalidad política."

13. Augusto Pinochet, *Discurso del 11 de septiembre de 1976.*

14. *Actas constitucionales,* no. 2.

15. *Declaración de principios;* and *Actas constitucionales,* nos. 2 and 3.

16. *Declaración de principios.*

17. *Objetivo nacional.*

Chapter 5

The Origins, Evolution, and Failure of Military Dictatorships[1]

For more than two decades, the Southern Cone has suffered the rule of military dictatorships, beginning with the coup d'état in Brazil in 1964, followed by the Argentine military regimes in 1966 and 1976, and those in Chile and Uruguay in 1973. These regimes have occasioned considerable political interest and an abundant literature on various aspects: the longevity of some of these regimes, the impact of their repressive brutality, their common features, and their uniqueness vis-à-vis other dictatorships or authoritarian systems in Latin America. Indeed, analyses of numerous divergent characteristics have occasioned a new focus in Latin American social sciences and have redefined the old themes of authoritarianism and democracy.[2] The new literature has focused on a variety of themes: general characterizations of these regimes; their repressive forms and the resulting preoccupation with human rights; their socioeconomic projects and role in the international capitalist system; new forms of relations between the state and civil society; the impact of these regimes on daily life; the redefinition of politics and the reorganization of social subjects; the structural transformations introduced into society; the forms of resistance and opposition; the failure of the historical projects of these regimes and their crisis; and the projects of change and transition toward democratic systems.

The dictatorships in Argentina, Brazil, and Uruguay have completed their cycles and now belong to a tragic past. The Chilean dictatorship is nearing its end, even though its final forms remain unknown. All these regimes have failed in terms of resolving the basic problems of society, which is to say that they have failed as national projects. But they have also failed in terms of their own parameters and goals, in terms of their hegemonic capacity. Yet

85

they have undoubtedly achieved a lasting impact on the future development of the societies that have endured them.

It might be useful at this point to attempt a synthesis or balance sheet of the characteristics of these regimes, their evolution, and the problems they bequeath to society at the moment of transition.

Authoritarian Capitalism: A Recapitulation

Going beyond the merely descriptive features of these dictatorships, they seem to have arisen out of certain historical processes. First, they were associated with sociopolitical crises in the so-called compromise state in these countries. The specifics of each crisis depended on the degree of active mobilization of the forces of change, especially popular masses who had acquired varying degrees of social or state power or subversive capacity. This mobilizing or activating, accompanied by considerable ideological radicalizing, was experienced by the dominant sectors and large middle sectors manipulated by them as a definitive threat to their world and their mode of domination, as a crisis of survival that had to be confronted with force at whatever cost. The social crisis thus crystallized at a relatively high degree of ideological and political polarization.

The emergence of these regimes and their subsequent evolution must also be analyzed in the context of another process that is sometimes visible and sometimes hidden. This process involves the modernizing, professionalizing, and ideological control of the armed forces subject to U.S. military hegemony. Incorporation of the Latin American armed forces into the military bloc led by the United States meant adopting new equipment and new standards of discipline and organization but also being socialized according to a new ideological perspective that redefined the role of the military in society. Playing a crucial role in this new perspective were conceptions taken from national security doctrine and counterinsurgency training: the vision of a society threatened by an internal enemy (either Communism or subversion), which requires a nonconventional total war in which the armed forces become the last bastion or the moral reserve of the nation. This perspective thus defined a latent but lasting political role for the military corps that would manifest itself when historical circumstances required.

The emergence and nature of these regimes are also influenced by the processes of restructuring capitalism at both international and national levels. Here I am alluding not to the previously supposed existence of a coherent capitalist project on a world scale, one that assigns precise roles to peripheral economies in a new system of division of labor. History has proven to be far more hazardous and complex than it has been envisioned by any such scheme. The tendencies followed by peripheral economies have not been those supposedly determined by an immutable project of accumulation demanding an authoritarian state to impose them.[3]

But it is a fact that the so-called compromise state experienced a political crisis, and its development model contradicted either the democratizing in progress or the requirements of internal accumulation and its place in international capitalism. For capitalist sectors, correcting this development model in terms of the excessively interventionist role of the state or redistributive extremes seemed paramount. Although no clear course developed in this direction, a certain consensus existed among these sectors about the necessity of restructuring and deepening capitalism without the democratizing interferences suffered until then. The political crisis and its triggering provided the opportunity to make this shift. Elsewhere on the international scale, structural phenomena, capitalist cooperation and coordination, and transformations in the financial system significantly affected the direction taken by the economic models of the military regimes. Without adopting a mechanistic and deterministic perspective, it can be seen that the type of crisis in local and international capitalism and the solution sought cannot be dissociated from the origin and trajectory of these regimes.

The military regimes of the Southern Cone have combined these elements according to each national history, but with no single element being the determining factor. All these considerations point to a useful perspective in analyzing these regimes, which is to view them as historical projects, albeit ultimate failures, for resolving crises in hegemony. Analyses considering only their political structure, military or repressive character, or capitalist aspect cannot be definitive. Rather, these regimes have constituted attempts to respond to a three-part question: How to contain change that has been threatening national capitalism in each country? How to transform society in order to create a new sociopolitical hegemony? And finally, how to maintain the system of domination even when it is not possible to transform society? Each question comes to the fore according to the phase that the regime is going through.

In an earlier chapter, I argued the necessity of perceiving a combination of two dimensions at work in the authoritarian regimes of the Southern Cone. The first is the antipopular reaction, a counterrevolutionary response to a sociopolitical crisis with a heightened popular mobilization and radicalization as well as considerable disarray in economic and political structures as a result of acute social polarization. This dimension consists of a reactive or defensive response by the dominant sectors of capitalism uniting with the armed forces, and it stresses repression in various forms: eliminating adversaries, violently dismantling popular organizations, and destroying political structures. Such repression is a defining characteristic of any dictatorship, and its intensity and duration depend largely on the extent of the preceding sociopolitical crisis and its level of popular organization and mobilization.

The second dimension, which I consider specific to these regimes, is their foundational intent—their project for reorganizing society as a whole, for founding a new order, and for restructuring the bases of national capitalism. By now it should be clear that this attempt at social refoundation is not to be confused with an effort that is purely restorative, even when it involves the regaining of former privileges and powers by certain social groups. The discourse within the dominant coalition expresses this foundational intent by accentuating criticism of the development model that prevailed in the decades preceding the advent of the new regime.[4]

The simple description of "authoritarian regime" alludes to only one aspect of the processes set in motion by the military coup and does not account for the "content" conveyed by this particular regime. It therefore seems important to assert the hypothesis (with the risks entailed) that what the state is attempting in such situations is late capitalist reestablishment or restructuring.[5] Without forcing these terms, three characteristics are being stressed here: first, the nature of an "attempt," not an overall result already attained but a problematic process with diverse parameters for measuring the degree of realization or advent of a new order; second, the violent character of the rupture with the preceding political order, with certain social classes and groups obtaining access to state power, and the nature of their attempt to create a new order; and the "late" character in terms of a nation's role in an established capitalist world system and a given phase of development and international division of labor, as well as its lateness in developing national productive, social, and political forces, in which anticapitalist barriers are represented by interventions of the compromise state resulting from the heavy pressure of organized, mobilized popular sectors.

A necessary relationship exists between the repressive and foundational dimensions to the extent that destruction of the preceding order requires employing the instruments of repression over a long period. Lengthy repression is needed not only because of the previous level of social and popular organization but also because the new order's crucial problem is the difficulty in creating a stable and consensual model for a relationship between state and society.

In the foregoing characterization, I have deliberately attempted to stay away from discussions of fascism or types of dictatorships in order to concentrate less on the form of the political regime and more on the nature of its domination, which cannot be divorced from this form of regime. We are dealing with a regime, but we are also dealing with processes that permanently redefine it. To emphasize only the dictatorial feature or the suspension of constitutional guarantees (*estado de excepción*) is to locate the problem only at the level of the political regime.[6]

In general, attempts at capitalist restructuring in late-developing societies disassociate capitalism from the goal of national development. Dominant sectors do not measure the success of capitalism in terms of its capacity to resolve large national problems or to "modernize" the nation as a whole. In this sense, when I talk about the viability of capitalist development and the regimes fostering it, I am referring only to capitalism's ability to reproduce itself as a social order, which is unrelated to success in national development. This observation leads me to note that the political impact of the "failures" of these regimes is a relative matter. What these failures may mean in terms of resolving the country's problems or achieving simple economic growth is one thing; what they mean in terms of ensuring effective domination is a very different matter. Nor is economic weakness necessarily synonymous with instability or political vulnerability. The possibility of partial or total success with this type of regime relates to neither technical successes nor unachieved solutions of national problems but to the resolution of the regime's problems of producing and reproducing a new social order.

The foundational dimension must also be understood in terms of a political project. Certainly, the great difficulty encountered by military regimes in establishing adequate systems of mediation between state and society and in overtly attempting to eliminate politics often leads observers to conclude that the historical project conveyed by these regimes takes as its natural political model the indefinite perpetuation of the military regime. Nevertheless, while the processes of institutionalizing tend to ensure the maintenance of the military regime as the context for the desired social transformations, they also aim toward a particular form of "transition." But the transition is not toward democratic regimes but toward forms that are suitably authoritarian. In such regimes, the military would cease to be the titular element of formal power, but mechanisms for participation and certain political arenas would be combined with state authoritarianism, institutionalized mechanisms for exclusion, and the protective power of the armed forces.[7] Such an arrangement might appear to be the political utopia of this historical project, yet it is not sought by all members of the dominant coalition. Some sectors support the continuation of the existing military regime, and this distinction between military regime and authoritarian regime polarizes the "hard-liners" and "soft-liners" within the coalition.

All this emphasis on the "content" of domination suggests one caveat—the avoidance of sociological or economic determinism because it will obscure the factors belonging to the "regime" aspect and therefore the political elements per se that have dynamics of their own and require thinking in more complex terms about the behavior of specific social actors. These actors are never mere manifestations of historical projects, and their behavior and interactions are more circumstantial and haphazard than could be inferred from what has been said thus far. Similarly, political processes are more than the mere result of confrontations between historical projects. This complexity becomes particularly evident in analyzing crises in military regimes or transition processes dealing only with a change of regime and not with other kinds of social change. The singular characteristics of the actors, which cannot be reduced to their class dimension, and the specifically political factors come to the fore in these situations. One problem confronting opposition to these dictatorships is the difficulty in concentrating on this purely political dimension in order to trigger and direct processes of transition. Continual reference to the problems of the "content" of domination divides the opposition into factions, delays the terminal crisis of the military regime, and postpones the transition.

The Evolution of Military Regimes

The evolution of these regimes can be traced in terms of the their two dimensions by indicating the major actors and the central *problématique* facing the regime and its opposition for each phase. According to the weight assigned to each dimension, a reactive phase can be distinguished from a foundational phase even though the repressive element is omnipresent throughout as an inseparable part of a military regime. The absence, weakness, or failure of a transformative dimension can cause the regime to evolve into a phase of managing recurring crises. In such a phase, the regime is adrift and, lacking proposals for society, makes the central issue its own maintenance and survival. Finally, a terminal phase can be distinguished, which is characterized by the triggering of a final crisis that raises the central question of how the major actors in the regime will manage their exit. The most probable outcome is that these phases will develop in sequence, one after another: the reactive phase tends to coincide with the moment of regime installation, the transformative phase with institutionalizing following the inaugural period, the phase of recurrent crises with the exhaustion or failure of the foundational dimension, and the terminal phase appearing as the result of accumulated crises. Except for the terminal phase, however, no set order exists for these phases. The reactive phase can coincide with the foundational phase, which can precede it to some extent. A regime can also pass directly from a reactive phase to one of managing crises or to the terminal phase; or in moments of crisis, the regime can reinitiate a transformative phase. Moreover, elements of one phase can always be found in other phases. The military regimes of the Southern Cone all demonstrate variations in this sequence.[8] But for purposes of analysis, I will treat these phases sequentially.

During the reactive phase, the central problem for the regime is how to eliminate its adversaries and, more generally, how to dismantle the fundamental mechanisms of the preceding society. Although the regime is not entirely consumed with this undertaking, the basic element of this phase is normally repression and the main actor is usually the armed forces. The foundational dimension remains obscured while various civilian groups debate over the regime's future direction. The repressive element becomes massive, brutal, and at times efficient and sophisticated and is protected by silence in society because the traumas of the crisis leading to the coup still encourage the complicity of large sectors. An atmosphere of generalized vengeance prevails at times. The ideology predominating in the regime is national security, and the legitimizing principle being claimed is victory in a war to save the nation from chaos and anarchy.

In this phase, the opposition consists almost entirely of the sector defeated by the military coup, although members of this sector are not the only victims of repression. The opposition's main *problématique* is to survive physically, and if possible, to maintain its organizational structure. The brutal regression unleashed by the repression makes human rights almost the only ideological theme of the opposition. As a result, the main actors opposing or criticizing the regime are those organizations, groups, and public figures who rally round to denounce violations of human rights and demand protection. These circumstances explain the dominant role acquired by the Catholic Church in some cases.

Features of the reactive phase, especially repression, are not exhausted in this period; they continue in one way or another during all the other phases and have their consequences. They weigh heavily during the terminal phase or processes of transition because these later phases must confront the problems created by information concealed during the reactive phase. This situation requires obtaining justice or settling accounts as well as dismantling the repressive apparatus.[9]

Passage from the reactive phase to the transformative or foundational phase (which may partially overlap) is occasioned by a combination of factors: exhaustion of the legitimizing principles initially invoked, consolidation within the victorious coalition of a dominant core that will run the state, and initiation of tasks and policies that go beyond being purely reactive or defensive to consider a new project for society. At this point, the regime's basic *problématique* is to define a development model, a new system of relations

among the various spheres of society, and to create a political model that
will emerge as the military regime's successor in the future. Its basic content
is provided (with variations) by the neoliberal economic scheme.[10] The
basic processes are those of institutionalization, in which the possibility of
politically institutionalizing prior to periods of crisis can significantly affect
regime stability.[11] This period is the triumphant phase of economic booms
or "miracles," in which everyone is encouraged to consume. It also involves
openings from above of limited spaces and managed plebiscites. During the
attempts to define and impose the new model of society, actors emerge in
the dominant coalition as partners with the military leadership, although not
without occasional strain. These actors include technocratic sectors, groups
of business owners, representatives of financial capital, and intellectuals who
provide the discourse and strategies. At this point, the dominant ideology
is no longer predominantly military, and concepts of national security
tend to fuse with ideas from civilian groups, especially those associated
with the economic ideology. A vision of the future now impregnates the
ideological themes.

From the perspective of a dictatorship, its process of institutionalization—that is to say, creating rules of the game in various spheres
of social life that express its project for society—is always two-sided.
One side involves a power that is consolidating. But the other side is a
space, however limited, where opposition groups can reorganize and social
movements can regenerate. Thus an ongoing tension exists between the need
to postpone institutional definition as long as possible for the sake of arbitrary
rule and the need to demonstrate a situation of "regularization" to the sectors
composing the dominant coalition as a whole and often to entities that are
exerting pressure, like the Church, international organizations, and foreign
governments. It is thus normal that processes of institutionalization are
launched in moments of crisis when, due to internal debate or external pressures, these regimes can no longer resort to arbitrary power and must frame
transformations according to specific rules of the game. Institutionalization
is also accompanied by changes in the legitimizing principles. Regimes no
longer invoke only principles of war or the presence of an internal enemy
but the need for a historical mission for reorganizing society, and a call is
made in terms of military responsibility for reconstruction.[12]

In all processes of institutionalization in regimes with these kinds
of historical projects, two levels can be distinguished. The first entails
elaborating rules of the game in various spheres of society. These rules
validate as norms the structural transformations already introduced and
establish systems of relations among individuals and social groups in a given
sphere. The second level involves political institutionalization, or the process
of establishing the rules of the game for the political leadership. Thus the

first level comprises relations within society, and the second comprises the sphere of the state and its relations with society. These two levels are closely related because they are part of the same pattern of social organization that is being imposed by one sector or group within the dominant bloc.

The regime's ability to make progress in the foundational dimension and thus try to resolve the crisis of hegemony suffered by the dominant sectors depends on various factors. A particularly interesting one is the formation within the bloc that emerged after the military coup of a hegemonic or dominant core. This core is understood here to be a sector capable of universalizing its interests within the dominant bloc and imprinting a direction or content on the historical project of capitalist restructuring and reinsertion by means of the state apparatus. The concept of hegemony employed here comprises the relations within the dominant bloc, not in the society as a whole. In other words, these regimes have a problem with internal hegemony in the dominant bloc that is initially resolved by military hierarchical legitimacy but must be reframed when facing tasks of governance that go beyond the pure exercise of repression. At this point, analysis must refer to particular characteristics of a specific bloc and to the mechanisms and processes of compromise, co-optation, and exclusion through which this hegemonic core is created.

Nor is internal hegemony the dominant bloc's only problem. Its relations with society as a whole cannot be reduced to the use of force, however brutal and extensive, especially during the installation phase of the regime. It is obvious here that we are not talking about a relationship of hegemony and that these regimes do not rest on consensus of any kind.[13] Repression in all its forms is an inseparable part of these regimes, and its ongoing presence in acts or threats and its continual resurgence, even during the more advanced phases of "normalizing" or consolidating the regime, demonstrate that repression is the most basic explanation of the regime's relative stability. But other factors must be considered as well. Some relate directly to force or repression, such as the generalized and internalized fear that leads to recognizing those in power and obeying them although without accepting them as legitimate.

Other factors highlight the foundational dimension, or structural transformations representing the sectoral and heterogeneous advent of a new order introducing a mix of old and new while dismantling social organizations and models of representation. In analyzing the diverse strata of the population, one finds partial loyalties and hegemonies. Certain themes evident in some sectors and latent in others tend to become generalized and permeate society as a whole, thus acquiring forms that have common meaning. Examples of this tendency are the themes of order, efficiency, security, and even the distrust of politics, although their degree of penetration in different social sectors varies greatly. Unlike other historical experiments that sought to mobilize sectoral or partial support in the service of general politicization, the new authoritarian regimes seek to maintain passive support and general demobilization.[14] Given their origin in a highly mobilized, polarized, and politicized society, this goal requires dismantling and fragmenting the social base. Rather than attempt to integrate consensuses and support into an overall model of society, these regimes try to find interests through disarticulation in order to make the situation seem acceptable and the alternative of change seem risky or threatening. Rather than mobilize support, these regimes seek to maintain it in latent form. Rather than inculcate a doctrine, they reinforce conformism and passivity by controlling communications media and using mechanisms of socialization. The idea being promoted is that "this is the way things are now" and one must adapt and play by the new rules of the game. This approach is especially evident in the processes of institutionalization.

But this partial penetration of a project for reorganizing society through structural changes clashes with its limited capacity for inclusion, with the limits of a dependent and repressive capitalism that exacerbates inequalities, marginalizes large sectors, and postpones indefinitely the aspirations of others. Even the moments of relative success and the "economic miracles," in which an attempt is made to legitimize the regime by its results, expose its limitations, imbalances, and contradiction of raised expectations. In such moments, various forms of social opposition movements reemerge that will subsequently manifest themselves in times of crisis.

The central *problématique* for the opposition in this phase is threefold: how to prevent the consolidation of transformations that entail a loss of former gains, how to create spaces in the various spheres institutionalized by the regime or in those that it does not control, and how to provide broad expression for many scattered forms of resistance. At this juncture, the world of political parties seems to be stuck in reverse gear in a debate between maintaining old identities and learning new forms of action and in attempts to reestablish ties with a rapidly changing social base. This backward motion explains why it is usually the new social bases and organizations or those being restructured (sometimes under the protection of organizations like the Church) that take the initiative in various spheres, without any unified political expression being perceived. In this phase, sectors that initially supported the regime passively and have been adversely affected by its policies begin to gravitate toward the opposition, at least to some degree.

Passage to the phase of crisis management usually results from failure in the foundational dimension, especially in the economic base. In short, the regime's limited capacity to incorporate and co-opt civil society combines with numerous economic factors to leave the regime with no project to offer society. Economic factors include the dogmatism and incompetence of technocratic teams, the absence of a substantial project for investment, extreme dependence on external financial capital for liquidity that tends to disappear, and the speculative and plundering character of the large economic groups formed under the protection of state policies. Subsequent developments that force recourse to reactive, but increasingly incoherent and exacerbating, policies include external debt, unemployment and recession, deterioration in production, and corporative groups who pressure a state that finds it difficult to take action. The regime's major challenges in this phase are how to put out fires here and there and to ensure the maintenance or survival of the regime beyond any transformative project. This phase consequently involves many losses for the regime: abandonment of the transforming impulse, weakening of the dominant core in directing the state, erosion of regime support by corporative actors who forsake group loyalty to defend their own interests and demands, isolation of the armed forces from other sectors in the dominant coalition, and erratic and inconsistent state policies. In the foundational phase, openings and liberalizations fit in with an offensive strategy for consolidating a regime secure enough to incorporate limited new sectors, but in the phase of managing crises, such moves represent either defensive maneuvers of co-optation to share the administration of failure and crisis or moves forced by a new society that is reactivating and mobilizing. The major ideological themes again aim at stirring up fears of a return to the past, but this time in a more disorderly manner.

The *problématique* of the opposition in this phase is to unify all discontent and resistance into a movement that avoids merely transforming the regime and impels it toward a final crisis. In this phase, civil society largely loses its fear and mobilizes actively, taking advantage of the regime's weakness and difficulties in making the repressive system permanent, the dream of the military elite. During this process, which has been called the resurrection of civil society,[15] the problem arises of how to unify opposition activity. This difficulty has two facets. One is the question of linkage between the social world, with its own dynamic of mobilization and organization and a certain resistance to political groups, and the political world returning to the public arena where old organizations and leaderships reemerge. The other facet, on the genuinely political level, is the problem of coordination among party forces that were once rivals, parties that despite their shared opposition to the regime maintain divergent and competing ideological and political projects. The possibility of a unified opposition proposal revolves around differing perceptions of the nature of the regime crisis and the content of a democratic alternative form.

It is evident that there are various methods of managing crises, ranging from attempts at direct regulation to a laissez faire attitude concerned only with staying in power. Moreover, these processes do not evolve in any predetermined direction. For example, a regime in a phase of crisis management can go back to its foundational dimension. Also, analyzing the evolutions of such regimes seems to cause a shift in focus from the regime and the overall processes to the rise and dynamics of particular social actors.

Yet loss of the foundational dimension does not necessarily mean that the regime will automatically enter a terminal phase. Regimes can rock along from crisis to crisis for a long time. This pattern is most likely in cases where the regime achieved some degree of institutionalization that was translated into mechanisms and stages before the crisis. During the phase of managing recurring crises, however, institutionalization is the only element shared by the sectors in the dominant coalition.

In the terminal phase, the central regime *problématique* is neither transforming society nor merely maintaining the regime but establishing conditions for the exit of the regime's major actors (somewhat like attempting to salvage the furniture from a fire) and fixing the basic elements of the alternative regime. Unlike other contexts, the existence of relatively modern and unified armed forces and diversified middle classes with their own ideological profiles make it highly unlikely that the terminal phase will involve an insurrectional confrontation and an internal military defeat.[16] The implication here is that this phase is defined by an institutional decision by the armed forces to retire from power and thus manage the conditions of their exit, or at least negotiate them. This decision to withdraw normally involves the military's internalizing its own failure.[17] Such institutional socialization of the military's failure can be provoked by an external military defeat, by an economic crisis that becomes violently acute, or by a perception of the ungovernability of society due to intensified social mobilization. During this terminal phase, a decisive factor is the shifting of sectors that were initially favorable to the regime toward the opposition camp.

At this stage, the opposition faces a double *problématique*: popularizing and channeling a process of social mobilization that will drive the crisis into the heart of the armed forces; and at the same time, coordinating at the highest level an institutional proposal for ending the regime that will facilitate the exit of the armed forces yet ensure a democratic regime.

The process of transition—the interregnum and passage between the military regime ending and the new democratic regime being born—will be examined later. Here I will note only that it is possible to go directly from a military regime to a democratic regime without any mediating transition phase with institutions of its own. In such a case, the basic processes of transition are accomplished under the institutions of the military regime in its terminal phase. The importance of distinguishing between the terminal phase and the process of transition is to point out that the social forces and actors that can provoke a terminal crisis and destabilize a military regime are not necessarily the same ones that can ensure a democratic transition.

In the evolution of the terminal phase, the theme of the alternative to the military regime—that is, democracy—takes on different meanings that are worth noting. *Democracy* is an ambivalent referent throughout various regime phases for the diverse actors involved, like a field of dispute with many meanings that are often contradictory. In the reactive phase, democracy is invoked as the main negative referent by the military regime and its dominant actors. They want to do away with democracy and its legacy and replace it with a "new order of institutionality" whose name and content remain unspecified. Meanwhile, the early opposition invokes the name of democracy as a system of guarantees against arbitrariness and violations of basic human rights, beginning with the right to live.

In the foundational phase, a new sense of democracy emerges from the regime: democracy is the goal that will be achieved after a long period of military rule, but it will be a new democracy (as opposed to liberal democracy and the democracy of the past), one featuring a restricted political arena for participation and representation and empowered with military protection and mechanisms of exclusion. Legitimacy and historical memory prevent the regime from calling this system anything other than democracy. Here, transition means the institutionalizing of an authoritarian and exclusionary pattern. In this phase, the opposition concept of democracy tends to combine the idea of regaining a system of civil liberties and political democracy with that of opposing the consequences of authoritarian domination (sometimes in conflicting terms).

In the phase of crisis management and the terminal phase, the transition to democracy appears to sectors supporting the regime as a defensive path to a system that protects the gains and privileges obtained under the dictatorship. But for opposition sectors, the transition means ending the military regime and establishing the institutions of classical representative democracy. This meaning is shared but broadened by other opposition sectors that define the democratic ideal as including organized popular participation at different levels and the transformation of society inherited from authoritarian capitalism according to pent-up popular demands. Thus it seems that the era dominated by the military regime requires of every opposition sector a definitive reevaluation of democracy as a political form of government to which to aspire. But the question remains as to the specific meaning that should be assigned to this value in other spheres of social life—that is to say, how to define the concept of democracy as not only a form of government but a struggle against domination.

The Consequences for Political Action

The project of these regimes has targeted as its main enemies the compromise state, populist society (by whatever name it is called), and a particular way of organizing social subjects and actors that favors political action and state intervention. The utopia to which these regimes have aspired would require eradicating politics, or at least organizing a political system with restricted participation that would exclude alternatives for change—that is, an authoritarian and conservative order. Thus the military regime was not the final objective but rather the necessary historical condition for realizing the structural and institutional transformations on which to build the future authoritarian political order, usually defined as "new democracy." The basis for these transformations came from the particular model of development and capitalist restructuring that was adopted in each case.

Beyond the failure of this project, the attempt at implementing a new society has undoubtedly had a significant impact on traditional styles of political action. I will first examine changes in the politics of the Left and then problems for the political opposition as a whole under these regimes.

Perhaps the main change for the leftist opposition has been the gradual merging of two ways of perceiving the situation, which are expressed in two sources or models of political action. The drama and spectacular intensity of the reactive dimension of the authoritarian regime have led important political and intellectual social sectors to conceptualize the ascendence of these regimes as a "defeat" of the popular movement. This conception is realistic, of course, but it tends to remain encased in a situation from the past. It speaks in the name of broken tradition and ruptured continuity, in which the present is only an extraordinary parenthesis and the future is merely the recovery of a momentarily interrupted trend. This interpretation assumes that the central task is to reorganize established actors and subjects whose natures have not changed. Society is always the same, just temporarily occupied by a strange enemy who will change nothing "essential" in it. The defeated talk more in terms of errors committed or denunciations of the enemy than of new contradictions and new fields of struggle and confrontation. The triumph of the enemy is perceived solely as the negation of former gains and victories, without emphasizing the search for opportunities and the meaning of the new struggles that are emerging. Each transformation introduced by the regime is denounced more in terms of the values, principles, and institutions of the past than in terms of appeals to new alternatives that involve overcoming the present seeking to impose itself and the past as well. This perspective's core of political action consists of "recovering" what was lost, "overcoming" errors, restoring established organizations by renewing relations with a social subject that maintains its identity despite repression, and calling for accords and alliances among organizations assumed to still represent these social subjects.

Behind this perception and mode of action lies unchanged what could be called the "classical source" of leftist politics.[18] This source is based on a series of assumptions: first, a society of domination with an already determined class carrying out a historical project of overall transformation systematized by a class vanguard who create class consciousness and call on other social sectors to "join in an alliance"; second, a state that is the only focal point of political action, a situation culminating in the seizure of state power; third, a party conceived of as the most politically conscious core, as the vanguard and detachment that unequivocally express the interests of its class, consisting of disciplined and homogeneous cadres and professional activists; fourth, political action that directly projects this party onto the rest of society and whose universe is "high politics" in terms of the state; and fifth, an established theory that serves as both principle of identity and guide for action in situations that can only be illustrations and applications of this theory. This classical source is not identified exclusively with one particular political line. It manifests itself in various tendencies that are offshoots of the same trunk, even when each one perceives itself as being "correct" and the others as "deviations." This characterization therefore includes the conceptions of both the reformist and the revolutionary Left.

It must be acknowledged that this vision of politics achieved great successes in Chile in the society preceding the authoritarian attempt to reestablishing the capitalist order. This vision mobilized masses and advanced the popular movement in its struggle for equality, justice, and the transformation of society. Even in the society emerging under authoritarian capitalism there remain important spheres of social life where this kind of politics will continue to dominate, given that the attempt to reestablish the capitalist order does not change every part of society but rather reorders them into a new totality. It is for this reason that I call this source the "classical" rather than the "old" conception and mode of political action. The point being stressed here, however, is that the classical source can no longer be the dominant conception and mode of political action. Even before authoritarian capitalism emerged, this model and conception of political action appeared to be suffering a crisis, although its partial successes and the vision of possible "overall" success close at hand postponed recognizing this crisis and stifled the development of a coherent alternative model. Only the subsequent dissolution of that society and the emergence of authoritarian capitalism revealed this crisis in the classical model and created new requirements for political action.

Contrasting with this mode of perceiving and conducting politics, which at times tends to obscure perspectives for rebuilding the popular movement, is a second point of view. This vision emphasizes not the "defeat" but the foundational aspect of authoritarian capitalism, the creating of a new social order and a new state. Coexisting in this new state are processes, actors, and structures from the past (although more as the result of inertia than as bearers of the future) alongside new actors and social subjects emerging in a relationship of continuity and discontinuity with the past. Struggles are defined not in terms of old principles and conquests but as contradictions, and identities are reconstructed day by day in terms of these new struggles and claims. According to this second vision, it is not the defeated who fight but the new actors who, in the name of its struggles in various spheres of society, call for civil society to be independent from the state and for the recreation of political organizations. Although the old struggles are recognized as part of past history, they are only a point of departure for the emergent subject's new identity rather than ghosts that interfere with it. The transformations introduced by the authoritarian regime are viewed as negating the great gains in whose name they must be resisted, but these changes are also viewed as the field that will generate new contradictions, new conflicts, and new actors in the social struggle. This view recognizes that society has changed, that the military regime is not a parenthesis that will end with everyone going back to "doing the same thing that they knew how to do" before, that society has become something new that is not purely a reconstruction of the past. The issue is therefore not to revive old organizations and methods of action but to recreate them according to the changed roles and functions of the various structures. According to this vision, the basic purpose of political action is to reorganize civil society, build new relations between politics and the social movement, and recreate organizations.

The conception underlying this vision is less formalized and less full of "certainties" than the classical source. A popular subject exists that must discover and establish itself through a long and complex process. Its extent and diversity of interests are not identified with a particular class as the sole depository of universal interest a class whose role in history is already fixed. Political action is being redefined, and every sphere of social life has a political dimension that is not defined only in reference to the state: "high politics" are not the only politics. No "theory of the party" determines the relation between political parties and the social movement. Instead, this relationship must be established in a historical context: where the principle of democracy is not compromised, where the party loses its fetishistic and religious character and its mainly instrumental value is emphasized, and where the party's identifying principle ceases to be a theoretical body or a homogeneous social base. The relationship with theory is also problematic.

"The" theory no longer exists because theory is not a monolithic block of truths that are defined forever. Rather, theory is only one of various points of departure that demand a rational and critical attitude, investigation of historical reality, and an apprenticeship in divergent theoretical fields. All these characteristics make this new modality of political action problematic. Moreover, this modality does not create a homogeneous political line but instead encompasses many diverse positions that arrange themselves in factions, tendencies, and organizations.

Many of the difficulties encountered by leftist opposition movements to authoritarian capitalist regimes derive from this ambiguity, from the coexistence of the classical and the new perspectives, the two conceptions and modalities just described. Structures and actors from the past survive without losing vigor, and new ones tend to emerge. Some battles are fought to prevent the arrival of a new order in certain spheres while others are fought amidst an already established order. Some elements resist what the military is trying to impose while others contradict what has already been imposed. Some defend what has already been won and is perceived as threatened while others seek vindication in future conquests. But this coexistence itself has already formed a precarious new order that has arisen out of the dismantling of the old order and the partial advent of the new. It is therefore difficult to bring into focus and project a clear image of a society altered in this way. Projecting a utopian alternative is even more difficult because the diagnoses are confused and alternative proposals are colored by the memory of the pre-authoritarian society. Thus the tension between the classical and the new modes runs through all political organizations and every detailed debate about which political line to follow.

Yet each source plays a particular role in the evolution of the military or authoritarian regime. During most of the repressive phase of the regime or its moments of crisis, the classical source or model of political action will tend to acquire greater force. But during the primacy of the regime's foundational phase, the emergent source or model will get its best chance to unfold.

In looking at changes in this type of regime not as internal shifts but in terms of what the opposition can do, it is worth recalling that the kind of politics practiced by the Left in the pre-authoritarian society now needs reformulating. As noted, the leftist political project generally consisted of organizing the popular and social base institutionally (mainly through labor unions), interconnecting these organizations with political parties through a strata of national leadership that served as intermediaries between organization and party, pressuring the state with claims, and proposing the alternative project of socialism. But under authoritarian capitalism, these organizational and party ties as well as their role as the contact with the state for making claims or demands have suffered substantial changes. Similarly, the invocation of socialism has lost its relevance. Thus it is impossible to imagine the pure "adaptation to new circumstances" by the former model or political project of the Left.

The temptation to adapt to the "new circumstances" is experienced by all opposition political forces, not just the Left. It is manifested in the tendency to consider political action and the struggle against a dictatorship as a unitary process in which the four dimensions of action (maintaining the organizational structure, eliminating the dictatorship, creating a postauthoritarian political alternative, and reorganizing civil society democratically) are viewed as a single line of action. This tendency in turn assumes that resolving any one of these problems will automatically solve the others. Thus achieving organizational survival is often assumed to mean democratically reorganizing civil society, or elaborating a consensus on a postauthoritarian alternative is viewed as resolving the problem of eliminating the dictatorship. What these regimes actually seem to demonstrate is a dissociation among these dimensions of opposition action, in which resolving the problems of one dimension does not imply satisfactory resolution of problems in other dimensions. Tensions also exist among the dimensions, inasmuch as each one favors different kinds of action and social forces.

Actually, it is possible to think of party and organizational maintenance or reconstruction as a "zero level" or minimum. The struggle to eliminate the dictatorship or provoke its fall can be thought of as a dimension that favors strategic problems and the forces capable of resolving them. The search for a postauthoritarian alternative can be thought of as the dimension that favors political organizations, pacts, and alliances at the elite level. Finally, in the dimensions of redemocratizing or democratically reorganizing civil society, three processes can be distinguished: constructing autonomous organizations and social subjects, resisting or obstructing transformations imposed by the dictatorship, and achieving democratic advances in society under the authoritarian regime. On examining the histories of opposition movements to this type of authoritarian regime, one realizes that in many cases the impossibility of eliminating or defeating a dictatorship does not mean that great advances were not made in the daily struggles to resist the transformations pushed by the dominant coalition, to create a popular force, and to achieve democratic gains within civil society.

Merely projecting the old political model of action onto the new circumstances created by the military regime can lead the opposition to favor dimensions of action such as rebuilding the parties functionally and seeking top-level political coordination to develop a postauthoritarian alternative. This approach seems to be the usual one, given the repressive conditions of the military "rupture" and the preceding political polarization. In the first period of the military regime, opposition action concentrates on these dimensions and on limited struggles against the regime's repressive measures and transformations. At this point, two implicit assumptions are operating: first, the illusion that the dictatorship will quickly collapse as a result of weakness, intrinsic contradictions, or international factors isolating the military regime; and second, a lack of awareness of the military regime's historical project of transformation. These two assumptions delay the debate over strategy and allow the tasks of democratically reconstructing civil society to be forgotten. Only after the illusions have faded does the debate over strategy tend to become important. It also comes to the fore with the generalized perception of a transformed and disarticulated society whose bases for organizing social forces and actors have radically changed.[19] For these undertakings, however, the classical model of political action is insufficient and unrealistic. Such undertakings demand new modes of action that are unknown to class politics. Under these circumstances, reestablishing the political opposition becomes unavoidable. But the critique of traditional politics should not fall into a sociological reductionism that ignores the strictly political dimension requiring elite, institutional, and instrumental phenomena as well as cooperation, coordination, and negotiation. These requirements are especially central to processes of transition, whose success basically depends on the primacy granted by various actors to specifically political aspects belonging to the "regime" dimension. This aspect is sometimes forgotten when talking about "refounding" politics.

The challenges that each dimension poses require functional forms and styles of action that are extremely varied and diverge from the linearity of traditional political action. The formula of social organization interlocking with the political parties that pressures the state—the populist formula—ceases to be the only, or perhaps even the predominant, formula for redefining the terrain of politics and its mode of action and organization. Yet although a political option must consider and address the four dimensions as a whole, the specific conditions of each military regime and the preceding society can certainly make one dimension a precondition for realizing the others. It is thus possible that in situations of extreme disarticulation, resolving the strategic dimension or the postauthoritarian alternative will require a long period of stressing the dimension of redemocratizing society (what I call the "invisible transition"), so that real social groups can be involved, not merely the top level of a highly socialized political class. Here again, one can see that when the reactive phase of the regime predominates, or in situations of crisis or transition, the appropriate dimensions of action are those favoring organizational forms and styles from the more classical or historical sources. But this observation does not imply postponing the tasks of reorganizing civil society, which are absolutely necessary due to the rupture with the previous world caused by a military or authoritarian regime. Conversely, predominance of the foundational phase of the military regime will necessarily correspond with predominance of the dimension emphasizing redemocratization of society, the creation of social subjects and actors, and political refoundation.

Transitions to Democracy

The problem of transitions from dictatorships to democratic regimes have been placed at the center of discussion by several developments: the failure of the military dictatorships, the struggles carried out by opposition movements, the international climate, and the eventual change of almost all these regimes to political democracies.[20] With this shift in focus, the major theme becomes democracy. Whether "the" alternative involves self-critical reformulating of a theoretical nature or imputing a general sense of resistance and struggle against the authoritarian regime, all such discussion seems to assume the operation of a natural law similar to the one that ineluctably destines a traditional society to become a modern society: according to this "natural law," the inevitable outcome of a military or authoritarian regime must be a democratic political order.

But "transition" and "democracy" are ambivalent themes that have different meanings according to the national context and its various actors. In this sense, it is important to maintain the distinction between phases of institutionalization and transition, even when their respective internal dynamics can lead from one to the other. *Political institutionalization* is understood here to mean the processes through which a given regime fixes its own rules and norms. It is usually the phase that follows the reactive period, its duration varying according to each case. *Transition* is understood as those processes by which a country goes from a given authoritarian regime to a distinct political regime.

In terms of the processes of political institutionalization, at least two major categories can be distinguished. The first includes the processes by which the regime simply passes from a dictatorship without rules to one that establishes its own rules, still maintaining the essential features of command organized at the time of the coup. The second category involves the processes that found a political regime differing in some respects from the command organized at the time of the rupture but maintaining the authoritarian pattern. The difference between the two categories is that the first case constitutes the self-regulated conversion of the "period of emergency" into a period of normalcy while the second involves an attempt to create a regime that can generate mechanisms for limited participation and resolve problems of succession internally without abandoning its exclusionary and authoritarian character. Both processes differ from those of transition in that institutionalization involves some form of regime consolidation, even when an appeal is made to new principles of legitimacy, while a transition involves a change from an authoritarian regime to a different kind (democratic or not), which can be more or less gradual according to the case. The "openings" (the creation of arenas for representation and participation) and the "liberalizations" or "détentes" (attenuation of the authoritarian or repressive pattern) can be formal or informal and take on various meanings according to whether they are part of a process of institutionalization or transition. Interconnections undoubtedly exist among all these processes, and what begins as institutionalization can lead to a transition and vice versa. It seems useful nevertheless to maintain the distinction for purposes of analysis.

Transition processes can respond to collapses caused by phenomena that may be either accidental or international. In such cases, the new regime being installed does not necessarily have any continuity with the political alternatives that were being set up in society and is therefore relatively unpredictable in behavior. The processes of transition that respond to internal causes can result from various sources: a process of internal erosion and disarray within the dominant coalition, a triumph of opposition forces, a process in which the dominant coalition is partially consolidating its rule by inviting various social sectors to participate in a new political order, or a combination of these factors. Forms of transition can range from some kind of insurrection to gradual programs for the medium or long term offered by the military regime, formal agreements between the forces of the dominant coalition and opposition sectors, or some combination. These aspects, however, lie beyond the scope of this book. What I wish to examine are some of the problems encountered in analyzing transitions in the regime type being studied here, especially in dealing with ongoing processes that have no predetermined outcome.

One problem is the tendency to dichotomize analyses of transitions from authoritarian regimes. Thus the dichotomies of rural-urban, underdeveloped-developed, and traditional-modern are now joined by the new dichotomy of "authoritarian-democratic." But viewing social processes as the development of phases or stages heading toward predetermined goals reduces social analysis to studying the "requirements" or "obstacles" for fulfilling these stages, thus limiting analysis of historical action to the way in which individuals or actors adapt or react to a history whose meaning they do not create. When starting with a postulated goal, meanings are assigned to actors and processes whose real significance can be totally different. Various contradictions and conflicts tend to be subsumed into "the" contradiction or conflict that is central in terms of the political regime—authoritarianism versus democracy—and are consequently not analyzed according to their own significance and potential. Struggles against a dictatorship in overall terms—for human rights, freedom from state interference, better living conditions, or satisfaction of basic needs—are not always viewed by their agents as fighting for a particular political regime. Imputing this meaning to all such struggles can therefore distort the historical truth about social demands and movements. To put it another way, the struggle for political democracy is only one of the struggles going on under these regimes, not "the" struggle. Analyzing the meaning and specific priorities of the struggle in each society requires shifting one's perspective from the dynamics of the regime to the diversified behavior of social actors, from the "alternatives" proclaimed by ideological discourses to the "demands" created in society. Thus democratization of society and transition to political democracy are processes that have rhythms, dynamics, requirements, and social agents that may or may not harmonize among themselves and may coexist without necessarily being associated.

A contrasting liberal conception, which also contributes to a particular dichotomy and a certain evolutionary vision of society, tends to perceive all the internal processes of authoritarian or military regimes that are called "openings" as indicators or points in a predetermined transition to a standard democratic regime. Again, the social dynamic is prescribed, and an "external" sense is imputed to the processes by a predetermined goal.

In sum, it is neither an immutable truth nor an inevitable historical consequence that the response to or way out of an authoritarian regime must be a democratic political regime. Neither the internal processes of the regime nor the nature of resistance and opposition movements expressing social demands assure such an outcome. The analyses of intellectuals and the aspirations of politicians may not define the outcome of social struggles, despite the best of intentions. The relationship between aspirations and outcomes is a field open to political action.

But despite all these perplexities and paradoxes, the democratic political order continues to be the form most favorable to the development of popular demands. Moreover, it tends to be the only universal and nonclassist or nonsectoral logic of a national type that can oppose particularistic authoritarian domination. The result is that today, unlike other moments in history, political democracy is valued as an end in itself rather than as a means to be abandoned when a better means appears. This view implies for many a thorough settling of accounts with a theoretical tradition that relegated political democracy to a historical means that could also be an obstacle to social transformation and therefore dismissed.

In speaking of democracy here, I am referring to a specific type of political regime and not to a form of society.[21] The democratic regime is characterized by several features: respect for basic human rights and guaranteed civil liberties, the rule of law, principles of popular sovereignty exercised through universal suffrage, alternation in power, political pluralism, competitive elections, the division of state powers, and so on. Thus when I speak of transition, I am referring only to a change of political regime that does not involve changes in other dimensions of society. It is evident that this definition poses the theoretical problem of the compatibility between a type of domination, a form or phase of capitalism, and a viable democratic regime. In other words, the problem is whether it is possible to dissociate a political transition from deeper transformations in society as a whole, given the particular nature of the military regimes being discussed and their having been a vehicle for a project of social reorganization that seems to contradict all forms of democratization. This problem, however, cannot be analyzed on a "structural" level because it requires studying the formation of political dimensions and forces and the way that they define their interests, values, and aspirations at given moments in history. Thus these transitions are not "revolutionary" because of the temporal dissociation between regime change and more general social change, between transition and overall democratization. This dissociation implies that political democracy appears as a precondition for democratization and structural changes in society, which are not part of the transition but part of the consolidation of political democracy once the transition has ended and political democracy has been established. The transition, then, lasts from the final crisis or terminal moment of the military regime until democracy is established. The distinction between the phases of transition and consolidation seems crucial because the factors, actors, and processes that compose these phases tend to be different, even when actors in some transitions raise issues appropriate to the period of consolidation. Such overlap is inevitable because of the mingling of concepts of democracy and democratization in these countries. Analysts and political strategists should nevertheless try to treat them as distinct issues.

If no "seizure of power" or internal military defeat occurs (no elimination or expulsion of those in power), then the decision is made by the armed forces to retire from power. But such a decision is forced or precipitated either by external factors or by popular and political pressure from opposing factions. This kind of transition entails a complex combination of four processes. The first is the breakdown and isolation of the governing core following the erosion of support from civilians who no longer feel that their interests require the continuation of the military regime. The second factor is popular pressure and mobilization oriented not only toward rebuilding social forces and organizations but toward massively supporting an institutional formula for replacing the dictatorship (such as elections, a plebiscite, or constitutional reform). The third process is a set of negotiations, explicit or implicit, between those in power and the political opposition regarding the institutional "exit," in which those in power seek to preserve their institutional interests, assure impunity for crimes committed, and maintain certain authoritarian enclaves. Meanwhile, the political opposition seeks a new constitution for the country, disappearance of these authoritarian enclaves, prompt and safe free elections, and the inclusiveness of the political system. Fourth, these transitions normally involve mechanisms that can resolve the conflict between the regime and the opposition (such as elections and plebiscites) as well as arbitrators acting above the interests of both sides, pressing for a democratic solution.

The Failure of Military Dictatorships and Their Legacy

The military dictatorships of the Southern Cone end or move inexorably toward their end as a result of a double failure. The first failure is their inability to resolve any important national problems, such as economic stagnation, external dependency, unemployment, growing inequality, misery, and disintegrating social relations. In those countries where a modernizing impulse previously existed, it has not extended throughout society as a whole, greatly aggravating internal polarization. But this failure in terms of national project also creates a failure in terms of a class or hegemonic project. These military regimes have actually failed in terms of their own parameters and dimensions. They have succeeded neither in decisively dismantling the preceding society nor in establishing a new political order as the culmination of the transformations introduced in society. In one form or another, politics have survived, and the old organizations and actors have achieved some degree of continuity with those emerging during the military regime. Thus the armed forces end up retiring to make way for relatively classical and familiar political forms.

But the failure of both the reactive dimension and the foundational dimension—the entire historical project of these regimes—does not mean that the societies involved have not suffered changes and transformations. Nor does the transition toward democratic regimes imply that there is nothing new under the sun or that everything picks up where it left off before the dictatorship. On the contrary, these regimes leave a profound imprint on societies that have been transformed and to some degree have ceased being what they were before.

This attempt at reestablishing the capitalist order is a problematic process that sets up for the dominant coalition what might be called a spiral of parameters. The first parameter is disorganizing the opposition forces as part of the process of taking power. The second step consists of introducing structural transformations in certain spheres of society that generate new forms of social relations. The third is expanding these new forms of social relations into society as a whole so as to ensure their survival. The fourth is consolidating and maintaining this new system of social relations through a consensual political order that establishes accepted rules for resolving limited conflicts within the new system.

Thus the transformation of society attempted by the project of re-establishing the capitalist order through the authoritarian regime attains different levels of accomplishments. One level consists of structural changes, the products of altering the development model, which are especially visible in the differential weight of economic factors in the agrarian structure and elsewhere.[22] Accompanying the changes in the development model are social transformations in various spheres. These transformations involve change at the institutional level itself that is expressed in both the political sphere and civil society. But this second level is not a mere reflection of the first, a simple adaptation to the requirements of a model of accumulation that can be explained in terms of the current phase of world capitalism. Although many of the institutional changes are undoubtedly part of this "adaptation," many are also politically, culturally, or ideologically rooted, and their logic must be sought in these realms as well as in the economic dynamic.[23]

In any case, the structural and institutional levels represent only the visible part of the iceberg. Even an exhaustive inventory of the changes produced on these levels, however spectacular they may be, does not necessarily account for what happens in the hidden part of the social iceberg. Perhaps it is here that the foundational or "revolutionary" nature of these regimes functions in reordering the way that a society is set up as a society, beyond the facts of its geography, population, and resources. Specifically, this process involves transforming the bases that make possible certain ways of structuring social forces and movements and eliminating a kind of relationship between civil society, political regime, and the state that was typical of various forms of populism and the compromise state. It is probable that in each case, the "backbone" of society (the manner in which social aggregates were evident as political-social forces and movements) has varied, as have its forms of disarticulation.[24] But the core of the transformations introduced by these regimes is the reformulation of modes of establishing political-social forces. It is possible that these regimes may stop halfway toward refoundation and become mere crisis managers, or simply fail before the emergence of any new society in a strict sense. But in any case, a death blow has already been dealt to the society that preceded the authoritarian regime in that the combination of the "old" with the "new" has already created a new type of society.

In this sense, social change seems to have proceeded in two different directions, according to the country involved. One direction involves an incomplete modernization in which an advance in industrialization, the presence of the state, and the creation of structural bases for the emergence of new social forces have combined with policies maintaining stagnation and the marginalization of broad sectors.[25] Even so, the existence of spaces for representation has allowed a certain complex comparing and combining of the old and the new. Social conflict during the regime's moments of economic and political crisis and in the transition takes the form of confrontation over the costs and benefits of this perverse kind of modernization. The second direction is characterized by stagnation and retrogression in industrialization, reduction of the state's role in society, and the elimination of all spaces for public representation.[26] This trend leads to a major weakening and to shrinkage of the structural and institutional bases for establishing the old sociopolitical forces and actors, without anything new emerging to fill their role. Here the problem arises of recovering collective identities and representation, and as a result, the theme of the transition to democracy is redefined as a process of rebuilding the nation.

With variations according to case, the destructive impact of the reactive dimension combined with the disarticulating effects of the transformative dimension leave a heavy legacy from these military regimes. Having to deal with it undoubtedly exacerbates the usual problems during transition from one regime to another because such a transition then coincides with a period when a new era or a new type of social relations and organization are being founded.[27] This situation is analogous to the challenge presented in the past by the collapse of the oligarchical order and the setting up of the middle-class order or the compromise state—both raise the issue of whether the social forces are capable of constructing this new order.

In this context, it is worth mentioning some of the challenges posed by the failure of these dictatorships as problems for consolidating a democratic system, difficulties that will not be resolved by the transition. For example, there is the problematic presence of the armed forces, who were not defeated in an internal confrontation and have preserved their organizational autonomy, institutional and armed resources, and capacity to exert pressure. Their weakness at the point of transition, sometimes due to an external military defeat, and their mandatory retirement from power in no way signify any substantial change in the armed forces' vision of society or their perception of their role in it. These armed forces have adhered to democracy only because of calculated interests or because they were forced to. They therefore remain a permanent threat to democratic stability, a situation that requires a thorough transformation of military forms of organization, socialization, and relations with political power. The crux of this transformation would appear to be breaking down military impermeability to civil society.[28]

This precarious kind of support for democracy is not limited to the military sector but spans key segments of civil society, especially the capitalist class. These sectors and the Right appear to be at most only tactically inclined toward a nonmilitary regime, in hopes of resolving under more favorable policies their problems stemming from the economic crisis. This attitude is attested by their behavior toward the repression and the elimination of liberties during the military regime and also by the absence or weakness of parties representing these sectors independently of military power and pressing for its end. Like the armed forces, these sectors represent the sword of Damocles hanging over a new democratic regime, which must also confront profound transformations of the capitalist system in order to count on popular loyalty and support.

Nor is the persistence of nondemocratic enclaves the only problem confronting regimes that succeed military dictatorships. They must also face crises in the development model and the legacy of a social organization produced by military power and a neoliberal economic scheme. A return to the economic model that characterized the compromise state seems unlikely to resolve problems of employment, dependency, growth, and redistribution. The drawbacks and bottlenecks that accompany the old model are already well known. Yet the neoliberal scheme attempted by the dictatorships has provided no solutions for these problems either. Thus the economic issue remains, and current critical awareness of the problems confronting industrial society will not allow naive or easy solutions to be floated with much success.

At the same time, these new regimes must resolve old problems on other levels that have been aggravated for decades as well as problems recognized recently by advanced societies: preserving the environment, creating spheres of collective participation and decision-making, recognizing the emergence of new social forces that initiate their own processes of liberation from old restraints and forms of domination, drastically changing the use of resources, redefining the relationship between state power and civil liberties, and so on. Nor can some of these challenges be postponed while others are overcome. All these pressures weigh simultaneously on the emerging democracies. Yet establishing a base for development, a model for social relations, and an image of what society wants for itself all involve a consensus that runs much deeper than simple agreement on the rules of the game or the institutions of political democracy. Moreover, the new regime must cope with an aggravating factor that did not exist when the development model was redefined in the 1930s: a democracy in which the masses have already consolidated. As a result, reaching a consensus on the model of development and social organization that favors the stability of the political regime is not easy.

This difficulty in turn raises the problem of relations among the social and political forces making up the democratic coalition opposing the military regime, a coalition whose accord revolves around confronting a common adversary. Ahead of this democratizing coalition, with its diverse motivations, lies the indispensable need to build a progressive coalition for transforming society that can ensure the viability of a new model of development and social organization.[29] This future coalition is still uncertain and includes sectors that in the past demonstrated antagonistic tendencies toward one another, such as certain middle sectors versus the popular masses, or in political terms, the parties of the Center versus those of the Left. Often, the processes of renewing and relinking political organizations to an emerging social base (largely made up of young people) stop halfway when the transition processes begin. Thus the internal renewal of politics and long-term cooperation and coordination to ensure democratic stability remain as pending challenges for regimes that are born when military dictatorships end.

NOTES TO CHAPTER 5

1. This chapter was based on a revised and enlarged version of my article "Transformación social y refundación política en el Cono Sur de América Latina," *Teoría* 6 (April–June 1981), a journal published in Madrid Spain. I have updated the English version by introducing various elements from the first chapter of my book *Dictaduras y democratización* (Santiago: FLACSO, 1984), which was published in a reduced version entitled "The Failiure of Dictatorships in the Southern Cone" *Telos* 19, no. 3 (Summer 1986). I have also added several paragraphs from the original Spanish version, *El proceso político chileno*, from Chapter 6 (which has been eliminated in this version) and Chapter 11.

2. See the references cited in Chapter 3.

3. See *La América Latina en el nuevo orden económico internacional*, edited by C. Portales (Mexico City: Fondo de Cultura Económica, 1983).

4. I will explore this point further with reference to the Chilean military regime in Part III.

5. The use of these terms may seem excessive in view of the weaknesses or the collapse of these regimes. In any case, I am talking about "attempts." The term *counterrevolutionary* does not account for the project of creating a new social order in that it alludes only to what I call the "reactive dimension."

6. It should be recalled that the term *political regime* is understood here as the institutional system of mediations between the state and civil society.

7. A military regime can be considered as a type of authoritarian regime. Or a regime can be called "military" when the armed forces directly control the power of the state but

"authoritarian" when the armed forces maintain patterns of repression and exclusion but are not formal officials of state authority, although they exercise some type of indirect control over it. Throughout this book, I have used the two terms interchangeably except when otherwise indicated. Passage from a strictly military regime to an authoritarian type of regime is what the Chilean authorities call a "transition." I prefer to term it *institutionalization* and reserve the term *transition* for the process of regime change.

8. As will be shown in subsequent chapters, the Chilean case demonstrates this evolution most clearly, with a primarily reactive phase between 1973 and 1976–77, a mostly institutional phase from 1976–77 to 1980–81 culminating in the Constitution of 1980, and a phase of crisis management since the middle of 1981. The period in Argentina following the Malvinas War is a classical illustration of a terminal phase. Brazil has evidenced a largely reactive phase some years after the regime's inaugural phase.

9. This point is illustrated by the terminal phase of the Argentine regime, which included the debate over detainees who disappeared.

10. See Alejandro Foxley, "Experimentos neoliberales en América Latina," *Estudios CIEPLAN* 7 (March 1982). English version: Latin American *Experiments in Neoconservative Economics* (Berkley: University of California Press, 1983).

11. This point has been illustrated in Chile by the establishment of a constitution prior to the economic crisis. The Argentine experience with the Malvinas War exemplifies the opposite—a crisis without previous institutionalization.

12. The concept of institutionalization is used here and throughout this book in a precise and restricted sense.

13. The concept of hegemony used in this book falls within the tradition defining hegemony as the capacity of a system of domination for establishing cultural direction and relative consensus beyond the component of coercion.

14. Some of the ideas presented here have been taken from the works of Juan Linz, without necessarily accepting all his conceptualizations. See in particular Linz, "An Authoritarian Regime: Spain" in *Cleavages, Ideologies, and Party Systems*, edited by Erik Allardt and Yrjo Littunen (Helsinki, Finland: The Academic Bookstore 1964); and Linz, "Totalitarian and Authoritarian Regimes," in *Handbook of Political Science*, vol. 3, edited by Fred I. Greenstein and Nelson W. Polsby (Reading, Mass.: Addison Wesley, 1975).

15. Guillermo O'Donnell and Philippe Schmitter, *Transitions from Authoritarian Rule: Tentative Conclusions about Uncertain Democracies* (Baltimore, Md.: Johns Hopkins University Press, 1986).

16. In other cases, as in Central America, the end of a dictatorship can coincide with the beginning of a social revolution.

17. It is also possible that this outcome can be foreseen in the previously established time frames for institutionalization, in which case the decision to retire must involve deviation from these time frames. Frequently, the passage to a terminal phase is triggered by a dramatic event, such as the Malvinas War.

18. I am basically referring to a Marxist Left like that in Chile. In other situations, the classical source derives from the populist Left, which introduces several variations.

19. The sequence outlined here can vary in each national case, but that would not necessarily alter my observations. What has been described fits the Chilean case, which I will elaborate in another chapter.

20. For a complete analysis of these processes, see the volumes edited by Guillermo O'Donnell, Laurence Whitehead, and Philippe Schmitter, *Transitions from Authoritarian Rule: Prospects for Democracy* (Baltimore, Md.: Johns Hopkins University Press, 1986). O'Donnell and Schmitter's *Transitions from Authoritarian Rule: Tentative Conclusions about Uncertain Democracies* is especially important for the discussion that follows.

21. I am attempting only a minimal conceptual clarification here, which explains the schematic nature of the observations that follow. These ideas have been developed in more detail in my book *Reconstruir la política: transición y consolidación democrática en Chile* (Santiago: Editorial Andante, 1987), chap. 1.

22. Some examples in the Chilean case that I will examine later are the shrinking proportion of the industrial working class in the working population, the smaller proportion of the middle sectors connected with the state, and the dwindling agricultural proletariat.

23. The changes in the systems of education, health care, social welfare, and labor relations are examples of institutional change in Chile that will be discussed in Part III.

24. In Chapter 1, I defined what I call the backbone of Chilean society.

25. Incomplete modernization seems to apply to Brazil in terms of structural transformations. See Fernando Henrique Cardoso, "Dependencia y democracia," mimeo, Mar. 1983.

26. The Chilean case illustrates this direction. See J. Martínez and E. Tironi, *Las clases sociales en Chile: cambio y estratificación, 1970–1980* (Santiago: Ediciones Sur, 1985).

27. The alternative is permanent instability.

28. This problem is illustrated by the policy toward the armed forces adopted by the democratic government in Argentina after Alfonsín took office.

29. This aspect is illustrated by the relations between Peronism and Radicalism in Argentina or by those between the Christian Democrats and the leftist parties in Chile.

PART III

The Chilean Military Regime and the Prospects for Democracy

Chapter 6

The Emergence of a Historical Project[1]

The Effects of the Crisis of Origin

The Chilean military regime seems to have fully manifested both the reactive and foundational dimensions typical of such regimes, even though the foundational dimension began to wane in 1981. As for the reactive or defensive dimension, the regime's primary objectives have been to block the radicalized popular mobilization from the Popular Unity period, to dismantle its organizational bases, and to establish "order." The legal and institutional formula employed by the regime has been the "state of emergency" in all its variations.

As described earlier, at the end of the UP government, Chile experienced a crisis that had two major components. One involved a breakdown in the capitalist system without its being effectively replaced by an alternative system. This process was manifested as much in operational difficulties in various spheres of daily life as in the overstraining of national government and its capacity to run the country. The other component of the crisis was expressed in the intensity of political polarization: the organizational level attained by popular sectors and their radicalization; intense mobilization of middle sectors for whom the political system had lost its legitimacy; and a deinstitutionalizing of political action by key sectors of the Chilean Right. This situation was compounded by several factors: the high degree of popular organization and mobilization, the capitalist class's fearful sense of losing all its power, the tacit or explicit support of the Right by middle sectors and the political Center (mainly factions of the Christian Democrats who supported overturning the political regime even while invoking democratic values),

117

and disarray in the capitalist system. This combination of factors produced at least three implications worth discussing.

The first is the range, depth, and duration of the repression, which reached the most extreme and brutal levels. The military aspects of this repression and its destruction of the prevailing order are well known, both in violating individual and social rights and in destroying the system of mediations between state and civil society—the political regime in its broad sense.[2]

The second implication is the crucial and radical role assigned to the tasks of "normalizing" or "stabilizing" the economy. This emphasis consequently obscured the specific nature of the project for capitalist restructuring and reinsertion in a situation where various directions were possible.

The third point is that the political polarization involved the tacit or explicit approval of the military coup by the Center (the Christian Democrats). Immediately afterward, some sectors of the Center lent their support to the military government in technocratic tasks although the official line of the Christian Democratic party proposed a collaboration that was conditional on certain issues relating to human rights, a proposal that was soon rejected by the military government.[3] One step at a time, especially when the repression targeted certain activist factions and leaders of the Christian Democrats, the party was traveling down what has since been called its "road to Damascus."[4] Prior to this time, the opposition had consisted basically of the Left. In effect, the time that the Christian Democrats spent on their "road to Damascus" was the time the armed forces needed to consolidate their leadership and resolve the problem of internal hegemony within the dominant coalition.

By the juncture in March and April of 1975 of the political situation and the launching of the Shock Plan (Plan Shock) for the economy, a clearer direction for this project of capitalist restructuring and reinsertion had apparently been defined at the top levels of the state.[5] It was at this juncture, in my view, that the dominant core solidified and began to run the state.

The Reactive Dimension

We will see later that no exact correspondence exists among periods of defining and transforming the economic model, the model of social organization, and the political model. The economic model was first given clear definition and some degree of direction around April 1975. Yet except for the direct repercussions of the economic model, what was ruling society was the purely reactive dimension, and at the level of political organization, the increasingly personalized military command.

The virtually unrestricted reign of repression is significant because it conditioned major elements of the political leadership, where a parallel existed between the process of concentrating and centralizing the repressive apparatus and that of consolidating the personalized leadership of Augusto Pinochet within the armed forces. Moreover, the heavy repression also shaped the kind of opposition that existed during the early years of the regime as well as some of the problems it subsequently faced. Thus a correlation exists between the regime's repressive characteristics and those of the institutionalizing carried out during the foundational phase. Also, when the regime gradually entered a phase of crisis management in 1981, this shift was reflected in the changing nature of the repression.[6]

Thus if the evolution of the repression is analyzed broadly, various stages can be distinguished, as has been substantiated in several studies.[7] The first stage began with the military coup and was characterized by massive repression that lacked overall coherence or technical coordination but was directed at the leaders, militants, and supporters of the UP government. At this point, there existed in Chile neither legal process nor judicial recourse for protection, and the population was often called on to participate in denunciations. In some areas, property owners even carried out acts of vengeance on their own. This kind of repression must be understood more as revenge than as a set of systematic measures intended to punish particular acts against the regime. This period witnessed thousands of assassinations, executions, and deaths by torture, all reflecting the arbitrary power of an unleashed repressive force that was still segmented in the several branches of the military.

As a result, there emerged the "technical necessity" of specializing and coordinating the field of repression. This goal characterized the stage that began in June of 1974 and witnessed the creation and expansion of the National Intelligence Directorate (Dirección Nacional de Inteligencia, or DINA). Gradually, repression began to be orchestrated by this centralized organization, which depended directly on Pinochet and tended to subordinate the intelligence and security units of the branches of the armed forces, although not without friction. During this phase, repression became more pointed and selective, combining secret kidnappings and murders with spectacular deeds intended to terrify the entire population by their visibility. DINA created major impact by various means: its unlimited escalation, its penetration into various spheres of society (like the educational system), its far-reaching operations affecting well-known individuals who were inclined toward the regime but critical of its repressive aspect, and public certainty of DINA involvement in assassinating General Carlos Prats and Orlando Letelier and attacking Bernardo Leighton. Eventually, however, combined pressure from the international community, the Catholic Church, and a few sectors within the regime led the government to dissolve DINA. In August 1977, it was replaced by the National Information Center (Central Nacional de Informaciones, or CNI). On paper, the CNI appeared to be an intelligence agency lacking executive powers, but in actuality, it emulated DINA in almost all its methods. The difference was that the disappearances ceased and the government, having learned something from DINA, attempted to incorporate into legislation measures that would allow the flexible functioning of the repressive organization. In this way, the government sought to "legalize" repression, even though this "legality" too was often exceeded.

Between 1977 and 1980, when the political model was being defined, repression became more responsive to the actions of the opposition and more capable of selecting its targets politically. It sought methods that would terrorize the populace and crush morale, which included executions justified by the pretext of confronting armed resistance. The search for "legal" adaptation to the necessities of repression was reflected in the new constitution submitted to a plebiscite in 1980, promulgated, and made effective as of March 1981. Its transitory articles suppressed the conventional forms of defense that had been unsuccessfully attempted by those involved in legal defense. The constitution also awarded the broadest of discretionary powers to Pinochet so that all kinds of repression could be employed without any judicial check or other control.[8]

If this summary view of the evolution of the Chilean repression is considered along with the nature of the reactive dimension in more institutional spheres, it is possible to see how this phase not only paved the way for institutionalization but also determined much of its form and content.[9] The official elimination of political parties was formalized in 1977, only a few months before the plan for political institutionalization was first announced. Labor unions and professional associations were not allowed to meet or elect new leaders until 1978. In the universities and the entire educational system, organizations not supportive of the regime were eliminated. Thus prior to 1978, except for the changes produced by the economic model, there was neither innovation nor new rules of the game but only repression, dismantling, and immobility. On the political level, no decisions were made even about the mechanisms for succession within the regime itself. Thus the economic transformation and the reactive phase predominated in every sphere of social life while a repressive apparatus gained momentum and the dominant core took hold. These trends were facilitated by almost total silence within Chilean society, the exceptions being the voices of the Church and those sectors under its protection.[10]

The Dominant Core within the State

As previously mentioned, a dominant core coalesced and consolidated for purposes of running the state that held together as such until 1981. The core's two components were the increasingly personalized and hierarchical leadership of Pinochet in the armed forces, which ensured management of the mechanisms of political power, and the technocratic group known as the "economic team" or the "Chicago Boys." This group was charged with managing the economy in the interests of the dominant capitalist groups and assuring the proper course for state policy. How can the combination of these two components be explained, especially their becoming a dominant core in a situation where state power at the moment of rupture was assumed by the armed forces as a whole?

First, the relative cloistering of the armed forces for several decades (due to the political regime's having established a series of legitimate mechanisms for resolving its conflicts), kept the armed forces from developing a consensual political project other than obedience to civilian rule. This attitude was expressed in the elaboration of the military's constitutionalist ideology. Military participation between 1970 and 1973 was insufficient to establish a political project beyond a "consensus for termination," once constitutionalist sectors had been purged or subdued. Although geopolitics, counterinsurgency doctrine, and national security ideology can furnish the armed forces with a self-image that is useful in moments of crisis and the appearance of a project, these sources cannot provide a program for governing that goes beyond repressive measures and some restructuring of the political regime. Such a program must be contributed by social classes or sectors of civil society.

Lacking an agreed-upon military program, the internal cohesion of the armed forces derives from its formal hierarchical structure, in which the legitimacy of formal leadership becomes crucial. Because governing requires making daily decisions and because in Chile the commander in chief and the highest authority in the military government are one and the same, this formal leadership tends to become progressively personalized in the absence of a consensual political program within the military. Herein lies a structural root of the personalization of leadership that requires no references to psychological traits or phenomena. In Chile, the growing personalization of leadership, backed by formal or hierarchical legitimacy, ended the process of deliberation that preceded and followed the military coup, making way for absolute verticality. Internal opposition and dissident groups in other branches of the armed forces (like that expressed by the Air Force to holding the national plebiscite in January 1978, which culminated with the head of the Air Force being expelled from the Governing Junta) have never succeeded in becoming coherent alternatives. All of them have claimed the same principle of legitimacy ("the spirit of 11 September"), but none of them seem to have been effective. The lack of intermediate alternatives and the risk of rupturing the internal cohesion and unity of the armed forces both favor perpetuating the status quo. Consequently, the "job" of disciplining the Army and the armed forces as a whole is as important as consolidating leadership at the state level, inasmuch as the stability of leadership is partially grounded in the dual principle of political authority and maximum military hierarchy. Although the growing personalization in Chile definitely clashed with some bureaucratic features of the military organization and generated dependencies that affected its traditional functioning, the significant rise in the economic and social status of the military, combined with the lack of coherent alternatives having any hierarchical legitimacy, mitigated organizational resistance to the personalizing process.

This personalization of leadership at the top level of government, which was paralleled by increasing subordination of the other branches of the armed forces to the Army, has evidenced several identifiable stages. The first was the succession of legal and institutional designations enjoyed by Pinochet: while always remaining Commander in Chief of the Army, he went from Head of the Governing Junta to Head of State and from there to President of the Republic. The last title was finally sanctioned by the Constitution of 1980.[11] The second stage witnessed the growing concentration and centralization of the repressive apparatus directly commanded by Pinochet, which culminated first in the creation of the National Intelligence Directorate (DINA) in June 1974 and then in its replacement by the National Information Center (CNI) in August 1977. The third stage saw the progressive elimination from the Army of those high officials who had been Pinochet's peers at the time of the coup. This turnover accentuated the vertical distance between the Commander in Chief and the newly promoted officers, who "owe everything" to Pinochet. These changes have been accompanied by a series of institutional transformations within the Army that have been detailed in other works.[12] Thus Pinochet's personalization of leadership has been accomplished through a combination of measures of force, management of the repressive apparatus, and legal and institutional formulas. All these actions were made possible by the cohesion of the armed forces, which were unified by hierarchy and internal organization rather than by agreement on a common political project. This process has not occurred without confrontation, however, especially in situations where the authority of the governing military junta was decreased by Pinochet's personal decisions, which were then ratified after the fact.[13]

As we have seen, the Chilean military leadership was, for historical reasons, incapable of offering a project after the rupture produced in

September 1973. The situation was compounded by the unreadiness of the capitalist class to propose alternative development projects. In the mid-1960s, various intellectual, management, and political sectors identified with the Right had begun to criticize the development style and the political regime in Chile in recent years for growing state interventionism, the cyclical nature of the economy, and excessive political mobilization, which was characterized as "demagoguery and anarchy." These rightist sectors went on record as favoring an authoritarian system of government and a drastic reorientation of the development model. A certain awareness existed among these sectors of the need for radical change in society, although the ideology of structural reforms and the democratizing tendencies of recent years prevented this viewpoint from being expressed in pure form. An incipient vision of this restructuring project was found in the "New Republic" program of Jorge Alessandri's candidacy in 1970. Thus the idea of a profound capitalist renewal combined with an authoritarian political transformation that would facilitate it (as opposed to a simple restoration of capitalism) existed long before the military seized power in September 1973. The idea was reinforced and catalyzed during the UP era, when it acquired some consistency as an ideology of "capitalist revolution" that opposed every form of reformist or revolutionary populism.[14] This ideological persuasion was also reinforced by the dominant economic sectors' sense of having experienced a definitive threat to their existence during the UP government. But when faced with this threat, these sectors had no vision beyond recovering their confiscated patrimony and privileges and ensuring future political conditions that would reverse the situation and avoid its repetition. For this reason, even when certain productive sectors (especially those involved in import-substituting industrialization and agriculture) later found themselves gravely affected by the economic model operating after 1974, they could imagine nothing worse happening in 1975 than what had already occurred under Popular Unity. Moreover, their expectations had been initially validated by the military government with the massive restitution of properties that had been nationalized or incorporated into the state by the UP government.[15]

The result was that when an acute political crisis occurred in early 1975, precise definition of the economic project of capitalist restructuring did not originate from the business class or its interest groups. It developed instead out of the consolidation within state government of the technocratic sector, whose members came from international financial organizations or universities and were fervent adherents of the doctrines of Milton Friedman and the University of Chicago School of Economics. Members of this technocratic sector moved progressively in and out of top positions in the dominant financial groups. Their leadership also sought to extend its management beyond strictly economic activities to all spheres of governmental decision making.

The growing dominance of this sector and its economic model in state management was not implemented without objections from other sectors of the dominant coalition, however, particularly from nationalist groups and productive sectors that protested either the dismantling of the state economic apparatus or the lack of protection for national economic activity. In voicing such criticisms, these sectors were counting on the support of a diffused perspective in certain military circles. Thus neoliberalism could not have become dominant without Pinochet's decisive intervention on behalf of the economic model from 1975 on. Paradoxically, the policies themselves as well as the ideology that inspired them seemed to radically contradict the military's consensual inclinations toward strengthening the state while remaining rather distrustful of excessive power held by an economic Right. This tendency required a few minimal concessions in the economic model and other relatively autonomous spheres.[16] But in the end, the model was imposed for several years, and Pinochet committed himself to it personally, despite its being the issue most debated within the dominant coalition.

This outcome can be explained by several factors. The economic model undoubtedly expressed the interests of certain fractions of the capitalist class, especially the financial sector. Also, mediation by the technocratic group in directing the state could be presented in 1975 as the only possible solution for an entire class that had recently feared definitive loss of power and now saw the possibility of economic recovery being stimulated by restitution and privatization of state enterprises. This possibility caused less privileged capitalist groups to accept the model too. Moreover, the model's internal coherence and appearance of having a scientific and universal logic unrelated to the discourse of any fraction allowed the military to present it as a system capable of arbitrating among sectoral interests. In addition, the technocratic sector, the apparent arbiter of particular interests in the name of general interests, held itself out as the guarantor of a key element needed for regime continuity: the increasing flow of private foreign capital that was indispensable for relaunching the Chilean economy in a situation of international political isolation. This inflow could also provide the armed forces with an extremely high level of military financing that fractions of the capitalist class would ordinarily consider unproductive or competitive with their demands on state resources, even though such spending was required by the military's corporatist demands, geopolitical vision, and repressive necessities.

Adding to these factors was the ideological force of a discourse that went beyond the purely political to link politics to a coherent model of society—that is, to a set of transformations in all of spheres of social life. The antistatist discourse of the model touched a nerve in various segments of the dominant coalition by presenting state intervention as necessarily tied to the politicization and the economic experience under Popular Unity. No other sector could offer all these elements to a military leadership with great resources of power but no plan for organizing society. Herein lie the reasons why Pinochet decisively backed the proposed economic model.

Thus the political history of the dominant coalition prior to the crisis of 1981 is the story of the affirmation of the dominant state core. This nucleus was created by an alliance between Pinochet's personalized leadership in the armed forces and economic leadership of a sector seemingly capable of arbitrating all capitalist interests, even though it strongly manifested the predominance of financial capital over productive sectors.

The Meaning of the Historical Project

What meaning did the dominant state core seek to impart to the project of capitalist restructuring that the military regime had to address? This foundational dimension was not limited to its purely economic aspects, in my view, but was also an attempt to reorganize Chilean society completely by force of state power. It was an attempt to create a new political order and a new form for representing society, its history, and its destiny—which is to say that it was an attempt to create a new cultural model. This project was not one of simple restoration because it sought to establish new bases for sustaining the development of capitalism, even after old classes or sectors had regained privileges lost in the years under Popular Unity and even under the Christian Democratic government.

On the economic level, an attempt was made to reverse the development model prevailing in recent decades (which centered on import-substituting industrialization and the predominant role of the state in economic activity) and to replace it with a "new model of outward-oriented development." This attempt implied reorienting production toward primary sectors and natural resource exports, drastically reducing the state's economic role as regulator and manager, and granting a preponderant role to the private sector. The last shift gave primacy to the financial sector linked to international capital and produced an increasing concentration of resources in fewer and fewer "economic groups."[17]

But equally significant as the transformation in the development model was the proposal of an organizational model for society. This proposal involved reversing the democratization process and replacing state control of opportunities with new patterns of distributing and concentrating them through the market. The effect was to enshrine a conception of society as a market in which stratification and segmentation appear to be a natural order, the principle of organized collective action is systematically rejected as leading to "politicization," and the state loses its identity as the focal point for social demands. Market principles would be enthroned in various social spheres, the regulative and redistributive role of the state would be reduced (although a vertical, authoritarian system of decision making would be maintained), and social demands would be fragmented and segmented in order to keep them from spreading.

Thus there were an economic model, a model of social reorganization, and a political model as well. The political model distinguishes the mature phase introducing transformations and requiring a lengthy military regime from a future political order having limited spaces of representation and participation but also preserving mechanisms to prevent changes in the established social order. Thus a military regime and a restricted and conservative democracy can be viewed as two phases of the same process, which has been denominated in the official jargon as the process of "transition."

The image of the society being attempted—its cultural model—was based on a negative assessment of national development in recent decades. The political system and the growing state presence were both perceived as the central causes of the "national decadence" (meaning economic stagnation and excessive political partisanship) that would have led to the loss of national unity. Although decadence culminated in the period between 1970 and 1973, the path had been paved by preceding governments. According to this view, the basis for national recovery was to be economic freedom (understood as private property), the only solid foundation for political freedom.[18] Such a foundation could be guaranteed by allowing the laws of the market to dominate in all spheres of national life. Hence came the symbiosis between a discourse that seemed extremely liberal and a profoundly authoritarian conception from the military sphere.

Internal Divisions

The specific meaning of the historical project was not defined unanimously, however, within the dominant bloc. Its meaning was questioned many times, building up to a crisis that began in 1981. Internal debate first centered on criticizing the economic model. Isolated voices from the business community defended the role of national production and state intervention. Some business associations also raised the argument of the model's high social cost.[19] These objections were joined by the criticism of self-proclaimed nationalist political groups calling for a more active role for the state and proposing corporatist mechanisms of participation that opposed both the preceding party system and the fragmentation imposed by the hegemonic project. But as noted, no other sector in the dominant bloc could offer an alternative economic policy as well as a coherent project for all levels of society. Several other factors also diminished the effectiveness of criticisms within the dominant bloc: the propaganda of economic "success," as measured by the government's own official statistics until 1980; the link established between economic policy and what were called "modernizations"; the lack of organization among the industrial bourgeoisie; the lack of debate within the military, except on specific aspects of economic policy; and general perception of Pinochet's unconditional support for the socioeconomic model. Indeed, only the emergence of a major crisis in 1981 revived criticism of the model. This time, however, it arose in a context where new business associations were staking out positions that were relatively autonomous of the government.

The other point of friction within the dominant bloc concerned the political model. In contrast to the economic debate that emerged early on, the debate over the political future was postponed for several years by the unanimity surrounding the suspension of constitutional guarantees and the requirements of the "internal war." Gradually, however, definitions of the optimum political model began to emerge in the wake of several developments, among them the fulfillment of the most urgent tasks of this phase, the preoccupation of some regime intellectuals with problems of succession and the future, and pressures from the international community and several national institutions, mainly the Catholic Church. These divergent definitions eventually caused alignments to form within the dominant bloc.

The importance in these regimes of internal division between "hardliners" (*duros*) and "soft-liners" (*blandos* or *aperturistas*) has often been stressed in the literature. Yet in a certain way, analyzing the Chilean reality from this perspective pays a price because it involves mechanically transferring a factor that had significant weight in other contexts. The difficulty has been compounded by the opacity of the phenomena and processes occurring in the political sphere.

Before expanding on this point, however, it seems appropriate to mention two distinctions. The first concerns the so-called openings (understood here as the creation of spaces for representation and participation) and liberalizations (understood as the attenuation of authoritarian control in various areas of social life). To be evaluated accurately, both must be placed in the context of broader processes. According to the context, they can be part of the institutionalizing of a military regime or a dictatorship, or part of the processes of transition to a different regime.[20] The second distinction is the point that the significance of the debate between hard-liners and soft-liners for the dynamic of a regime or its transformation depends on various factors, two of which will be mentioned here. First, this debate is meaningful only if social actors are represented and incorporated who have their own resources of power or influence, rather than being limited to discussions among intellectuals attracted to military power. Second, the nature of the political spectrum is important because the nonexistence of a political Center or an alliance between an existing Center and the soft-liner sectors has always been the precondition that allows the soft-liners to set themselves up as an alternative to the regime.

In Chile a sometimes rancorous debate took place over institutionalization among the various civilian sectors clustering around military power. Some asserted early on the bankruptcy of democracy and its universal crisis in the West, and they proposed ideas such as perpetuating the military regime indefinitely or searching for formulas of a corporatist nature. These voices included some of the major critics of the economic model.[21] Other groups conceived of the military regime as a historical precondition for creating a new kind of society but also as a transition to a political model of limited democracy with the protective participation of the armed forces.[22] At certain times, this current of opinion included the defenders and promoters of the economic model. But the connections between the economic debate and the political model must not be exaggerated in elucidating the meaning of this conflict among regime sectors because in Chile this debate took place for both factions within the context of the same *problématique* of institutionalizing the military regime. The one point not open to question was the continuation of Pinochet's leadership. Methods of his staying in power could vary, and individuals could therefore opt for maintaining the power constituted in 1973 at full strength without introducing institutional modifications or for proceeding with institutionalization, which would allow the regime to look more respectable abroad. But one can scarcely describe those who sought institutionalization under Pinochet through various legal formulas as "soft-liners" or *aperturistas*.

In any case, none of the sectors in the dominant coalition could frame an alternative when obvious crises were not occurring. The nature of the political spectrum made matters difficult, with the Center occupied by the Christian Democrats who were clearly situated in the opposition camp. Any alliance with the soft-liner sectors ran the risk of splitting the Christian Democratic party and was therefore vetoed. Neither could the soft-liners, who were not in the middle of a crisis, align themselves with a Center that set up conditions threatening the very foundation of their project of domination—its model of socioeconomic organization.

Nor did the period between 1973 and 1980 witness any debate involving players who were autonomous of state management, like the bourgeois actors or the middle-class business associations that played such an important role in bringing down Allende. These actors were identified with a regime that still appeared to them to be the ultimate solution to a threat perceived as definitive, or else they were too wrapped up in their corporatist adaptation to the economic model. Although these actors made their voices heard at particular moments of debate, no clearly shared positions emerged that could be put forward as an alternative to provide a societal base for the debate among the factions surrounding state power. The same can be said of the military corps. Consequently, the debate between hard-liners and soft-liners (or whatever one wishes to call them) was a disagreement that lacked meaningful roots in the regime's social base or in the military until 1980. The debate was thus reduced to influential groups within the regime who were therefore incapable of providing an alternative to it and had to content themselves with the ideological struggle for positions of power. As a result, the division between hard-liners and soft-liners had no significance in terms of what has been called a "liberalizing coalition" or dynamic of transition.[23] Rather, this division of opinion was restricted to the *problématique* of institutionalization and was resolved by Pinochet's decisions on this process. The significance of the division among these sectors was thus limited to the possibility of its reemerging in moments of regime crisis or its potential role in some future coalescence of the Chilean Right.[24]

I have attempted to point out systematically the existence of cleavages within the Pinochet regime. The greatest opacity seems to have existed within the armed forces, where certain reservations were manifested about policies that would reduce the role of the state or denationalize public enterprises. But these reservations did not emerge clearly and were instead relegated to the relative marginalization from decision making that Pinochet has imposed on the armed forces.

Notes to Chapter 6

1. This and subsequent chapters are based on the following works of mine: *Procesos políticos en un régimen autoritario: dinámicas de institucionalización y oposición en Chile, 1973–1980* (Santiago: FLACSO, 1980); "Evolución política del régimen militar chileno y problemas de la transición a la democracia," paper prepared for the project "Transitions from Authoritarianism and Prospects for Democracy," Latin American Program, Wilson Center, Washington, D.C., 1982; and "Modelo y proyecto políticos del régimen militar chileno," *Revista Mexicana de Sociología* 44, no. 2 (Apr.–June 1982). The English version has been updated.

2. For analysis of the repression, I have relied on the work of Hugo Frühling, particularly his article "Repressive Policies and Legal Dissent in Authoritarian Regimes: Chile, 1973–1981," *International Journal of the Sociology of Law* 12 (1984).

3. An important group of Christian Democratic leaders and activists radically opposed the military coup. On this subject, see the documents presented in the news magazine *Análisis* 5, no. 43 (March 1982).

4. Guillermo O'Donnell, *Reflexiones sobre las tendencias de cambio en el estado burocrático autoritario*, CEDES Documento de Trabajo (Buenos Aires: CEDES, 1976).

5. Compare T. Moulián and P. Vergara, "Estado, ideología y políticas económicas en Chile," *Estudios CIEPLAN* 3 (June 1980).

6. All these themes will be dealt with in the following chapters.

7. Here I am closely following Frühling's analysis in "Repressive Policies and Legal Dissent in Authoritarian Regimes." He warns against a certain schematic tendency that rigidifies a fluid process into stages when elements of one phase are actually present in another.

8. On the Constitution of 1980, see *Constitución Política de la República de Chile*, March 1981. A critical analysis is found in *Las críticas del Grupo de los 24* (Santiago: APSI, 1981). On Transitory Article 24 of the constitution, which invalidates the right of habeas corpus, see A. Gonzalez, "Constitución política: disposición 24 transitoria," *Mensaje* 30, no. 300 (July 1981).

9. On labor unions, see G. Campero and J. A. Valenzuela, *El movimiento sindical chileno en el capitalismo autoritario* (Santiago: ILET, 1981); and VECTOR, "Movimiento sindical: política laboral, tendencias, iglesia, campesinos," *Revista de Talleres* 2 (June 1981). On the universities, see L. Silver and J. P. Mery, "Las universidades chilenas y la intervención militar," 2 vols., mimeo, Santiago, 1975.

10. In this sense, centrist groups that directed news magazines like *Ercilla* and later created the weekly *Hoy* did not embark on their "road to Damascus" until 1976.

11. On this evolution, see Genaro Arriagada, *El marco institucional de las Fuerzas Armadas* (Washington, D.C.: Taller Seis años de Gobierno Militar, Wilson Center, 1980). The combination of the positions of chief of state and chief of the Army seems to be a distinctive feature of the Chilean case.

12. A. Varas, "Fuerzas Armadas y gobierno militar: corporativización y politización castrense en Chile," *Revista Mexicana de Sociología* 44, no. 2 (Apr.–June 1982); and G. Arriagada, *El marco institucional de las Fuerzas Armadas*.

13. These confrontations between 1973 and 1980 culminated with General Leigh and the staff of Air Force generals leaving. This set of events represented the widest split to date in the top political leadership, but it also demonstrated the power at Pinochet's disposal to require the armed forces as a whole to support his positions in a disciplined, subordinate manner.

14. On this subject, see A. Varas, *La dinámica política de la oposición durante el gobierno de la Unidad Popular*, FLACSO Documento de Trabajo (Santiago: FLACSO, 1977).

15. Data and references on the return of funds and businesses can be found in H. Vega et al., *La situación económica de los trabajadores, 1973–1979*, Serie Estudios Económicos, Documento de Trabajo no. 1 (Santiago: Vicaría Pastoral Obrera, 1980); and J. Crispi and J. Bengoa, "El modelo neoliberal y las transformaciones agrarias: algunas lecciones de la experiencia chilena," CECADE mimeo, Mexico, 1981.

16. Examples of this tendency are the regime's maintaining state control over the nationalized copper mines (despite excessive indemnity payments) and liberalizing future exploration, and in another sphere, expanding state involvement in preschool education.

17. Of the extensive literature on the economic model, I will cite only a few works: Vega et al., *La situación económica de los trabajadores, 1973–1979*; Alejandro Foxley, "Experimentos neoliberales en América Latina," *Estudios CIEPLAN* no. 7 (March 1982); Tomás Moulián and

P: lar Vergara, *Estado, ideología y políticas económicas en Chile*; and Aníbal Pinto, *El modelo económico ortodoxo y el desarrollo nacional* (Santiago: VECTOR Ediciones Especiales, 1981).

18. See Chapter 1, note 4.

19. One who raised this argument was Orlando Sáenz, former president of the Society for Industrial Development (Sociedad de Fomento Fabril, or SOFOFA), a group of industrial leaders.

20. This possibility will be illustrated in Chapter 7.

21. "Hard-liners" or "nationalists" have expressed their points of view in columns in the newspaper *La Tercera*. Some individuals having this perspective came out of the fascist movement known as Country and Liberty (Patria y Libertad), which was important between 1970 and 1973. Many are linked to military officers connected with DINA. Several have been associated with the Corporation for National Studies (Corporación de Estudios Nacionales), directed by Pinochet's daughter, Lucía Pinochet. Still others have been government advisors or participants in various government commissions.

22. These sectors' concepts are those expressed in the Constitution of 1980. Some of the main elements are groups involved in running the economy, a sizable number of mayors appointed by the regime, the association sector coming out of the Catholic University Student Federation (Federación de Estudiantes de la Universidad Católica, or FEUC), and certain groups associated with the influential rightist newspaper *El Mercurio*. These elements have also coalesced around magazines like *Realidad* and institutions like the New Democracy Group (Grupo Nueva Democracia). Important internal differences nonetheless exist between hard-liners and soft-liners.

23. Guillermo O'Donnell applies these terms to the cases in which the transition has already begun. See O'Donnell, *Notas para el estudio de procesos de democratización política a partir del estado burocrático autoritario* (Buenos Aires: CEDES, 1980).

24. It should be recalled that after the 1973 coup, the National party dissolved itself. Some elements of the political leadership of the Right became advisors to the regime, members of state commissions or councils, or regime ambassadors. A small number moved toward a centrist opposition. Except for these few, leaders of the Right have publicly declared their loyalty to the regime on such occasions as the plebiscite of 1980, at least until the crisis that began in 1981.

Chapter 7

The Processes of Institutionalization

The Pressures for Institutionalizing

In earlier chapters, certain generic factors were pointed out that exert
pressure for institutionalizing and relegitimizing the military regime. I will
now examine certain more specific factors.

Implementation of the economic model affected many sectors that
had initially supported the military government but gradually became
dissatisfied with the continual blocking of their claims and demands. These
sectors were already perceiving the threat that gave rise to the regime as
remote, and they felt frustrated by their lack of access to decision-making
levels and by the effects of the economic and legal reordering. Protests
were expressed not only by business sectors adversely affected by economic
policy but also by the organized interest groups that had been central to
the overthrow of President Allende. This phenomenon, however, grew out
of more than economic roots. Various influential groups, some linked to
economic interests and others acting as the government's political advisors
and intellectuals, coalesced around the nucleus of personalized leadership
and technocratic neoliberal management. Once the first stage of unanimity
concerning the overt and generalized repression had passed, a discussion
sprang up among these groups about the future of the regime, its stability,
and its permanence. A heterogeneous mix of doctrinal and ideological
sources mingled in a debate that was at first internal but gradually became
public. This situation required reordering the regime's sources of political
support because its initial legitimizing principle had lost some value and
because the uncertainty about regime stability was creating restlessness and
a potential for scattering.

Another necessity facing the regime was that of responding to growing opposition to the regime, in which the Catholic Church and international pressure played significant roles.[1] Moreover, any response to Chile's progressive isolation and to multiplying voices of opposition could no longer appeal only to the crisis of the past.

Finally, certain discernible exigencies were being imposed on the institutional political system by the transformations introduced into society. Many of these transformations required particular rules of the game and relatively stable institutions that were not suffering from an unpredictable future, as was the case in education and labor relations.

None of these necessities—the erosion among supportive sectors, the demands of a growing opposition, or the functional exigencies of certain social transformations—could be resolved solely by means of the elements characterizing the political regime during its first phase. Political repression and control could not continue to be the only visible elements of relations between the state and civil society, nor could counterrevolutionary legitimacy be claimed any longer. The regime needed to relegitimize itself in the eyes of its supporting sectors and society as a whole. It also needed to institutionalize the transformations initiated in order to fulfill them in other social spheres. Both necessities required that the regime progress from being a dictatorship without rules to one that establishes its own rules. If this analysis of the particularities of the historical project and the regime conveying it is correct, then the precise meaning of this process of institutionalizing is twofold, in terms of the categories enunciated in earlier chapters.

Institutionalization in Society

Beginning in 1978, an attempt was made to resolve the delays in political-institutional transformations and in social organization by means of the first of the officially designated "modernizations." The Labor Plan (Plan Laboral) contained the legislation that allowed labor unions to organize and bargain collectively.[2] From this point on, institutionalizing at the level of society encompassed various social spheres and was presented by the regime as a series of "modernizations" that included labor relations, health care, education and social security, agricultural modernization, and changes in state administration and the judicial system. Both the method and nature of these modernizations reveal certain interesting features.

In terms of method, the establishment of regulations had its starting point in several crises precipitated in certain social spheres. One example was the antecedent of the 1978 Labor Plan, in which the threat of a boycott by U.S. labor unions created a commotion in dominant circles; another example was the 1980 legislation on universities established after focal points of student mobilization had emerged. When such crises emerged, the government would form a commission whose members were known to be loyal to the military regime (despite their being mostly civilians) and would entrust it with preparing legislation on the matter. Usually, the work of such commissions would be filed away for a long time until new conflicts broke out. Then the government would restudy the problem, set aside the presentations made by the commission, and in short order dictate legislation based on a study conducted within Pinochet's inner circles. Thus an extremely personalized pattern was set for creating regulations, one that lacked representation of the interests of the various sectors affected. The results were then officially accepted in the name of a universality rising above special interests.

In terms of content, regulations attempting to transfer the principles of market competition to new spheres tended to converge with norms derived from military currents. The first set of regulations sought to unburden the state of its responsibility for social services, to introduce the primacy of private groups with greater resources, and to weaken the role of representative organizations in resolving conflicts.[3] The second set of regulations sought to guarantee the exclusion of "dangerous" ideological or political sectors and to maintain the repressive capacity of the state.

Thus the process of social institutionalization contains both an element of responding to crises in the political situation as well as one attempting to lay a new foundation. The latter element seeks to stabilize the more durable features of the regime. In this effort, strictly capitalist visions are combined with concessions to the military mentality. This mingling explains the ambivalence inherent in the design of these transformations combining the omnipresent market element and the authoritarian role of the state. Ambivalence also characterizes the actual execution of the transformations, when the original content tends to be distorted or modified by various pressures. Such pressures can arise from military sectors, from interest groups within the spheres where the transformations are being implemented, or from centers of influence identified with nationalist positions (which are usually circumvented). This ambivalence becomes especially significant in moments of crisis, when it tends to weaken the leadership capacity of the dominant core directing the state.

Institutionalizing at the level of society succeeds to the extent that it manages to create a new order with its own mechanisms of reproduction, one in which the various sectors participating submit to its impositions. In this sense, significant variations occur according to the sphere being transformed. It is possible that some of these transformations will not outlast the military regime, even when they have significantly affected current forms of social relations or conditioned modifications that a new regime might introduce. In other spheres, the institutional transformation will appear to have consolidated a new kind of social relations that, if not irreversible, will continue to affect the society after the regime ends, particularly in fields like social security and education.

But a process of institutionalization is measured by more than its capacity to create a new order. It is also measured by its capacity to dismantle social relations and the system for creating social and political actors.[4] Thus even when no new system of relations has been created that is legitimate and capable of self-reproduction, it is still possible that the former modes of action characterizing social behavior and its ideological images and invocations will become irrelevant. In such a case, resisting these transformations in the name of an old social order can sacrifice the ability to rally support. There is always a period during institutionalizing when resistance manifests itself more as a corporatist demand in the name of old gains than as a conflict growing out of new contradictions generated by the system, in response to which alternative projects and proposals can be framed. Thus the dissociating dimension of the process of institutionalizing makes the opposition's task more difficult.

Structural Changes and Their Effects

It is evident that both the development model and the processes of institutionalization described above have brought about significant changes in Chilean society and its national profile. This overall change, regardless of the degree of irreversibility, poses a new set of conditions for establishing social actors and political action itself. Without getting into the debate surrounding these changes, let us recall some of their features.[5]

In terms of the development model, several important features can be cited: reorientation of production according to the de-emphasis on productive sectors (especially industrial sectors) and the strong expansion of the service sector; reduction of the state's role as economic agent; growing concentration of wealth in a small number of big conglomerates; capitalist penetration in the rural areas; and dominance by the financial sector accompanied by growing dependence on international financial capital.

Structural changes have also had major impact on various social sectors: a consistently high level of unemployment; impoverishment of the working class and occupations around which the union movement was historically organized; disarticulation and pauperization of the peasantry; transformation and diversification of the middle sectors that lost important elements of their identity, such as their ties to the state and opportunities for educational improvement; restructuring of the dominant classes due to the predominance of the financial sector, and so on.

Institutional transformations tend to manifest and reinforce these changes.[6] And all of the effects described above have repercussions on social organizations, especially on popular social organizations, which must confront processes of fragmentation that diminish their size, affiliation, and consequent capacity to coordinate and exert pressure.[7]

Finally, it is evident that individual and collective behaviors and strategies also tend to undergo changes. Except at the highest political levels, the most frequent change consists of a certain destructuring of collective behavior into an incoherent pattern in which elements drawing on the past to affirm identity intermingle with partial internalization of fear, conformism, adaptive or defensive patterns, and so on.

As a result, no well-defined new social subjects or consistent new behaviors and ideologies have emerged. Chilean society under the military regime has been characterized instead by unprecedented disarticulation and attempts at restructuring and combining with the new elements. This outcome cannot be divorced from the repressive dimension of the regime and the dismantling of the "backbone" of Chilean society and its sociopolitical system. The attempt to find a substitute for this backbone brings up the subject of the processes of institutionalizing the regime politically.

Political Institutionalization

As previously indicated, the process of institutionalizing at the level of the society is closely related to the process of political institutionalizing, which is understood as establishing the rules of the game for political leadership, state management, and the relationship between state and society. In March 1974, only six months after the military government assumed power, the regime published its *Declaration of Principles* (*Declaración de principios*).[8] This document affirmed that the regime would not be a mere parenthesis between a destroyed democracy and its restoration. But the political formulas for reorganizing and creating a new purified democracy remained shrouded, with only vague formulations borrowed from Catholic corporatism being intimated. At this time, no formulation existed for any political project other than the pattern of government and command generated by the military coup.

No meaningful debate took place within the regime about the political future until 1976. During this period, the reigning priorities were to personalize Pinochet's leadership in the armed forces and the government and to maintain the repressive hold over society. This entire course of action sought legitimation by invoking the "internal war" and the "international siege."

In 1976, when the regime had completed three years of military government and DINA's campaign had reached its greatest extent and impunity, an attempt was made to legitimize the military regime and enthrone it permanently in Chilean society. This intent was expressed by the promulgation in September 1976 of the provisional constitutional guidelines, the so-called *Constitutional Acts* (*Actas constitucionales*). This document contradicted to some extent the work of the Ortúzar Commission, which had been created in December 1973 to prepare a new constitution. By 1976 national security ideology was dominating official discourse, which was asserting that the methods of liberal democracy had failed and that the military regime was the only solution to the Marxist aggression confronting Latin American countries. The *Constitutional Acts* were an attempt to bestow constitutional status on the governing military junta (Junta Militar de Gobierno) and on the legal formulas that had allowed repressive operations in recent years. Once again, however, the subject of constructing a new democracy remained wrapped in obscurity.[9]

This attempt to institutionalize military power at a time when international and Church pressures were intensifying precipitated internal discussion about the future political model. The advent of the Carter administration and the announcements by several Latin American governments that they were initiating some form of transition to democracy placed the topic of democratization on the agenda. Yet meanwhile, bold assassinations perpetrated by the security services (like that of Orlando Letelier) and the increase in disappearances and other forms of repression were provoking strong denunciations from the Church. All this controversy caused a debate among the groups favoring the regime and led Pinochet to announce in July 1977 a political strategy called the Chacarillas Plan.[10] This plan set up various phases for the regime, which was to culminate in 1985 with power being transferred to civilian sectors by extremely restricted and exclusionary democratic mechanisms that combined representative systems with military appointments.

But the vagueness of the plan's political mechanisms and its conditioning the time frame on advances in socioeconomic transformations revealed it to be a typical recourse for avoiding crisis by reordering debate within the regime and by countering pressure from international organizations, foreign governments, and the Church. The plan nevertheless reaffirmed the transitory character of the military regime even while attempting to found a new institutional order. Left behind was the project for making the military regime permanent, which had been sketched in embryonic form in 1976. The Chacarillas Plan was instead a means of gaining time by postponing specific formulations for transition but announcing the advent of a particular kind of democracy within a "prudent" period of time. Proclamation of the plan rekindled the debate within the regime regarding new institutional forms even though they were limited by the plan. This debate was accompanied by a modification in the methods of repression, with the CNI replacing DINA in August 1977.

Pinochet responded to the internal debate—the product of discontent, discrepancies, and anxiety about the future regime—and to international pressure by intensifying his personalistic pattern. This personalization left its mark on all aspects of political institutionalization, as can be seen in the arbitrary management of relations with civil society. A significant illustration of this pattern was the first national plebiscite (*consulta nacional*) held in January 1978. This event, which was staged under the pretext of addressing Chile's international isolation, sought to legitimate transition to the "new institutionality" under Pinochet by resorting to a thoroughly manipulated "popular will." This same personalistic pattern was similarly expressed in confrontations within the armed forces, as when Pinochet insisted on holding the national plebiscite despite the open opposition of the Navy and the Air Force and when he removed General Leigh from the junta by retiring most of the Air Force Corps of Generals in 1978.

Debate intensified after publication of the Ortúzar Commission's report in October of 1978,[11] which proposed a preliminary draft of the new constitution for review by Pinochet and the governing junta. This debate deepened the disagreement between those who wanted to postpone political institutionalization by constitutional means in order to keep the military regime in power indefinitely and those who wanted a long-term constitutional definition that would reintroduce elements of democracy and resolve the political and economic problems of international isolation. As noted, this disagreement involved no alternative to Pinochet's leadership, thus limiting the debate to the question of whether or not institutionalizing his leadership was necessary and establishing time frames.

Pinochet's resistance to time frames was countered in 1980 by the imminent need for a decision. The entities created to deal with the matter had issued their reports, and internal debate on the political future was polarizing. Moreover, major symptoms of disarray in the repressive apparatus were creating a climate of generalized insecurity that was being reported even in the media supporting the military regime.[12] Faced with this situation, Pinochet reacted quickly and characteristically: he revamped a constitutional project, taking elements from reports by the Ortúzar Commission and the Council of State (Consejo de Estado), and called for a plebiscite in one month's time to approve his revision. This forceful response put the lid on internal debate, exposed the lack of alternatives within the regime, and temporarily settled the disputes. Concessions to "hard-line" factions included the continuance of the military regime until at least 1989 (with possibilities for being prolonged until 1997), preservation during this period of discretionary repressive capacity, and relegation of the governing junta to a purely legislative function. At the same time, "soft-line" factions were mollified by the fixing of time limits on the military regime and the creation of mechanisms that would restrict political openings once the regime ended and preclude the possibility of basic changes in future economic and political institutions.[13]

It is evident that the plebiscite called by Pinochet demonstrated all the characteristics of a political act of this type of regime: an oppressive propaganda campaign on the behalf of the government and significant restriction of opposition propaganda; general intimidation of the population, especially in the poor urban neighborhoods (*poblaciones*) and sectors farther away; unilateral presentation of a single option (a definitive constitution, an eight-year transitory statute, and ratification of Pinochet as president for eight years with the possibility of another eight years) while limiting the choice to flat rejection without any alternative proposal; absolute government control of the entire electoral process combined with a complete lack of guarantees for the opposition; the lack of electoral registers for control and means of independent appeal; and various forms of fraud during the voting process that altered the results.[14] Detailed analysis of the results would therefore be irrelevant, especially because the extent of the fraud is difficult to calculate. What is interesting to analyze is the significance of the 1980 decision in the context of political institutionalization.

In one respect, the plebiscite temporarily resolved the crisis within the dominant coalition and established a framework within which divergent internal factions had to operate lest they open the Pandora's box of repoliticizing the armed forces. Although the solution did not eliminate internal disagreements, it placed them within a framework viewed as legitimate by the various factions of the dominant coalition. This internal legitimacy subsequently played a crucial role in moments of crisis, especially within the armed forces.[15]

It is nevertheless important to point out that although the constitution imposed via the plebiscite and promulgated into law in March 1981 represented a triumph for Pinochet and the sectors closest to him, it also created several problems for his personalized leadership. The Constitution of 1980 effectively placed limits on Pinochet's discretionary power and made solutions to crisis situations (like the inopportune calls for the national plebiscites in 1978 and 1980, or removing most of the Air Force generals in 1978) subject to regulations in the future. Thus breaking these rules (which was always a possibility) would involve a step backward in the institutionalizing process and would rekindle debate within the regime, especially in the armed forces. Yet one portion of Pinochet's discretionary power was left untouched—his power to manage repression. This approach explains why the difficulties encountered in implementing the foundational dimension have been compensated by intensifying the repression. Another problem for Pinochet's leadership created by the constitution is that the same mechanisms devised to solve the "succession question," which could have allowed Pinochet's election as president in 1988, also created a political space for debate within the armed forces. This institutional framework thus worked in Pinochet's favor until 1988 but then created serious problems for him that might yet lead Pinochet to break with his own institutions and risk a counterreaction by the armed forces.[16]

A second dimension of the plebiscite worth analyzing is its significance for Chilean society as a whole and for the opposition. In this regard, the enormous abnormalities and irregularities that occurred before and during the plebiscite have already been noted. Yet the plebiscite can still be perceived as a success for the military government, not in terms of active loyalty to the regime but in the regime's capacity to disarticulate society, propagandize the traumas and terrors of the past, create uncertainty about alternatives, and manipulate passive conformism. All these "successes" were closely related to monolithic control of certain mass media and the physical and psychological intimidation of opposition groups.

In terms of the political opposition, the plebiscite marked the culmination of its efforts to unify and mobilize. At the same time, the plebiscite underscored the limits of the opposition. What became evident was the opposition's difficulty in reaching social sectors that were not loyal to the regime but behaved according to their characteristically passive conformism.

The Political Project and Model

The last dimension of the political institutionalization sanctioned by the constitution that needs to be analyzed is its political model. The constitution actually validated two political models. The first is what is officially called the "transition model," which merely preserves the pattern set by the coup of 1973—a military regime with strong repressive and personalized features.

Although the Constitution of 1980 regulated the power of authorities, it granted Pinochet maximum personal discretion in managing repression and eliminated the few remnants of protective mechanisms that still existed.[17]

These two features (combined with a few changes made in 1983) have continued to characterize the prevailing political model along with the absence of any formalized system for processing social demands. At the top level, in fact, there existed only a set of very loose ties between the government team in charge of economic management and the dominant financial groups until 1981. This relationship gradually became closer through the exchanging and rotating of positions between the public sector and the economic groups. Ministers, subsecretaries, directors of services, and even technobureaucrats were constantly shuttling back and forth filling government appointments and positions in banks or financial institutions, private management firms, and study groups associated with these organizations. This informal rotation system gave these sectors an immense advantage in terms of information, influence, and access to decision making until the system was destroyed by the crisis of 1981.

Meanwhile, other social sectors that lacked a political arena for representation and any office or official to address were forced to await personal decisions by the chief of state. With sectors of business leaders or professional associations, protests and claims took the form of public declarations or press conferences whose final objective was an interview with Pinochet. The protests of opposition sectors were manifested in more radical forms like hunger strikes or land seizures by groups of urban poor. But these methods too have lacked a specific official or office to address and have instead played a more testimonial role in stimulating group cohesion rather than effectively exerting pressure. The military government's policy has been either to repress such manifestations violently or, if their sponsors are protected by Church, to ignore them. At more local levels, the municipalities can serve as interlocutors for very specific kinds of demand. But these local governments too have reflected the overall pattern in the lack of mechanisms for representing and processing claims and the personalizing of limited power held by mayors designated by the military government.

The only institutionalized space or formalized system for processing demands during this period has been that created for collective bargaining by organized labor. But even this system is narrowly limited because the rules of the game leave labor union organization in a state of disarray that makes it impossible to elaborate demands going beyond individual companies. Moreover, any attempts to transcend these limits in order to restore the labor movement to its role as a social actor with national relevance have been severely repressed. In other social spheres, the formalization of channels of expression has been narrower still or simply nonexistent.[18]

Other factors that must be considered are the severe restrictions placed on communications media and the absolute control of mass media.[19] These conditions have kept dissident sectors isolated and reduced almost totally to making simple denunciations. Efforts at coordinating or linking an already diminished capacity to express opinion to any defensive or offensive collective action have been violently quashed.

The crux for the military regime seems to be to suppress systems of broad representation and mechanisms for making claims. No sector of society can speak in the name of the general good. This suppression is related to the transfer of basic state functions to market mechanisms. As a result, claims referring to problems of labor, health care, education, social security, housing, and other areas have lost their traditional state referent and must be channeled into "private" entities managed by the dominant capitalist interests. This transfer has had major consequences for the social and political opposition. Absence of a political arena or space where larger social demands can be represented and the precariousness of the arenas for corporatist demands partially explain the conflicts between the military government and the Catholic Church.

The above features of the political model help explain why all announce-ments and efforts to create an organized political movement in support of the regime have failed. Such efforts have been continually derailed by the exclusionary or restrictive features of social policy and the reduction of the state's redistributive role. The same circumstances have limited the capacity of massive appeals and mobilization. In sum, the goal of depoliticizing and fragmenting demands by eliminating their collective character is contradictory to pro-regime initiatives.[20] This situation led civilian sectors supporting the regime to favor organizations like research centers, editorial publication committees, and similar entities until 1983, when rightist political organizations were finally established. Supportive civilian sectors have since coalesced around these groups to disseminate their ideas and attempt to influence state decisions. For the latter purpose, these sectors also relied on the so-called legislative commissions of the governing junta.

As for the regime's penetration into society, which would ordinarily be the task of a political movement, it has been partially realized at the sectoral level by the National Secretariats (Secretarías Nacionales) that provide training services and organizational resources. Penetration has also been facilitated by appointed mayors who have wielded unrestricted power over municipal services.[21] While processing decisions and plans made by the military government "from the top down" can be carried out with relative efficiency (although it cannot achieve total coverage of the social base), processing demands of the base "from the bottom up" through these local mechanisms tends to be limited to demands arising from sectors linked to the military government.

The political model described above appears to be the necessary precondition for a social transformation. But it is not proposed as a definitive or complete model, only as necessary for a transition to another stable regime.

As already indicated, consensus within the dominant bloc favored prolonging the military regime for a lengthy period. This consensus, however, has tended to break down on the subject of a political model to succeed the military regime. Minority factions have sought to maintain the prevailing scheme indefinitely because only under these conditions could their presence, positions of power, and influence be preserved. Others have viewed the so-called transition period as a time of preparing for new political institutions that would emphasize corporatist features and avoid the most salient features of liberal democracy. Finally, the hegemonic project that evolved over the years within the dominant bloc has envisioned a type of authoritarian regime called "authoritarian democracy," which is characterized by restricted participation, exclusionary mechanisms, and the protective power of the armed forces. The institutional features of this project were manifested in the Constitution of 1980, but aspects pertaining to the political structuring of actors and their dynamic were left obscure. This lack of definition and the competition for positions of power have been the areas where alternative visions within the dominant coalition have sought to prevail. Of interest here are some of the basic features and assumptions on which the future political model is based.

The political model to which the military regime seems to aspire combines a critical vision of recent national history with a particular conception of theory or political philosophy. In terms of national history, the military mentality's paradigm seems to be nineteenth-century Chilean society, with continual invocation of the memory of Diego Portales (one of the founders of the Chilean state). This view envisions nineteenth-century Chile as an orderly society managed in an authoritarian manner, in which enlightened sectors employed mechanisms for regulating their conflicts that did not affect the legitimacy of the system. In contrast, the political society of the twentieth century, especially in recent decades, is perceived as dominated by statism, politicization, and party divisions that were condemning the nation to stagnation, fragmentation, and chaos.

Consistent with this historical vision is a certain theoretical conception that views political freedom as possible only on the basis of economic liberty, which is defined around private property and the free play of the market. But the market of individual competition is not only the economic requirement for political freedom—market mechanisms also provide the foundation for the political system. The resulting fragmentation of the decision-making process converts it into an aggregate of individual calculations that make recourse to collective action and the coalescing of demands unnecessary or irrelevant. This view presumes a society comprised of segmented decision markets. The state's role as economic agent is constantly reduced as is its redistributive capacity, yet the state's potential for defending the rules of the game in an authoritarian manner is strengthened. Also envisioned is a political arena of representation limited to the options offered within these rules of the game. According to this conception, a reduced state is a stronger state not only because it is more manageable but because it avoids the proliferation of political actors seeking to influence decisions that no longer belong to their reduced sphere.

This project's utopian dream is to make organized collective action, politics, and change in society totally irrelevant. But because this goal can never be automatically guaranteed by transforming the market into the general principle of social life, recourse to authoritarian and military power and to exclusionary mechanisms will always be necessary. Such an arrangement requires more than merely strengthening executive power and limiting counterweights. It is also necessary to assign a permanent guardianship to the armed forces, to exclude ideological political currents that can be considered prejudicial to the established order, and to establish the independence of certain economic decisions from political power. Moreover, all these requisites must be constitutionally sanctioned. Thus although this scheme recognizes a political arena and a representative sphere, they are reduced in their decision-making capacity and limited to sectors considered "acceptable" in society.[22] This political model has been described variously as "restricted democracy," "authoritarian democracy," or "protected democracy."

The viability of this project depends on satisfying various conditions as well as maintaining the military regime's longevity and stability. At least three other conditions seem especially important. The first and most essential is the genuine transformation of society in all spheres according to the principles of market competition, reduction of state influence, and fragmentation of demands. This course implies not only institutionalizing these principles in each sphere but their maturing fully into a new type of social relations, which is to say that it requires success in the reorganizational dimension. The other two conditions for viability are linked to political aspects: first, creating a new and autonomous political leadership as a successor to the military regime; and second, co-opting if not the political Center or part of it, at least important elements of its social base—the middle sectors. The evolution of these conditions will be discussed in the following chapters.

Thus a political project has emerged from a perspective that differs from the model of the military regime, although the regime is a necessary precondition for it. Within this project are mingled and harmonized neoliberal conceptions of society as a market, fashionable critiques of the "ungovernability of democracy," and key elements of national security ideology.[23] The project's radical departure from the "compromise state" and the regime that prevailed in Chile until 1973 is that it makes no attempt to base regime stability on consensus via the political party system. Stability is sought instead in an adaptation between a transformed civil society and an institutional system that is both "inherent" in this transformation and protected by military power.

In sum, the processes described can be defined as institutionalizing a personalized political-military leadership that, in turn, points toward the future institutionalization of a regime that is authoritarian but not military. Starting with the promulgation of the constitution in 1981, a decision was made to confront the *problématique* of going from a military regime to a conservative political order that would be consistent with the transformations taking place throughout society. Thus the internal disagreements existing until 1980 have been reduced to a struggle for influence while the military regime remains in force and seem to lack any larger significance except in moments of crisis.

But we are dealing here with a long-term gamble that involves enormous risks. The possibility of creating a new order for civil society buttressed by a corresponding political model inevitably encounters several problems. The first is the extreme vulnerability of the material or economic base, its limited capacity for growth, and its restricted redistributive dynamic.[24] When these limitations confound the expectations created by official propaganda for the economic model, pressures and claims build up that keep alive potential recourse to organization and politics. Although old organizational forms can be dismantled and protest can be segmented, these methods do not eliminate the threat of future reorganization and mass mobilization. Second, structural and institutional transformations can be imposed, but they do not directly guarantee a change in value systems and loyalties. At least a full generation is required for such profound change to mature, and even then loyalty to a new order will not be assured, despite participation in it. The presence of an opposition, however repressed it may be, continues to nourish perception of a potential alternative.

All these obstacles and difficulties have been manifested within the dominant coalition and lie at the root of what will be examined in the next chapter: the crisis of the foundational or reorganizational dimension of the regime, its stagnation, the weakening of the will to dominate, and the primarily "negative" success of the process of transformation. The last factor reveals the regime's greater capacity for dismantling a previous order than for generating a new one, a characteristic that has resulted in frequent cycles of repression.

Notes to Chapter 7

1. Church opposition to the regime will be analyzed later. An especially significant document is *Nuestra convivencia nacional*, which was issued by the National Episcopate (Episcopado Nacional) in March 1977, following the government decree dissolving the Christian Democratic party. International pressure was created particularly by the votes taken in the UN General Assembly condemning violations of human rights in Chile. See also Heraldo Muños, "Las relaciones exteriores del Gobierno militar chileno," *Revista Mexicana de Sociología* 44, no. 2 (Apr.–June 1982).

2. On the "modernizations," see Pinochet's messages of 11 Sept. 1978 and 11 Sept. 1979. A complete "dossier" can be found in *Chile-América*, no. 74–75 (Dec. 1981), published in Rome. On the Labor Plan (Plan Laboral), see VECTOR, "Movimiento sindical: política laboral, tendencias, iglesia, campesinos," *Revista de Talleres*, no. 2 (June 1981); and G. Campero and J. A. Valenzuela, *El movimiento sindical chileno en el capitalismo autoritario* (Santiago: ILET, 1981).

3. The regulations concerning labor unions, student organizations and professional organizations illustrate this point. See Campero and Valenzuela, *El movimiento sindical chileno*.

4. This point applies to the agrarian question. See Jaime Crispi Soler, "El agro chileno después de 1973: expansión capitalista y campenización pauperizante," *Revista Mexicana de Sociología* 44, no. 2 (Apr.–June 1982). On the regulations relating to reducing the role of the state, see P. Vergara, "Las transformaciones del Estado chileno bajo el régimen militar," *Revista Mexicana de Sociología* 44, no. 2 (Apr.–June 1982). On the labor movement, see Campero and Valenzuela, *El movimiento sindical chileno*. This point also applies to the student movement.

5. This discussion by several authors can be found in the conference papers "Para una nueva política," *Margen: Revista de Filosofía y Letras* 3 (1982), published in Santiago. In addition to the works already cited by J. Crispi and J. Bengoa, G. Campero and J. A. Valenzuela, H. Vega, and A. Pinto, see R. Lagos, "La nueva burguesía chilena," *APSI*, no. 101 (June 1981); P. Vergara, *Autoritarismo y cambios estructurales* (Santiago: FLACSO, 1981); F. Dahse, *El mapa de la extrema riqueza* (Santiago: Aconcagua, 1979); and the "dossiers" published in the *Revista Mexicana de Sociología* 44, no. 2 (Apr.–Sept. 1982) and in *Amerique Latine* 6 (1981), published in Paris.

6. On labor relations, see G. Campero and J. A. Valenzuela, *El movimiento sindical chileno*. On changes in social security, see J. P. Arellano, "Elementos para el análisis de la reforma previsional chilena," *Colección Estudios CIEPLAN* 6 (Dec. 1981). On education, see Rafael Echeverría, "Política educacional y transformación del sistema de educación en Chile a partir de 1973," *Revista Mexicana de Sociología* 44, no. 2 (Apr.–June 1982); and G. Briones, *Las universidades chilenas en el modelo de economía neo-liberal, 1973–1981* (Santiago: PIIE, 1981).

7. VECTOR, "Movimiento sindical: política laboral, tendencias, iglesia, campesinos"; and G. Campero and J. A. Valenzuela, *El movimiento sindical chileno*.

8. See Junta Militar de Gobierno, *Declaración de principios del Gobierno de Chile* (11 Mar. 1974).

9. This point is emphasized in Pinochet's message of 11 Sept. 1976, which accompanied the promulgation of the *Actas Constitucionales*, cited in Chapter 4.

10. The Chacarillas Plan was named for the place where Pinochet delivered his speech on 9 July 1977. On the international pressures during this period, see H. Muñoz, "Las relaciones exteriores del Gobierno militar chileno." Prior to the plan, the political parties that had not been proscribed in 1973 were officially dissolved, and new restrictions on freedom of information were promulgated.

11. The commission was named after the individual who presided over it.

12. In July 1980, the Council of State (Consejo de Estado), a consulting body created by the military junta and controlled by Pinochet through appointments, delivered its report to the junta. During this period, a young man kidnapped in a group of students was killed by a team from the security services and a high Army official was assassinated.

13. On the Constitution of 1980, see Chapter 6, note 8.

14. With all these antecedents, the government announced the following results: 67.06 percent in favor; 30.17 percent against; 2.77 percent invalid votes; and electoral participation by 93.1 percent of the eligible voters. If any meaningful comparison can be made with this kind of election, the results of the national plebiscite on 4 Jan. 1978 were supposedly 75.04 percent in favor of the government and 20.32 percent against it. Thus from one plebiscite to the other, the pro-government votes had increased by 26,551 and those for the opposition by 760,217. On the irregularities of the plebiscite, see P. Aylwin et al., "Presentación ante el Colegio Escrutador," *El Mercurio*, 3 Oct. 1980.

15. The concept of "internal crisis" refers here to the social and political coalition in power.

16. The transitory articles of the constitution established that in 1988, a candidate designated by the commanders in chief of the armed forces and the Carabineros and elected in a single-person plebiscite would assume the presidency. If the commanders in chief could not agree on a candidate, the National Security Council would have selected the person. Had this candidate won in the plebiscite, he would have assumed office in March 1989 and Congressional election would have been held one year later. Because Pinochet was appointed candidate and defeated, he will continue as president for one more year until a competitive presidential and parliamentary elections are held. (See *Postscript*.) Such an election, however, may exclude leftist groups and candidates according to Article 8. The Congress to be elected has its powers drastically curtailed and a significant proportion of the Senate members being appointed. Moreover, the definitive articles of the constitution make modifying the constitution almost impossible. The veritable immutability of the constitution and the rules on succession beginning in 1989 have led some regime sectors to plan constitutional revisions, which have been resisted by Pinochet. His defeat in the plebiscite might lead the junta itself to propose a change in the rules of succession.

17. See Transitory Article 24. See also A. González, "Constitución política: disposición 24 transitoria," *Mensaje* 30, no. 300 (July 1981).

18. For example, until 1983 the only student organizations permitted at the universities were those supporting the government. Regarding the situation of labor unions, see the pertinent bibliography cited in Chapter 6.

19. Decrees 1281 and 2146, published in the *Diario Oficial* on 29 July 1981, and Transitory Article 24 of the constitution exemplify official control of information. Television, which reaches the largest audience, is allowed to broadcast only official positions. But several written means of communication have emerged, some protected by the Church, and have achieved limited circulation. Periodicals with a critical slant, an example of limited freedom of speech, have been consistently taken to court, threatened, or closed. Since 1983, however, more opposition journals and magazines have begun to publish, although continually under threats and court orders; in 1986 a few opposition newspapers started circulating.

20. In moments of regime crisis, this theme has been resurrected by nationalist sectors, sometimes in response to Pinochet's vague references to a civilian-military movement.

21. On occasions like the national plebiscites in January 1978 and September 1980, these organizations have shown their efficacy. National secretariats have been established for women, youth, and professional and business associations, in addition to the Directorate of Civilian Organizations (Dirección de Organizaciones Civiles). These organizations, the municipalities, and the organization of mothers' centers (*centros de madres*) directed by Pinochet's wife, Lucía Hiriart, supervise a certain amount of social work by upper-class women who support the regime in several poor urban neighborhoods.

22. Separation of the spheres of representation is manifested in the many barriers and restrictions established in the constitution, which prohibit relations between social and political leadership. See note 16 of this chapter describing certain characteristics of the constitution. Also see note 8 of Chapter 6.

23. See Norbert Lechner, "El proyecto neoconservador y la democracia," *Crítica y Utopía* 6 (March 1982), published in Buenos Aires; and Michel Crozier et al., *The Crisis of Democracy: Report on the Governability of Democracies to the Trilateral Commission* (New York: New York University Press, 1975).

24. This point is confirmed by the complete disintegration of the economic model in 1982. On its vulnerability, see Aníbal Pinto, *El modelo económico ortodoxo y el desarrollo nacional* (Santiago: VECTOR Ediciones Especiales, 1981).

Chapter 8

The Crisis of the Foundational Dimension

The Evolution of Military Regimes

As has been shown, a military regime does not evolve in a linear succession in which the repressive phase is followed by an institutionalizing phase and then by a transition to an authoritarian or some other type of regime. A direct succession is precluded not only by the interconnection already pointed out between the first two phases but also by the possibility of interruption or diversion by crises in the regime. These crises can vary greatly in type and may be provoked by external factors, problems within the regime, or the dynamic of confronting the opposition. Here it should be noted that crises *in* the regime, including those involving changes at the top level, must not be confused with a crisis *of* the regime or a terminal crisis. In this sense, it is helpful to recall the asynchronic development of a crisis in which, for example, a sharpening of tensions and contradictions on the economic level is not necessarily reflected directly on the political level.

A dictatorship can survive from crisis to crisis by making defensive or reactive adjustments and by restructuring short-term alliances. In such cases, the lack of an alternative that can universalize discontent helps prevent a terminal crisis. Thus a dictatorship that defines itself in purely reactive terms as well as one that attempts to reorganize society can both become mere crisis managers. Some features characterizing a regime in this phase are the weakening of its capacity to transform society, the single-minded search for regime survival, the breaking up of the dominant core, recourse to partial solutions, erratic conduct of state government, and fragmentation

149

and breaking away of its sectors of support. In sum, the attempt to direct society as a cultural whole comes to an end, as does the foundational impetus. A regime that is transformed into a crisis manager may endure over time and may undergo changes that lead to redefining the meaning of its original historical project, or it may suffer so much breakdown that it moves rapidly toward its end. This outcome may or may not be fomented, catalyzed, or intensified by opposition forces.

Toward a Regime of Crisis Management

This section will attempt briefly to clarify the *problématique* characterizing the Chilean military regime since 1981, when it experienced a collapse in the foundational dimension and moved toward becoming a regime of crisis management. But the regime was not yet perceived as heading toward a terminal crisis.

As indicated, the 1980 plebiscite and the promulgation of the constitution with its transitory dispositions in March 1981 culminated the phase of political institutionalizing of the regime. By this point, the most obvious tensions within the dominant coalition seem to have been resolved in favor of Pinochet's leadership. Moreover, this resolution took place at a time when the regime was touting the success of its economic model (according to its own official indicators) and when the inauguration of the new Reagan administration appeared to be a positive signal for Latin American military regimes. Adding to this climate of political and economic triumph was an intensification of efforts to transform and reorganize, particularly in the key areas of the universities and social security. Meanwhile, the political opposition had ended a cycle of its own in September 1980 and appeared powerless.

Several months later, however, the extreme vulnerability of the economic base chosen by the regime as the foundation of its historical project was revealed by the bankruptcy of one of the most important economic groups involved in speculation, the CRAV Group (Grupo CRAV). The bankruptcy of this group proved to be an omen of the generalized economic crisis to come in 1981 and 1982. Another significant event was the murder of several bank employees in Calama during a robbery, which was perpetrated by high local officials of the National Information Center (Central Nacional de Información, or CNI). This event demonstrated that the expanded repressive apparatus had become so powerful that it was exceeding any social control. The Calama crimes and other police-related political crimes implicating the security apparatus in 1982 also showed the effects and the magnitude of repressive penetration in society.[1]

The failure of the neoliberal economic model to resolve the problems of growth, investment, employment, and an increasingly unjust distribution of national income had been obscured until 1981 by apparent success according to certain indicators publicized by the government and, above all, by an international economic situation that allowed an excessive flow of foreign capital into Chile. This capital was dedicated purely to financial speculation and luxury consumption based on growing indebtedness. The collapse of this financial climate, combined with the dogmatism and incompetence of the "economic team," laid bare the profound weaknesses hidden beneath the triumphant official discourse. What had been called the "Chilean miracle" showed its true face: increasing economic concentration in the hands of a few groups engaged in irresponsible plundering and speculative manipulation, one of the highest external debts in the world, destruction of national means of production, acute economic stagnation, unemployment totaling almost 30 percent, and the lack of an economic project with solid investment bases for the future.[2]

The economic crisis that unfolded and worsened during 1981 and 1982 had major political effects. It revitalized the debate about the economic model, but now the voices of groups close to the center of power were augmented for the first time by diverse business associations and organized interest groups. A majority of the sectors in the dominant coalition lost faith in the economic model's capacity to succeed. Doubt led to growing isolation of the technocratic team that had been one element of the dominant core directing the state, thus weakening the team's capacity to govern and causing its progressive disintegration.[3] Meanwhile, demands on Pinochet multiplied, and he introduced readjustments here and there to alleviate the pressures. All these events made it impossible to preserve unscathed the socioeconomic model followed until then. Even so, no coherent substitute emerged, despite a general distancing from the team who had implemented the model.

All these events could only lead to disorientation and a crisis in the expectations of the sectors constituting the regime's base of support. The triumphant image dissolved, the regime's capacity to transform society shrank, sectoral interests became fragmented and antagonistic, the political debate over the foundational model sharpened, and repression intensified.

In 1983 a turning point occurred in the crisis of the military regime's transformative project.[4] The crisis in the economic model was affecting large sectors of the middle classes, in some cases multiplying their debts, in others diminishing their bank deposits and savings. This trend alienated these middle-class sectors from the military regime. The resulting relative isolation of the government produced a genuine opening in which organized opposition sectors could publicize their protests and discontent without risking a massacre.

In May 1983, the Copper Workers' Union (the main labor union in Chile) changed its first call for a general strike to a call for a national day of protest. Protest was manifested by Chileans staying home from school, partially disrupting daily activities, briefly demonstrating in downtown Santiago, honking car horns, banging pots and pans, and turning off lights at a prearranged hour. The massive success of the first day of protest surprised both the government and the opposition and inspired the latter to repeat this form of social mobilization, with some variations, during the following months. The first national day of protest and those that soon followed united middle-class and popular sectors on the same side of a political confrontation for the first time in several decades, an alliance that accounted for the massiveness of the protests. This cooperation was later eroded, however, by government efforts to co-opt some business associations economically (mainly through renegotiating debts and making other limited concessions) in order to dissuade them from participating in the mobilizations. Cooperation was also mitigated by middle-class fears of the radical forms of mobilization manifested by youth groups in the poor urban neighborhoods.[5] The result was that subsequent mobilizations became concentrated among more militant groups of youth, students, and especially urban poor sectors, which were being dominated strongly by the military regime. Two other factors should also be mentioned: the repression unleashed against the large labor organizations, first against the Copper Workers' Union (Confederación de Trabajadores del Cobre) and later against the National Workers' Command (Comando Nacional de Trabajadores), which included various broad labor organizations; and the appearance of political parties on the scene when the first protests effectively transferred the leadership of the protest movement to the parties.

But this shift took place at a time when the political opposition needed to get organized and define a precise strategy vis-à-vis the weakened government. Various elements contributed to the opposition's inability to come up with a detailed unified proposal for ending the regime: the debate over abstract models of transition; the notion that the regime's fall was imminent; old ideological and functional identities that led to mutual exclusions; and absolute confidence that social mobilizations alone would lead either to regime collapse or to the armed forces abandoning their loyalty to Pinochet in order to negotiate an exit with civilians. These debates ignored the legitimacy granted by the military to the Constitution of 1980 and the military and political leadership awarded to Pinochet by the regime. In any case, because the opposition lacked a single solution or formula for ending the regime and beginning a transition, the general goal of "Democracy now" (apparently the minimum opposition consensus) failed to become part of a coherent strategy or set of intermediate goals that could maintain a high level of mobilization and force negotiation with the regime. As a result, efforts to mobilize ran out of energy and were reduced to outbursts of agitation by the most activist militant groups.

The government's initial response represented the intensification of purely military logic—a repressive response that did not take into account the political impact of what was happening. The consequences were repression in the poor urban neighborhoods and the detention and exiling of political and social leaders. But beginning with the fourth day of protest in August 1983, this military logic, which had proven unable to prevent continuing mobilizations, was reinforced by a political logic. The political approach had two goals: to regroup dispersed civilian support for the regime and to try to encapsulate the opposition within the regime's institutions by opening a minimal space for limited expression. This "opening" materialized through the efforts of Minister of the Interior Sergio Onofre Jarpa, the highest leader of the Right under Allende who had dissolved his party (the National Party) at the time of the coup so that the Right could fuse with the regime. At the request of the Catholic Church, the newly appointed minister initiated a "dialogue" with some opposition sectors, but it was doomed to failure because the government was disinclined to make any political concessions and the opposition lacked uniform expectations in this regard. Thus the dialogue was not really an opening but a minimal liberalization—informal, erratic, reversible, and accompanied by high levels of repression.

Several months later, the government began to make adjustments in the economic model to calm the business sector, which had been severely affected by the extreme measures of the "Chicago" model. But after a year, the government ended the opening by decreeing another state of siege following a protest that came close to achieving a generalized shutdown, and also because the regime had failed to unify the Right and to encapsulate or neutralize the opposition. By the middle of 1985, however, international pressure—particularly the threat of the United States limiting its loans—led to the state of siege being lifted. The opposition then attempted to relaunch the protest movement with massive demonstrations, while reinforcing political differences and contradictions in a configuration of varying ideological coalitions that made collective manifestations increasingly difficult.

In 1986 a new sociopolitical organization was founded, the Civil Assembly (Asamblea de la Civilidad), in which professional associations predominated but joined forces with labor unions and, formally at least, with sectors in the poor urban neighborhoods. The Civil Assembly attempted to overcome the exclusion of sectors of the Left imposed by rightist groups opposed to the regime, particularly the Christian Democrats, and to organize an extensive plan for mobilizations. After the Civil Assembly successfully halted much daily activity in July 1986 (even though it did not involve the worker sectors completely), the government imprisoned the leaders of the Civil Assembly. The organization's efforts were further frustrated by other opposition set-backs: in August arsenals were found that were attributed to the Manuel Rodríguez Patriotic Front (Frente Patriótico Manuel Rodríguez), the armed organization closely associated with the Communist party; and in September, the same organization made an unsuccessful attempt on Pinochet's life. The climate during the aftermath allowed the government to decree another state of siege and thus shut down the opposition's space for public expression.

At the beginning of 1987, the government again lifted the state of siege and embarked on deepening its political institutionalization by means of the so-called political laws. These regulations dealt with the future electoral system, political parties, and related aspects, all of which allowed establishing rules of the game for a limited and exclusionary political participation within the framework of the Constitution of 1980. These laws also looked toward the 1988 plebiscite in which the commanders in chief of the armed forces were to propose a single candidate for a yes or no vote. This advance in political institutionalization was accompanied by two other complementary processes: Pinochet's national campaign to keep himself in power as the only possible candidate, and increasing legal repression of opposition organizations and channels of expression to prevent them from interfering with the timetable and plan set forth in the constitution.[6]

In sum, the government initially confronted the crisis with a merely repressive logic that neither regulated nor actively intervened in the crisis. Since 1983, however, the government has been consciously managing the crisis to ensure regime survival and continuity according to the institutional design and timetable set forth in the constitution. This strategy has entailed various efforts: combining "closings" with formal or informal liberalizing measures (the return of exiles, erratic acceptance of public demonstrations, and so on); deepening institutionalizing measures that allow for transition from a military regime to an authoritarian regime; maintaining the pattern of personalization to ensure Pinochet's continued dominance; rejecting any kind of negotiation with the opposition and any political arena for confrontation other than the 1988 plebiscite; and continuing to employ repression, whether by proscriptive terms, intimidation, or terrorist operations (like cutting the throats of Communist leaders in 1986 or assassinating twelve persons in one day in 1987).

If the main political goal has been to ensure the continuity of regime institutions and Pinochet's leadership, the main socioeconomic response to the crisis has been economic stabilization. This goal has been approached by renegotiating the external debt according to the rules imposed by the

International Monetary Fund and privatizing state enterprises (both under very good terms for foreign capital) as well as by partially alleviating the indebtedness of leading capitalist sectors in Chile.[7] Political and economic goals have relegated social transformations to a secondary level of importance. Moreover, these efforts have encountered such enormous resistance that they have been partially attenuated.[8]

Meanwhile, social mobilizations and the opposition's public profile succeeded in several ways: by reinjecting politics into Chilean society, overcoming collective fears, partially reorganizing civil society and sociopolitical actors, and in forcing the government to make room for politics (albeit an informal space) and to yield some economic concessions. In other words, the opposition forces have changed the panorama of Chilean society and the regime, even though they have not succeeded in creating social actors who are autonomous of the political sphere or in triggering a process of transition.

Political Alternatives and the Limits of the Crisis

The military regime's entrance into a phase of crisis management has been characterized by a crisis in the regime's foundational dimension, as defined initially in 1975 and subsequently by the process of social institutionalization.

Certainly, a regime that enters a phase defined more by crisis management than by the capacity to transform society will be subject to increasing erosion in support and breaking away of sectors that previously backed it. What is distinctive about a phase like this (which can last a long time) is that each internal sector tends to lose its loyalty to an overall project and instead favor its particular interests: the elite in power seeks only to stay in power; the armed forces worry only about their internal unity and a certain level of control over the crisis; civilian groups push for the corporatist struggle without worrying about maintaining the overall scheme, and so on. Such dissociation of interests leads to irreversible readjustments and a kind of "general stalemate" that can seriously diminish loyalty to the regime. When the regime found itself facing this situation, there were various political solutions that could have maintained the regime's essence even while implying its relative transformation.

One possible solution was to incorporate the armed forces into the decision-making process, from which they have been marginalized by Pinochet during the military regime. This solution might have resulted from a narrowing of Pinochet's room for maneuver, from his firm decision not to open a political arena for resolving competing interests within the dominant coalition, or from the armed forces' growing preoccupation with the economic crisis. Thus such incorporation would have appeared to be a recourse for managing the crisis, restructuring the core directing state policy, and internally relegitimizing governmental action despite loss of support and increasing discontent. But the effects could also have deepened the political crisis in the regime in two ways. On the one hand, the most probable effect of incorporating the armed forces into the decision-making process is that the military mentality would have tended to introduce criteria for state intervention and to have definitively dismantled what had been accomplished without providing a coherent replacement model. On the other hand, there would have been a tendency to isolate the armed forces institutionally from the other sectors of the dominant coalition. A final probable outcome would have been growing politicization of the armed forces, which is usually accompanied by internal divisions and loss of cohesion. Thus all these outcomes could have accelerated a final crisis.

But a crisis in the armed forces has a rhythm and stages of development that do not necessarily correspond to those occurring in the economy and in civil society. In effect, the armed forces need time to internalize the regime's failure as their own. Moreover, the "internal" legitimacy of the constitution and the large corporate and individual benefits received by the military have counteracted the triggering of a crisis leading to a military exit.

A solution of this kind was partially and briefly suggested in 1982, but it was not thoroughly played out. Pinochet resisted this solution because it would have narrowed his discretionary capacity even further. In all probability, this solution would have been one last recourse before a terminal crisis, but even then it would have occurred over Pinochet's objections. Such a situation did not come about, however, and only in 1988 did the armed forces obtain the political initiative to propose a candidate for the presidential plebiscite, and even then they chose Pinochet.

Two other possibilities for restructuring the dominant core were to incorporate more functionally into state governance the business sector, which has traditionally been dominated by the "economic Right" or its representatives, or to lean toward "hard-line" or "nationalist" sectors. The first approach might have appeared to impose too many conditions on a personalized leadership that did not want to renounce its discretionary power. The second approach would have aroused enormous resistance within other sectors of the dominant coalition. Moreover, it would have further isolated the state nucleus within the dominant coalition and would have had to confront the nonexistence of a coherent alternative project that could unify the economic, political, and cultural dimensions into a single model for society.

An intermediate solution that could have been adopted was to create spaces and mechanisms for processing demands. But this course would have required a minimal political arena for channeling and regulating conflicts, and Pinochet has repeatedly rejected any form of political "opening" that lacks constitutional justification. In this sense, the so-called opening did not involve establishing an arena for representation but only tolerating an informal and reversible political space, as when measures of partial relief from the pattern of repression were followed by repeated hardening. Given the strength of Chilean political groups, a real opening would have threatened the regime with the risk of becoming uncontrollable.

The other possible means of transforming the regime while maintaining its essential nature (which could have been attempted independently or in combination with other formulas) was to make changes in the "content" of its policies. This populist temptation has arisen at various points in the regime's history, especially during periods of crisis, but it has been undermined by the lack of a popular base of support as a result of government confrontations with unions and middle-class business and professional associations. Moreover, if the social base of this potential populism had been the poorest and most disorganized sectors, the lack of resources would have precluded the necessary redistributive aspect. In any case, some elements of a limited populism reappeared in 1987, tied to Pinochet's campaign to be designated as the candidate in the presidential plebiscite.

None of these solutions were discarded a priori, but all of them became merely short-term maneuvers for gaining time. Thus what effectively occurred was a kind of adaptation that combined military logic with political logic without any new transformative project. But this adaptation subordinated changes in the governing team and policy content to other goals: to maintaining the essential features of the economic model, now devoid of its triumphant aura; to meeting the requirements of the external debt that had been contracted; and to strengthening the conditions that would permit keeping the regime and Pinochet in power according to the plan established by the Constitution of 1980.

Why did the exhaustion of the foundational dimension lead to some transformations within the military regime but not cause its final crisis? Setting aside opposition factors, the regime's having imposed a process of political institutionalization, time frames, and mechanisms before a crisis arose in its socioeconomic model worked in the regime's favor. Such accomplishments create an internally legitimated framework for resolving conflicts that in crisis situations permits the problem of time frames and transition mechanisms to be perceived as having been resolved. This framework has been the main tool relied on by the regime when its transformative capacity stalls or diminishes. From this perspective, the Chilean military regime has enjoyed an advantage over similar regimes. In one sense, it is evident that the military dream of going from the military regime to a new authoritarian order has been undermined and that the regime's capacity to transform society in this direction and to dominate the process have diminished significantly. In another sense, all sectors of the dominant coalition rely on this common code of time frames and mechanisms embodied in the constitution, and any attempt to revise it would unleash a dynamic that would be hard to control.

The New Features of the Political Model

What changes in the political model of the regime—in its real functioning—came out of its passage to this new phase, defined here as the crisis of the transformative project? As noted, its basic feature has been the introduction of politics into social life. Thus this phase has involved the regime's adding the logic of political calculations to the logic of military action. It has also witnessed the presence of opposition political actors in public spaces despite the fact that no political arena has been established. Consequently, confrontation occurs between the government and the opposition but without any regulated institutional space for it. The next chapter will analyze the changes introduced by this phase in the opposition's course of action. Here I will discuss the new elements introduced within the regime.

The first feature was the unfolding of a new pattern of internal dissent. Business and professional associations that had remained to some degree identified with the dominant core of the state apparatus began to act autonomously by confronting the technocratic component of the regime. The emergence of dissidence within the capitalist class and middle-class sectors dispelled the image of unity projected by the dominant coalition. Moreover, dissent no longer occurred only as debate among political elites, as did the debate between "hard-liners" and "soft-liners" until 1980. Dissent now expressed the social interests of broad groups with considerable capacity to exert pressure.

The evolution of internal dissent varied between socioeconomic groups and groups that were strictly political subsectors. Socioeconomic groups included at least three distinguishable factions. The first was the dominant capitalist core—represented mainly by large business associations, including the Federation of Manufacturing and Commerce (Confederación de la Producción y el Comercio), the National Agricultural Society (Sociedad Nacional de Agricultura), and the Society for Industrial Development (Sociedad de Fomento Fabril), and by some medium-sized business sectors, or what is generally called the "economic Right." These sectors favor corporatist interests strictly and question economic policies that affect them, but they have basically supported the military regime without questioning violations of human rights or pressuring for democratization. They have manifested Chilean capitalists' traditional lack of any ideological political project beyond simple maintenance of their privileges. Finally, these sectors have pledged themselves to support the institutionalization of the military regime and Pinochet's leadership. This stance does not imply that they will not adhere to the rules of the game if a democratic regime is established in the future, but it does suggest that they will not participate in destabilizing the dictatorship or in triggering a transition, although they could back a transition if it became imminent. In any case, these sectors' strong criticism of the government's economic policy during the crisis and until 1984 was reduced to limited questioning after postcrisis adjustments incorporated most of their demands.

The second socioeconomic sector consisted of associations of medium-sized and small entrepreneurs and merchants, truckers, public transportation workers, and middle-level employees. It should be recalled that the political importance of these sectors dates back to period when the Chilean political system was dismembered during the UP government. Because these sectors lack a clear political identity, they can provoke crises and important changes through their impact on the military but cannot ensure that such transformations will be democratic. The political ideology of these sectors contains contradictory elements: a persisting sense of injury suffered during the UP era, general loyalty to the military regime but growing discontent with its policies, and little clearsightedness regarding the future political model. The confusion among these emerging social actors inhibits them and makes their political behavior unpredictable. Moreover, their unity is mainly defensive in favoring sectoral interests that are often contradictory. The government has sought to neutralize these sectors by minimal, timely concessions when they have threatened to join the protest mobilizations.

A third socioeconomic sector consists of the professional associations that mobilized against the UP government and initially supported the coup. During the transformative phase of the regime, laws were promulgated that greatly weakened these organizations in an effort to fragment them. These factions are more susceptible to party influence, although their politicization is relatively ambiguous. Since 1983 the professional associations have begun to define themselves more clearly as part of the opposition. This trend has resulted in the replacement of their leaders, nearly all of whom now identify with the opposition parties.[9] They have also served as the main leaders of the Civil Assembly, which instigated important mobilizations like the work stoppage in July 1986.

As for the political groups attached to the regime, it should be remembered that when the military coup occurred, the Right dissolved the National party in order to merge completely with the regime. Thereafter, its activities were limited to organizing debate among influential groups as to the best means of institutionalizing the regime. Many rightist leaders have served as government appointees or advisors. Starting in 1983, however, an attempt was made to overcome the fragmentation of the Right in unifying efforts that expressed the Right's basic alternatives of becoming the political heir of the regime, pledging itself to regime institutionalization, or filling the role of a democratic Right. The last alternative implied betting on a democratic transition that would be institutionally agreed upon, which would have required establishing ties with opposition sectors of the Center.[10] In 1987, faced with the imminent "political laws," especially the one on political parties, various rightist groups closer to the regime formed the National Renovation party (Partido de Renovación Nacional), which excluded the more recalcitrant nationalist sectors as well as those occupying democratic positions somewhat further from the regime. It is probable that the more democratic sectors of the Right will remain marginalized from this party's attempt to fill the void left by the classical Right while taking advantage of the opportunities provided by the institutional legacy of the military regime.[11]

The second new feature of the political model relates to the government's pattern of responding to the crisis, especially at the highest levels. A rupture occurred in the dominant core of state governance, which was manifested in the dismembering of the "Chicago economic team" and its being gradually removed from higher positions in state government.[12] Yet this disintegration in the dominant core of the state and the decline of the "Chicago team" have not been accompanied by any coherent replacement for the technocratic team. The attempt to incorporate the armed forces into directing economic policy in a more decisive, albeit partial, fashion in mid-1982 met with enough failure to relegate this solution to an uncertain future.[13] Nor has recourse of a functional nature been sought from the business sector, the political Right, or "nationalist" sectors. At most, Pinochet has incorporated various individuals from some of these groups, carefully avoiding the impression that they constitute some form of "representation." This approach has simply reinforced Pinochet's role in directing the state, although he has become more and more isolated. But Pinochet can still count on the unlimited support of the armed forces, which have no political project other than the Constitution of 1980 and their hierarchical and institutional loyalty.

Beneath the level of discourse on permanent ratification of the economic model and its policies, however, modifications were introduced that yielded a set of incoherent contradictions, which blurred the model's logic. These changes and partial adjustments affected the entire sphere of economic policy as well as other areas where the foundational model was being implemented. Such modifications were not part of a larger plan or an overall vision but were instead defensive measures oriented toward economic stabilization, external requirements of the foreign debt, or pressures from certain social sectors. Paradoxically, various partial responses to the crisis have transferred most of its costs to popular sectors yet have entailed greater state intervention in the economy,[14] even when they involved further dismantling of state production and thus contradicted a basic principle of the socioeconomic model implemented since 1975. On the political level, the government's actions have been oriented toward implementing the institutions set forth in the constitution, reducing opposition activity, and ensuring conditions that would allow regime maintenance until 1989 and beyond. Until then, nevertheless, the logic of the military regime will coincide with the logic of Pinochet's personalized dictatorship.

Conclusion

The crisis in the foundational project left the regime with no mission other than political survival according to the pattern of institutionalization set forth in the Constitution of 1980 and defensive adaptation to the new situation created by the economic crisis. Thus the regime was simultaneously attempting to maintain certain essential features of the economic model while undermining its coherence by the responses made to pressures from the regime's coalition of support and from society in general. The dominant core of state government was not replaced, rather, the pattern of Pinochet's personalized power was reinforced.

Meanwhile, politics reappeared in Chilean society, a development that reactivated political parties and produced a confrontation between the regime and the political opposition despite the lack of a regulated arena for such conflict. But the opposition did not succeed in transforming its social force into a political force that could convert the administrative crisis into a final regime crisis and transition process. The reasons for this failure will be examined in the next chapter. Other contributing factors were the type of regime institutionalization prior to the crisis, the personalized leadership's capacity to maneuver, Pinochet's dual legitimacy in the eyes of the armed forces (political as well as institutional-hierarchical), and the gradual, but uneven, erosion of the supporting coalition. Nevertheless, the issue of maintaining or ending the regime and possible strategies for achieving these goals became the major subject of debate and planning by Chilean political actors.

Notes to Chapter 8

1. Moreover, in mid-1981 a national workers' organization made a successful attempt to broaden social demand, this time without the protective mantle of the Church, in presenting the national petition (Pliego Nacional) compiled by the National Trade Union Coordination (Coordinadora Nacional Sindical). The harshness of the reaction against this sector and the sharpening of repression in 1981, which were reinforced by constitutional regulations permitting arbitrary management, demonstrate that stagnation in the efforts to institutionalize is almost always coupled with an intensification of repressive activity.

2. On the nature and origin of the economic crisis and recession, see Aníbal Pinto, "Razones y sin razones de la recesión," *Mensaje* 31, no. 307 (Mar.–Apr. 1982); and P. Vergara, *Auge y caída del neoliberalismo en Chile* (Santiago: FLACSO, 1985). A synthesis can be found in N. Flaño and R. Sáez, *El modelo económico neoliberal frente a la crisis: Chile, 1981–1985*, CIEPLAN Notas Técnicas (Santiago: CIEPLAN, 1986).

3. This team first faced the business sector as a whole and then the large financial groups. The team's presence in the cabinet of August 1982 was significantly reduced, and it disappeared altogether from the cabinet of February 1983.

4. I have dealt with the following aspects in more detail in my book *Reconstruir la política: transición y consolidación democrática en Chile* (Santiago: Editorial Andante, 1987). I have discussed popular mobilizations at length in my essay "Popular Mobilizations and the Military Regime in Chile: The Complexities of the Invisible Transition," in *Power and Popular Protest: Latin American Social Movements*, edited by Susan Eckstein (Berkeley and Los Angeles: University of California Press, forthcoming).

5. Examples of radical forms of mobilization are the "barricades" and bonfires set up in the poor urban neighborhoods. The Manuel Rodríguez Patriotic Front (Frente Patriótico Manuel Rodríguez), which is closely associated with the Communist party, planned national power blackouts to coincide with the national protests, as described in my article "Popular Mobilizations." For a descriptive analysis of the cycle of protests, see G. de la Maza and M. Garcés, *La explosión de la mayoría: protesta nacional, 1983–1984* (Santiago: ECO, 1985).

6. Repressive operations have been unleashed against militants of insurrectionary groups that have proved to be veritable massacres, as in the case of the four Communist leaders whose throats were cut. Also, communications media have been shut down, their boards of directors and reporters jailed, and social and political leaders have been imprisoned. In 1987 a law was promulgated complementing Article 8 of the constitution that broadened political proscriptions and extended their control over the media.

7. See N. Flaño and R. Sáez, *El modelo económico neoliberal*.

8. This point is illustrated by the changes in university policy and by suspension of efforts to transfer control over the educational system to municipal governments. Both instances were strongly resisted by students and teachers.

9. See my article "Estado de sitio y elecciones en la sociedad," *Mensaje*, 34, no. 340 (July 1985), Santiago.

10. Various groups have been fighting over the role of heirs to "Pinochetism": some ultranationalist sectors versus the Independent Democratic Union (Unión Democrática Independiente, or UDI), enjoying strong intellectual influence on the regime and occupying mayoral positions throughout Chile, a faction somewhat like the political arm of the "Chicago economic model" and the Labor Front (Frente de Trabajo), led by Sergio Onofre Jarpa. Staking out an intermediate position has been the National Union (Unión Nacional), which brought together under new leadership important sectors of the old National party. Another political faction consists of former party leaders who reorganized the National party, which is attempting to fill the role of a democratic Right yet stay out of the opposition coalition. Still other smaller groups on the Right, the Republicans and the Liberals, have joined the opposition.

11. Creating a problem of viability for the National party are the National Renovation party (Partido de Renovación Nacional), which merged with the Democratic Union, the Labor Front, and the National Union. The new party tends to be dominated by those favoring regime continuity, who have adopted the Constitution of 1980 as their political model. This tendency was illustrated by the appointment of a former UDI activist as minister of the interior to direct the implementation of the "political laws" ensuring Pinochet's continued rule. This move isolated those sectors favoring constitutional change as a minority within the new party.

12. In January 1983, the state intervened and liquidated several financial entities in an effort to dismantle the two large economic groups that had developed under the protection of the regime itself. This change of course was followed by a cabinet being named that included no one from the "Chicago team."

13. The cabinets of December 1981 and April 1982 reflected a strengthening of the military presence.

14. An example of this outcome has been state intervention in the financial sector.

Chapter 9

Political Opposition to the Military Regime

The crises experienced by the military regime and most of its development have not resulted from any action by the opposition. Rather, these crises have reflected internal strains, contradictions, and conflicts—problems created by the government's own acts rather than barriers erected by the opposition. Such a view does not imply, however, that there has been no opposition or that the opposition can be evaluated solely in terms of its irrelevance or failures. In this chapter, I will discuss only the opposition to the Chilean military regime that is political in nature.

The Opposition under Authoritarian Regimes

Political opposition to such regimes involves an inherent paradox. It seems natural to analyze any opposition movement in terms of its capacity to provoke or accelerate the regime's fall, that is, to eliminate and replace the regime, not just replace an administration while maintaining the government, as occurs in democratic governments. Yet history seems to demonstrate that authoritarian regimes do not always fall because of the efforts of the opposition, even though the opposition's existence may have been very important.[1] Thus just as the success of these regimes can be measured by various factors or limited achievements rather than by the fulfillment of their historic project or mission, so the value and success of opposition forces are measured not only by the collapse of a regime or by the total replacement of its mission but also by partial successes. Such achievements may include a variety of endeavors: creating relatively free spaces; launching new courses of action; defending certain rights, persons, and organizations; maintaining hope for an alternative government; instilling in new sectors traditions that offer the hope of an alternative; making gradual inroads into the regime itself; and organizing and animating sectoral resistance in various social spheres. Although the opposition continually risks total immobilization, it cannot always escape the paradox inherent in being a historical movement that denies, denounces, and challenges the regime yet cannot stop the regime's consolidation and legitimation.

During the early years of an authoritarian regime, the opposition can only be defensive in nature because its priorities must emphasize the simple physical survival of persons and organizations. This defensive posture is required of both the political apparatuses per se—the parties—and the social movement and its organizations, all of which the regime is attempting to repress, eliminate, disperse, or dismantle. During the course of this phase, two important phenomena tend to appear that help shape the opposition and continue to develop later. The first is the emergence of spaces that become an alternative for the political arena, like those created under the protection of organizations of broad legitimacy, mainly the Catholic Church. Second, sectors are incorporated into the opposition that initially supported the coup, explicitly or tacitly, but did not identify totally with the regime. This process gives the opposition a relatively heterogeneous character that leads some observers to speak of "oppositions" rather than a single opposition. The time required for this process actually facilitates consolidation of the regime in power and its dominant core.

But the political diversity of the opposition is not the only factor that encourages talk of "oppositions" and raises the issues of the "unity" and the "alternative" represented by the opposition. As will be shown, the impact of political organizations varies significantly according to the national experience that preceded the authoritarian regime, the degree of these organizations' interrelatedness with social movements, and the vigor and autonomy of civil society. It is interesting to observe that in the alternative arenas and the spaces created by the social institutionalization of the regime's project (and as a result of its contradictory relation with this process) the diversity of the social movement is recreated. Whether this process involves political organizations surviving from the previous government, those emerging from political institutionalization, or those appearing around the edges, the inherent characteristics of the authoritarian regime create tension between the tendency toward an elitist politics and the relative proliferation, dispersion, and search for autonomy by these social organizations. Somehow, the spaces created in these regimes lead to a social movement being established from "below," while the more or less traditional activities of political parties tend toward a social movement being set up from "above." Within both processes there exists a problematic convergence.

Both the opposition's political diversity and this problematic convergence between political parties and the social movement reduce the opposition's capacity to establish itself as a real political "actor" for some time. Rather, these factors convert the opposition into a "space" for partial convergences, which explains why opposition behavior tends to be adaptive and reactive to the dynamics generated by the dominant bloc.

As noted, the course of action adopted by the opposition to these regimes has several main thrusts. The first is elemental—the survival, maintenance, and regeneration of organizational structures. The second thrust, which seems the most obvious, is the struggle to overthrow the regime. The third seeks to elaborate and prepare a future alternative to the military regime, while the fourth deals with the issue of democratizing society. The democratizing thrust manifests at least three goals under a military regime: to create and organize social actors who can express the autonomy and dynamic typical of civil society; to resist the transformations that the regime is attempting to impose on society by creating obstacles to state policies; and to achieve at least partial victories and advances in creating democratic spaces.

As noted, the history of these regimes and the opposition to them reveal a dissociation occurring among these dimensions, with the result being that the problems resolved and the successes achieved in one area do not necessarily correspond to resolutions and successes attained in others. The opposition may have failed in its efforts to overthrow the dictatorship yet have succeeded in maintaining its political organizational structure. It may have established a political alternative to the regime and yet lack the means to precipitate the transition. The opposition may have made civil society more democratic while having failed in its attempt to change the regime. The opposition may also bring about the overthrow or the fall of the regime without having achieved any degree of democratization in the aspects outlined. Moreover, it is possible that various sectors of the opposition may emphasize different goals or that during its evolution, these emphases may become displaced. Therefore, analysis of the role of the opposition in a given military regime should never take a one-dimensional approach, even when the opposition's rhetoric tends to stress the objective of overthrowing the regime.

As suggested earlier, many of these themes raise the classic problem of the "unity of the opposition." There is a tendency to attribute the continuity of a dictatorship or military regime to this lack of unity. What is certain, however, is that the durability of a dictatorship is often due to many factors that have little to do with opposition unity, which by itself is not necessarily a determining factor in ending a dictatorship. Moreover, the opposition's diversity can often enhance its capacity to bring together divergent social sectors that oppose the regime. But it is also certain that political parties, which have lacked relevance under the military regime, will enter the public arena at given moments and tend to become the crucial political actors. Such entrances seem to coincide with moments of crisis within the regime or attempts to define its future. In these instances, opposition unity becomes a key factor in accelerating the regime crisis. But here I am referring to neither ideological unity nor functional or programmatic unity. Rather, all these dimensions tend to divide the opposition and be expressed in terms of exclusions. Actually, opposition unity is required only on two particular matters: consensus on the formula for a political solution to end the military regime in operational and institutional terms, and agreement on the operations and mobilizations required to "push" in the direction of the proposed formula. But this accord cannot exclude any significant actor who could diminish the opposition's mobilizational strength. In other words, a time comes when the party level must predominate, and it must be achieved by transforming social demand into political demand for a regime change, which partly depends on having resolved the problem of linking party structure with society.

The Central Problems

The element that seems crucial in comprehending the problems of the opposition in Chile is the elimination of the political "arena." This assertion seems an obvious one in analyzing any repressive authoritarian regime. Yet actions such as eliminating or restricting public spaces, persecuting dissenters, and attempting to eradicate politics do not have the same effect in all instances of authoritarianism. Although these approaches are built into this type of regime, their consequences are not always the same. The Chilean case fits the historical pattern in which the political party arena becomes the main means for a social movement's self-realization. At such a time, a class, group, or social category recognizes itself as more than a simple, relatively homogeneous aggregation. It has become a movement that is pursuing goals and interests as well as the means through which these interests can compete for realizing and universalizing themselves. It should be recalled that in Chile social organizations like labor unions or student movements became social actors precisely because of their interests in common with politicians and their relationship to the state.[2] Under the Chilean military regime, however, these organizations were deprived of the political elements that gave them national relevance and were reduced to their corporatist dimension.

Whatever the sociohistorical reasons that assigned this role to the political party system (as described in the first chapter), the result is that when the political arena is eliminated, the consequences inflict more than a simple defeat. This approach destroys the basic means for organizing the popular movement and its most significant nuclei. In such instances, eliminating politics represents much more than a simple reactive or defensive measure of repression. It also takes on a basic dimension of reordering society because the process of redefining political space forces a reestablishing or renewing of the social movement, which takes a long time. As a result, party structure must remain frozen once it has been alienated from the political regime under which it established its basic relationships with the social movement. Party organizations do manage to renew themselves eventually and survive, despite the repression unleashed against them—the deaths, exiles, disappearances, and imprisonment of leaders and party activists. But to the extent that public spaces are opened, the parties tend to lag behind the social movement and to experience great difficulties in becoming part of the social fabric because they must operate clandestinely. In this circumstance, the political "supply" does not meet the social demand.

This phenomenon tends to be aggravated by the other characteristic of the Chilean regime analyzed here: its attempt to reorganize all of Chilean society from top to bottom. The regime's ultimate logic has been to eliminate all the structural bases that had allowed any form of class-based or popular activity to develop. In this sense, a number of regime measures went beyond simply attempting to repress and eliminate all opposition: the move toward "outward-oriented" development; progressive elimination of redistributive intervention by the state; the fragmentation of production; the unrestricted reign of market mechanisms not only in the economy but in all spheres of social life; and elimination of the "participatory" interferences of social organizations. This "activist" thrust of the regime introduced the series of structural transformations and concomitant processes of institutionalization already discussed. Not all transformations have achieved the success expected by their promoters. But one need think only of the Labor Plan, the transformations of the educational system, the various privatizations, or the drastic changes in the agricultural sector to realize that social stratification, the makeup of classes, and their behavior and values all tend to be altered by such policies. The structural bases on which worker, student, and peasant movements were built, or on which the relations between the middle classes and the state were established, are changing. Thus the society in which all the familiar political parties developed is now disappearing. Not only have political conditions and spaces changed (which enormously hinders party activity), but the entire society is changing, along with the structural conditions under which social movements and their political expressions are generated. This change is occurring not in the sense of modernization or development but through a kind of decomposition of the preceding system.

The situation facing the political party system in Chile is also an ambivalent one. In one respect, the survival and activities of the parties are indisputable facts. When some political space was opened in 1983, the same parties whose elimination had been sought reappeared and became valid and legitimate participants. This outcome is partly explained by the historical-structural reasons already discussed: the existence of a party spectrum with firm roots in society that encompassed more than a limited politicized minority and became the preferred channel of mediation between society and the state, and a thriving culture established at the national level with identifying symbols.[3] But the reemergence of the political parties is also explained by the characteristics of a regime that, in order to eradicate political parties, would have to resort either to genocide or to totalitarian control through mobilizing and fanaticizing its supporters. The intent to depoliticize is a double-edged sword, for it freezes and solidifies already existing structures. Thus, eliminating the political arena converts society's new organizations into the natural sphere of activity for political parties. The necessity of working clandestinely actually reinforces existing party organizations by hindering the creation of new structures and networks. Moreover, the lack of political space prevents the renewal of leadership and strengthens the symbolic value of the old leaders as the only point of reference for the wider public. Thus except for the Right (which renounced its own political identity in order to fuse with the leadership of the military regime and only recently seems to be attempting independent political reintegration), the Center and the Left in Chile have maintained their functional and symbolic identities.

In another respect, elimination of the political arena and the introduction of social transformations have together created severe problems for parties attempting to readapt (setting aside the question of their viability). These problems have challenged the parties' capacity to reestablish themselves within the social movement and become significant actors. Throughout the first phase of the regime, the basic goal was necessarily to maintain party structure, concentrating on ways to preserve and develop internal organization. But this emphasis also led to persistent problems of self-affirmation and continuity, hindered perception of what was new in society, and rigidified theoretical reelaboration by freezing it in the political language of old formulas and categories. On examining the internal and interparty debates and public statements during the first phase of the military regime, it becomes evident that old concepts predominated in the themes, theoretical references, and language. Only later, as new public spaces opened and modes of repression changed, did new themes begin to flourish and what was new in society begin to permeate the parties. Even then, the new themes spread only slowly and vaguely, often dressed in old rhetoric and operating within an organizational structure or spectrum that remained basically unchanged. The spheres not controlled by the regime—those generated by institutionalizing at the social level and those emerging from the protection offered by the legitimacy and relative immunity of the Church—all function as alternatives for the political structure sought by the social movement. But the political parties move with difficulty within these new spaces because the rules for social action have changed substantially.

Yet despite all that has been said, it should be remembered that in other countries as well, funeral orations were read for political parties that later proved to be alive and well. Despite years of authoritarianism and its impact on society, Chilean political loyalties have been essentially maintained, and resurrected political symbols have proved capable of again uniting social sectors supposedly transformed radically by profound structural changes. The ambivalent status of the political party structure in Chile is illustrated by two phenomena. First, it is undeniable that some autonomous organizations in civil society emerged in spaces not controlled by the government, spaces created by "substitute" actors, mainly the Catholic Church. But it is equally undeniable that party militants and activists played a key role in breathing life into these organizations. Second, although events in civil society were crucial in determining the configuration of the opposition and although political organizations merely reacted to changes inflicted by the regime until 1983, the party structure played key roles in certain situations and in social mobilization. But the ideological and organizational features that the opposition inherited precluded the necessary cooperation and coordination. This legacy also impeded formulating a consensual proposal for ending the regime that could channel social mobilization.

As a result, during the authoritarian regime in Chile, the opposition has faced two major problems: first, the problematic convergence between political structures and the social movement; and second, the need to reorganize the political structure and build interparty coordination around a formula for ending the regime. The second problem has hindered efforts to launch a transition process. But the solutions to both problems are closely interrelated in the Chilean situation.

The Evolution of the Opposition

Analyzing the evolution of the political opposition to the Chilean military regime reveals that its course of development until 1980 emphasized maintaining and renewing its organizational structure as well as creating a united front that could offer an alternative to the regime. Except for a small minority, the opposition stressed these goals over eliminating the regime. The other aim of establishing social goals and actors was also relegated to subordinate status. The debate over strategy was replaced by certain myths predicting the inevitable fall of the dictatorship, and the restructuring of civil society became somehow identified with the restructuring of political parties.

The first wave of opposition to the regime consisted of social and political sectors of the Left who had been defeated by the military coup. But they were unprepared for the magnitude of the repression that ensued—the killings, detentions, disappearances, threats, and exilings of leaders and activists, as well as the systematic attack on leftist political organizations and popular and student social organizations. This multifaceted repression made the physical survival of opposition leaders and activists and the preservation of a minimal organizational structure almost the only possible goals.

During the first weeks of military repression, an actor of fundamental political significance emerged—the Catholic Church. After initially calling for "reconciliation," the Church began to serve as the locus in society where information could accumulate about the repressive character of the regime and where abuses were denounced, minimal demands for survival were channeled, and strategies of judicial defense were developed to deal with this power that was violently imposing itself.[4] Moreover, the Church became the only place where social organizations could regroup and voice opposition. As for the tension created between the Church as a space for convergence and its logic as an autonomous actor, this difficulty will be discussed later.

The same aspects of the repressive system that eventually impinged on the Christian Democratic party and blocked its initial attempts at conditional collaboration with the military combined with growing perception of the true character of the government to encourage the party to join the opposition. This outcome defined the main *problématique* of the opposition as how to coalesce when sectors of the Left (mainly in the Socialist party) initially rejected any form of collaboration with the Christian Democratic party while other groups (such as the Communist party) sought its collaboration.[5] During this period, debate centered on forming broad or antifascist coalitions and determining the best alternatives to the military regime. But the opposition's main accomplishment turned out to be creating spaces that combined party presence with individual initiatives. One example was the Constitutional Study

Group (Grupo de Estudios Constitucionales, or Grupo de los 24), which was initially dedicated to preparing an alternate constitution but became instead an arena for dialogue among different sectors of the opposition.

This process of convergence culminated with the plebiscite in 1980. Although the Center seemed to predominate publicly, most of the opposition's social backing actually came from leftist sectors. The degree of mobilization achieved at this time, especially in popular sectors traditionally associated with the Left, reached its highest point since the coup, a peak that would not be surpassed until 1983.

But the plebiscite also marked the end of efforts to revitalize and unify party structures inherited from the democratic period. The issues that came to the fore next were such problems as how to end the regime and how to reorganize a society profoundly transformed by regime efforts to dismantle it. The possibility of violently overthrowing the regime was brought up by the exiled Communist party leadership, which caused its estrangement from the Christian Democrats and a realignment in the structurally fragmented Left.

Only after the plebiscite in 1980 did the theme of overthrowing the regime dominate opposition debates, thus reflecting the internal shifts occurring within the opposition. But this change occurred just at a time when the regime had reached its height, when the social transformations imposed by the regime were becoming evident. By this time, traditional points of reference for political organization and activity seemed to have lost their meaning, and the need to create new sociopolitical actors appeared to be the top priority. Without such organizing, the parties' survival might become irrelevant, and the issues of overthrowing the regime and developing alternatives to it would remain elite debates lacking the power and influence to unite Chileans. Thus defining strategy and redefining social actors and themes became the opposition's priorities during the period following the plebiscite.

Since the 1980 plebiscite, four significant phenomena have emerged.[6] First, the Communist party's new emphasis on insurrection began to orient its strategy and activities, especially in the poorest neighborhoods. Second, the Christian Democratic party's redefinition of its leadership made it more inclined toward reaching an understanding with the Left, although it still rejected an all-encompassing agreement with the Communist party. Third, tendencies toward renewal were strengthened in the Socialist camp, which has also experienced a unifying trend among its more traditional factions. The fourth phenomenon has been the development of spaces, organizations, events, and opposition activities generally revealing a dual thrust toward party identification at the elite level and greater autonomy at the intermediate and base levels.

As already indicated, the 1982 collapse of the economic model, the centerpiece of the military regime's entire political project, forced the regime into a phase of crisis management, although the economic crises were not severe enough to provoke a terminal crisis. The major phenomenon of this phase was, in my view, the massive irruption of a protest movement expressing popular and middle-class discontent. The first protest in May 1983 originated more from the large labor unions than from the leadership of the political parties. But these first protests caused the regime to initiate a "political opening" that was erratic, informal, reversible, and accompanied by high levels of repression. The purposes of this opening were to rebuild regime support and to encapsulate and channel the opposition. The opposition entered the public arena by organizing large ideological coalitions, which caused the party centers to become further removed from the social bases that had supported the first protests.[7] As a result, these social bases gradually dwindled down to groups of students and working-class youth. Although these youth groups are the most active sector, they are also the most difficult to channel and represent. Moreover, the lack of any opposition strategy for ending the regime led to ongoing destabilizing activities that had no political backing. Also lacking were transition formulas for negotiating with a military power that was rejecting any move in this direction. As noted, this impasse caused the "opening" to be closed at the end of 1984, when a state of siege was declared that lasted until the middle of 1985; it was later renewed from September 1986 until January 1987. In 1987 the regime began to implement the "political laws" required by the Constitution of 1980, thereby making a restricted and exclusionary party system official.

Within the opposition movement, the problem in the last few years has been how to overcome the fragmentation produced by divisions among parties. Several initiatives have emerged around the concept of a "single opposition," but none of them have prospered because they have emphasized either the functional aspect or ideological-doctrinal issues. The most important initiative was the one promoted by the Archbishop of Santiago, Cardinal Juan Francisco Fresno, whose role suggests the difficulties in achieving cooperation among political leaders. In August 1985, various groups, some very close to the military regime, signed the National Accord for the Transition to Full Democracy (Acuerdo Nacional para la Transición a la Plena Democracia). Although this accord represented the broadest agreement yet reached among civilian sectors under the military regime, it was weakened by a lack of consensus on timetables and mechanisms for ending the military regime. The accord was also weakened by having excluded those sectors of the Left represented in the Popular Democratic Movement (Movimiento Democrático Popular), especially the Communist party. An attempt was made in 1986 to overcome some of these deficiencies by signing another document that included new groups. But some of the accord's original participants did not sign the new agreement, and it continued to exclude the Communists and significant factions of the Socialists. Moreover, the Democratic Alliance (Alianza Democrática) suffered several defections, and the Popular Democratic Movement was replaced by the United Left (Izquierda Unida), which still excluded one Socialist group. Thus concerns about preserving identities and leaderships, as well as tactical calculations regarding alliances and exclusions, have taken priority over developing a coherent and consensual strategy of transition.

The regime's so-called political laws revived the debate over the opposition's options. The imminence of the 1988 plebiscite led most of the opposition to propose "free elections." This goal was initially formulated by one group of individuals, but eventually nearly all the opposition parties pledged themselves to it and created interparty committees to promote this goal. For the first time, the opposition put aside its abstract debates and confronted an alternative option to the regime, although without specifying any mechanisms. As part of the call for free elections, the opposition launched a campaign for enrolling voters in the registers, as required by regime law. Thus in the plebiscite in October 1988, the opposition finally managed to confront the government in the electoral arena. The initial refusal of some Socialist factions and the Communist party to participate in enrollment yielded to a more realistic position that ended disagreement in this regard, at least. The theme of free elections gave way to debate over alternative courses of action following 1988 plebiscite. All these considerations have placed the opposition on the terrain of developing feasible strategies, an area where pragmatic cooperation—without exclusions—is not only necessary but possible. Regarding the law on political parties, which could institutionalize an official, but illegal, party system, opposition debate has not yet reached a consensus and risks new divisions on this issue. In any case, the opposition's increased realism and convergence concerning alternatives for ending the regime reveal two weak areas: slowness in responding combined with a reactive character, and a tendency to lose touch with social mobilizations just at the times most favorable to converting them into a massive mobilization aimed at specific goals of regime change.

A latent problem that has faced the opposition throughout its evolution is the question of how to reconstruct its identity according to new conditions for organizing social actors and how to become an alternative to the regime. This problem arises because the rupture of the previous means of organizing sociopolitical actors has been accompanied by a persisting political party structure inherited from different social conditions, a structure that can therefore no longer rely on its past relationships to the social movement and the state. This difficulty explains the opposition's slowness at political regrouping as well as its having to work through a variety of inherited organizations. The Chilean opposition has evolved out of two sources. One consists of political organizations, and the other of what might be called the "social opposition," as expressed through popular-sector organizations that are mainly groups of workers, urban poor, and students. These groups are trying to make room for their claims against persecution and repressive threats and are attempting to broaden the nature of their demands without losing touch with social bases that are fragmented and plagued by problems of daily survival. Among these groups, a highly complex process of redefinition is occurring via reorganizing groups and social actors, which is producing change in the relations between parties and social movements. But only with difficulty can this process crystallize into an act of political refoundation.

The problem facing the opposition is extremely complex. It seems to suggest the paradox that the very conditions and characteristics that allowed a strong and stable democratic regime to exist in Chile have turned out to be the same factors that limit the activities and regrouping of the political opposition during an authoritarian regime. Yet in crisis situations—when the regime is disintegrating or experiencing critical moments of political self-definition—these same characteristics once again demonstrate their value. All these problems will now be examined in terms of the main political actors in the opposition.

The Political Actors: The Center and the Left

The *problématique* of the political Center, meaning the Christian Democrats, until the regime's crisis of 1981–82, can be summarized briefly. With important exceptions, the top officials of the Christian Democratic party, other sectors of the Center, and many of their supporters explicitly or tacitly approved of the military coup in September 1973. Several subsequent factors, however, have propelled the Christian Democrats toward the opposition camp: the new regime's prolonging restrictive measures indefinitely; the repression impinging on Christian Democratic party leaders, activists, and sympathizers; and growing perception of the true nature of the regime. In the process, the Christian Democratic party had to confront a long-standing problem of its own—the party's political isolation and its difficulty in establishing solid alliances. The Christian Democrats were becoming more and more radically opposed to the regime's political agenda, its overall plan, its high degree of ideological and functional structuring, its autonomous and "alternativistic" political plans, and its centristic messianism. Yet such opposition did not make the Christian Democratic party the natural field of attraction for moderate sectors of the regime (known as *blandos* and *aperturistas*) nor for sectors disillusioned with the regime. The reason was that the Christian Democrats lacked a coherent strategy with respect to such sectors. At the same time, the Christian Democrats' old distrust of the Left, the group that shared the party's opposition to the regime, combined with the Left's disunity regarding the Christian Democrats to preclude any stable agreement between the two groups. Indeed, the lack of agreement, especially with the Communist party, has been viewed by the Christian Democrats as a means of lining up political support elsewhere.

Moreover, the Christian Democratic party is the opposition sector that, because of its multiclass makeup, has the least-structured relationship with any single social base and therefore needs an open political system to sustain its bases of support and ensure its political viability. Yet the Christian Democrats' demand for a return to a democratic regime as a postauthoritarian alternative was not accompanied until much later by coherent formulas for ending the military regime nor by any broader plan for change that could solidify political democracy. On a strictly political level, several factors enabled the Christian Democratic party to cohere ideologically and then predominate within the opposition movement: the party's ties with other national and foreign centers of influence; its support among middle and popular sectors; its greater possibilities for public activity; and its affinities with the Catholic Church, which have allowed the party to capitalize politically on Church actions. But the problems just outlined counteracted these factors and made the political behavior of the Christian Democrats basically reactive, thus raising questions about the ability of the Christian Democrats to bring together those sectors that comprised the party's representative base.

After the 1980 plebiscite, the Christian Democratic party found itself an organization with resources and a public presence, but one whose capacity for representation appeared to be seriously damaged. This realization initiated a lengthy process of internal restructuring and debate concerning party leadership. The normal temptation in the political Center to seek spaces within the regime that would allow its survival and growth had been thwarted by the previous experience of many of the other sectors comprising the Center. These sectors had already discovered the repressive nature of the regime directly as a result of their links with a long ideological tradition that is critical of capitalism. Also working against the Christian Democrats' reaching an understanding opposition sectors were old ideological and organizational barriers that hindered reaching solid agreements with the Left. These obstacles included the fear of being overrun by the Left, distrust of the Communist party, the self-perception of being the alternative to the "Left and the Right," and so on. For all these reasons, the Christian Democratic party was not the place to rebuild a political Center that could serve as an intermediary and a transition from the military regime while welcoming the groups dissenting or detached from the military regime. But neither could the Christian Democratic party exercise any systematic leadership of the political opposition by establishing an alliance with the Left. As a result, until 1983 the Christian Democratic party appeared to be an actor with expectations rather than one consciously participating in a historic movement. This lack of purpose, however, did not prevent large numbers of activists from encouraging social opposition movements.

But as it turned out, the deepening regime crisis in 1982 coincided with the resolution of the problem of party and national leadership following the expulsion of the president of the Christian Democratic party in 1980 and Eduardo Frei's death in early 1982. These events, combined with an internal restructuring and reintegration of the party with major social bases (labor and professional groups), allowed the Christian Democratic party to broaden its capacity to unify supporters and become the visible focal point of regime opposition and an eventual transition process.

After the first protests in 1983, the Christian Democratic party broke out of its isolation to play an active role in organizing a political coalition that included sectors of the Right, Center, and Left (the Democratic Alliance) but excluded the Communist party and some Socialist factions. In the following years, the Christian Democratic party joined in several multiparty agreements within the opposition, including the National Accord and the Movement for Free Elections (Movimiento por Elecciones Libres), although always insisting on the exclusions noted. All these actions suggest that a significant learning process has taken place. But it remains to be seen whether the Christian Democratic party will prove capable of understanding that a transition process must avoid excluding significant actors and that a stable democratic solution for Chile requires a progressive coalition that will ensure socioeconomic transformation, which in turn calls for the active participation of the Left. This necessity will require the Christian Democratic party to abandon its isolationist tendency in relation to the Communist Left.

As is well known, the parties and organizations of the Left suffered most from the repression, with the persecutions, prohibitions, and exilings of key leaders weighing most heavily on leftist groups. Thus the first priority for leftist party structures was to ensure their own survival and recovery after being torn away from the social movement and dismantled. This challenge was addressed in various ways, according to each party's capacity to respond.[8]

Thus the Left constituted the first and most radical opposition to the military regime. It is probable that members of the Left lacked any awareness of the regime's capacity to prolong its rule. Throughout the first phase of the Left, themes of survival, self-affirmation, and continuity were stressed, although the language and symbols were adapted to new realities. The next stage (which varied from organization to organization) emphasized self-criticism of past accomplishments, although such critiques referred almost exclusively to procedural errors and only tangentially to fundamental elements and leftist formulation of its historic mission.[9] For a long time, initial calls for "establishing broad anti-fascist coalitions," "democratic recovery," or "resistance" (according to the party issuing the calls) were repeated with neither variations nor precise references to changes in the Left's political goals. But eventually, the theme of allying with the political Center and reestablishing ties with movements in civil society (a process paralleling the regime's consolidation) became the dominant issues for a new debate among factions of the Left.[10] This shift seemed to mark the end of the expectations during the first period regarding the intrinsic weaknesses of a regime that was moving quickly toward its own collapse. This shift was also evidenced at the time of the plebiscite by the emergence of a debate about using violence to end the regime. Some sectors of the Left that did not belong to the UP coalition, such as the Movimiento de Izquierda Revolucionaria (MIR), had staked out an insurrectionary position from the beginning. But it was the Communist party's change of course in September 1980 that caused this theme to permeate and reorder the debate within the Left as a whole.[11]

The earlier developments paralleled other processes occurring throughout the Left, which were the combination of old unresolved problems and new challenges resulting from broad social changes effected by the military regime in recent years. From an organizational perspective, perhaps the most significant of these changes was the disappearance of Popular Unity as a political coalition. Its demise revealed a fragmented party spectrum in which new alignments coalesced around the two sources of political action on the Left.

The Communist party, despite its capacity for survival and growth, has continued to manifest ambiguity and duality in its traditional line of political action and its incursion into insurrectionary tendencies pointing more toward revolution than toward a political outcome. This unresolved ambiguity has reinforced both the Communist party's political isolation and the Christian Democrats' excuse for excluding it from political agreements. It remains to be seen whether the traditional factions of the Communist party will succeed in returning to the classical party line, but doing so will require an end to exclusions that only reinforce the insurrectionary sectors. The Socialist party has displayed multiple fragmentations in which party boundaries have not seemed to be based on real political options but have instead reflected a history of inertia. The parties that emerged out of the Christian Democratic party and became integrated into the Left at the end of the 1960s and during the UP era have achieved some influence in certain public forums. But they have lacked the necessary presence in broader social sectors and consequently face the threat of becoming unviable organizations.

Overall, efforts to reorganize and reestablish political parties remain confused and caught in crystallized organizational structures. This outcome may be the result of the fact that all the organizations of the Left are pushed and pulled by another duality: the coexistence of a concept of politics and political action dominant in the 1960s and early 1970s alongside emerging new political concepts and styles that emphasize popular remobilization and redefinition of relations between social movements and political parties.

Let us now consider the coexistence of the two sources of political action within the Left.[12] The classical source, which dominated all Chilean leftist organizations in the 1960s and early 1970s, is based on more orthodox Marxist-Leninist ideology. But another model of political action evolved on the Left as a result of the defeat of the popular movement in 1973, the critique of past socialist experiences, and the lessons learned during the early years of the dictatorship. The coexistence of these two sources of political action within the Chilean Left has produced asymmetrical organizational forms. The classical source manifests itself mainly through the Communist party and secondarily through a few socialist sectors and the MIR. The nontraditional source is manifested in various groupings: in broad sectors of the Socialist parties, in sectors of parties that broke away from the Christian Democrats like MAPU (Movimiento de Acción Popular Unitaria) and the Christian Left (Izquierda Cristiana), and in large independent sectors of the Left. But the emergent tendency lacks the functional unity needed to become a political force that could redefine the politics of the Left. The alternatives here are either simple rebuilding of the party structure that existed in 1973, thus reunifying the Socialist party, or a genuine political redefinition that could broaden political appeals beyond party boundaries and shape a new focus within the Left. Such redefinition would involve a profound renewal of the political leadership and a radically new panorama of Chilean politics. It remains to be seen whether the political leaders' sense of responsibility to the nation will prevail over the inertia of the old structures.

Alternative Spaces and Actors

The dismantling of the political arena and the relative neutralization of political party structures are connected with the Catholic Church's emergence as a political-social space and an actor of primary importance.[13] To some extent and in certain phases, the Church acquired the role of being an alternative for the political system. In the earlier period, the Church's activities consisted of protecting and defending sectors that were being physically persecuted and repressed. But from the outset of the regime, the Church emerged as the only organization with enough legitimacy to address the military establishment in the name of the general good and the well-being of the nation. The reduction of public space by the regime was gradually countered by a corresponding expansion of the Church's own space as well as a growing and sometimes monopolistic presence of the Church in that public space. The Church's relative immunity derives from its legitimacy for political authorities who identify themselves as Catholics and claim to be the defenders of the Christian world.[14] But it is the Church's legitimacy for society in general that determines its capacity to become a refuge. The two factors together explain why the Church could take on activities and new forms that were unheard of when the social movement was able to express itself directly.

Some kind of organizational dimension is also evident in this situation. In responding to the void left by banned social organizations and to attempts to fragment Chilean society, the Church seems to have provided an organizational space for representing "general" interests and demands, a space analogous to that provided by the political system before the military crackdown. An ideological-cultural dimension is also evident in that the most organized ideological expressions of Chilean popular and social movements emerged in the context of a development model and a political system profoundly altered by the military regime. This void could not be filled by the ruling group's ideology because the regime's bases of legitimacy are too shaky to allow its ideology to predominate. Nor could popular elements readily express themselves in terms of the old ideologies or even become part of a new system. Instead, the Church provided an ideological space where its broadest concerns could help integrate and universalize the interests, aspirations, and demands of popular sectors.

To evaluate the Church's dynamics and its potential for action, one must keep in mind the dual character of the Church as a space and an actor. First, relations between the ecclesiastical hierarchy and the military government have been marked by a progressive estrangement. The Church's initial criticism of the excesses being committed by the military government did not deny the "legitimacy" of the regime's origins, but Church criticisms gradually broadened until they were eventually directed at the very foundations of the regime. Yet estrangement does not always imply a complete break. The relations between church and state in Chile are far more complex. The direct intervention of the Church in protecting individuals and organizations has led it to negotiate with the military government and publicly acknowledge what the Church views as partial advances. These negotiations have often guaranteed the independence and legitimacy of the Church's intervention by affirming its validity as intermediary, but they have also provided tactical advantages and valuable time for the government, an outcome that has deepened the estrangement in the long run.

Moreover, internal differences among separate factions of the ecclesiastical hierarchy have required the Church to maintain a certain image of unity that sets up an ongoing game of concessions. Hierarchical relations are in turn affected by pressure from the male and female clergy who deal directly with popular sectors suffering from repression and the regime's stringent economic model. These clergy consistently urge the hierarchy to take more radical stands against the government. The third dynamic comes from the ecclesiastical structure's new forms of organization, which interconnect with and incorporate diverse social sectors, many of whom had no significant relations with the Church prior to this period. Such entities, which include Church groups that are relatively independent from the highest levels of the hierarchy, tend to reflect (although in a refracted manner) the intergroup conflicts and competition previously found in the political arena. Finally, in the dynamic of the relations between the Church and the political movement itself, various initiatives reveal a game of succession and substitution in which the Church tries to appear to be unidentified with this movement, especially the Christian Democrats, with whom the Church has the greatest ideological affinities.

This whole complex of factors explain why the Church may offer itself as a space and an alternative actor for the political arena and political actors but can never assume this role in the identical manner or in simple terms. Because the Church's traditional dimensions and dynamics endow it with a logic of its own, the Church's logic cannot be reduced to the logic of political spaces and actors.[15]

Thus Chilean opposition to the military regime cannot be reduced either to political parties or to the hierarchical Church as an alternative space. A whole range of social opposition exists that includes base-level organizations, labor unions, Christian communities, human rights organizations, student and women's movements, and other groups. Moreover, cultural opposition includes artists, independent research centers, think tanks, and so on. But to discuss each of these opposition factions and their complex relations with the political organizations would far exceed the scope of this study.[16]

Conclusion: The Dual Responsibility of the Opposition

The problem of the disintegration of the "backbone" of Chilean society—of its former mode of organizing around sociopolitical themes—has been compounded by the problem of the survival of the political party structure inherited from the previous democratic regime. This combination has shaped the particular set of difficulties facing the opposition and has redefined the meaning of politics in Chile. It cannot be denied that during the years of military rule, something critical has happened to politics in Chile. Politics have been reshaped by soldiers, technocrats, the Church, certain communications media, intellectuals, some social organizations, and only marginally by the political parties themselves until 1983. The key political actors of the period were not the major players in the political game until 1973. Since 1983, however, the parties have played a more significant role, although with all the difficulties discussed, which have made it hard for them to assume a leading role in precipitating a final regime crisis and a process of transition.

But one can neither point to the proliferation of totally new and autonomous social movements nor deny that wherever some social stirrings have existed, one or more parties have been involved in their origin or development. Political parties may be distrusted and criticized, but their presence in Chile continues to be undeniable. In sum, social movements have not grown out of a void of political parties.

The military coup in Chile in 1973 brought together two processes: the exhaustion of one era of political action and the disintegration of the backbone of Chilean society have coincided with the imposition of a regime establishing new requirements for traditional political action. This combination has given rise to two contradictory tendencies. Some Chileans believe that participating in politics involves constructing a new backbone based entirely on civil society, and they thus consider all other political action to be mere illusion without substance. They recognize no role for parties or would delay any such role, envisioning instead of some kind of emanation occurring from social movements. For others, participating in politics means reconstructing the old backbone, but under new conditions. Everything else is relevant only to the degree that it can be reduced to the "true" politics that never change. According to this view, the role of the parties, which are conceived as the synthesis of society, is omnipresent, and everything else is subordinate.

In reality, the political leadership has a dual responsibility, and neither duty can be subsumed under the other. This responsibility is to reestablish politics, to create a new form of relations between civil society and the political system, and to construct a new backbone that will provide viability and stability for any democratic alternative while trying to precipitate a final regime crisis via institutional opportunities and the force of social mobilizations. This goal, however, entails cooperation and coordination on specific formulas for transition without excluding any significant actor in the opposition. In other words, it entails responsibility for setting up a democratic transition and rebuilding the Chilean political system.

Notes to Chapter 9

1. In developing my ideas, I have relied on the very useful discussions held in the seminars entitled "Chile: Six Years under Military Rule" (1980) and "Transitions from Authoritarian Rule and the Prospects for Democracy" (1980–81), which were organized by the Latin American Program at the Wilson Center in Washington, D.C.

2. These organizations differ from the business and professional organizations that consolidated during Popular Unity, when they exceeded the bounds of the political system, as discussed in Chapter 8.

3. See Arturo and Samuel Valenzuela, "Partidos de oposición bajo el régimen autoritario chileno," *Revista Mexicana de Sociología* 44, no. 2 (Apr.–June 1982).

4. See Hugo Frühling, "Repressive Policies and Legal Dissent in Authoritarian Regimes: Chile, 1973–1981," *International Journal of the Sociology of Law* 12 (1984).

5. The evolution of Chilean leftist documents can be traced in the journal *Chile América*, published in Rome.

6. The paragraphs updating the analysis from 1983 to 1987 are taken from my book *Reconstruir la política: transición y consolidación democrática en Chile* (Santiago: Editorial Andante, 1987).

7. Various ways of grouping opposition parties have been tried, but instead of achieving a multiparty coalition that would unite all opposition parties, such groupings have encouraged ideological and exclusionary elements. In 1983 the following coalitions were organized: first, the Democratic Alliance (Alianza Democrática), made up of the Republican party, the Liberal party, the Social Democratic party, the Christian Democrats, the Radical party, the Popular Socialist Union (Unión Socialista Popular), and the Briones or Núñez sector of the Socialist party; second, the Popular Democratic Movement (Movimiento Democrático Popular), comprising the Almeyda sector of the Socialist party, the Communist party, the Movement of the Revolutionary Left (MIR), and other smaller groups; third, the Socialist Coalition (Bloque Socialista), which included the Socialist Alliance party (Partido Socialista de la Alianza), the Christian Left, MAPU, MAPU Worker-Peasant (MAPU Obrero-Campesino), the Socialist Convergence (Convergencia Socialista), and some independents. The Socialist Coalition was dissolved two years later. Subsequent attempts have been made at further regroupings led by personalities of various tendencies, as in the cases of PRODEN (Proyecto de Desarrollo Nacional) and Democratic Intransigence (Intransigencia Democrática), but their attraction has been only opportunistic or circumstantial. The most important effort at regrouping the parties has been the National Accord (Acuerdo Nacional), which was established in mid-1985 at the request of Cardinal Fresno. The National Accord includes the parties of the Democratic Alliance, two rightist parties (the National party and the National Union party), and the Christian Left. In 1986 the National Accord was joined by various Socialist groups and MAPU, although the National Union party and the Christian Left withdrew from this enlarged coalition. All these coalitions are known as "referents." On the Left, the Socialist party withdrew from the Democratic Alliance in 1987, and the Popular Democratic Movement was dissolved. The United Left (Izquierda Unida) was then created, which included the Communist party, the Socialist party (the Almeyda faction), the MIR, a faction of the Radical party, the Christian Left, MAPU, and other smaller socialist groups.

8. The Communist and Socialist parties and the MIR were the groups most affected, although the Communist party's capacity to reorganize, which derives from its earlier history, was greater. The remaining parties of the Left were affected to lesser degrees.

9. This stage was analyzed in Chapter 2.

10. The idea of forming a political coalition with the Christian Democrats, in various

versions, has met with different responses from the parties of the Left. These responses have gone through stages, with the largest consensus emerging during the 1980 plebiscite and in recent years. In general, the greatest reservations prior to 1980 were expressed by the Socialist party and the greatest acceptance came from the Communist party. Since then, some Socialist sectors have established various alliances with the Christian Democrats, such as the Democratic Alliance, the National Accord, and the Movement for Free Elections (Movimiento por Elecciones Libres), while other Socialist sectors and the Communists have been excluded or self-excluded from these coalitions.

11. In September 1980, the Secretary General of the Communist party asserted the need to engage in all forms of struggle, including forms of "focused violence". This pronouncement created problems within the party because of its deviation from the party's traditional line and also provoked heated debate among leftist political groups. Since that time, the Communist party has been dominated by insurrectionary tendencies linked to sectors of youth, new party contingents in poor urban neighborhoods, and an autonomous organization created by the party—the Manuel Rodríguez Patriotic Front, which has been responsible for radical activities like power blackouts, the attempt against Pinochet's life in September 1986, and the introduction of arms into Chile. In 1987, however, general perception of the unfeasibility of the insurrectionary strategy and agreement among all opposition sectors on a political exit and enrollment in the electoral registers led the Communist party to heed this consensus. This decision has reinforced the more political sectors of the Communist party, although the party has not broken its ties with insurrectionary factions.

12. For a description of these two modes of political action, see Chapter 5.

13. See Brian Smith, *Old Allies, New Opponents: The Church and the Military in Chile, 1973–1979*, Latin American Program Working Paper no. 68 (Washington, D.C.: Wilson Center, 1980).

14. The Church's immunity has been relative, however, in that some representatives of the Church, especially priests and activists in popular sectors, have suffered during various waves of repression.

15. This logic has manifested itself at times of major crisis in the regime and the opposition, when the Church has gone beyond defending and condemning to play a clearly political role on at least three occasions. In 1980 the Church pointed out the illegal conditions established for the constitutional plebiscite, although it could not capitalize on the consequences of its stand because the opposition was participating in the plebiscite without any clear consensual strategy on how to discredit it. In 1983 the Church promoted a dialogue between the government and sectors of the opposition but abstained from playing the role of a mediator who would push for a certain outcome. In 1985 the Church had to break up opposition inertia by promoting establishment of the National Accord, but this approach prevented the Church from playing the role of arbitrator between regime and opposition because the Church appeared to be identified with the opposition. In all these instances, I am referring to the actions taken by the highest levels of the Church's hierarchy, the Episcopal Conference and the Archbishop of Santiago.

16. Some of these sectors are discussed in my article "Popular Mobilizations and the Military Regime in Chile: The Complexities of the Invisible Transition," in *Power and Popular Protest: Latin American Social Movements*, edited by Susan Eckstein (Berkeley and Los Angeles: University of California Press, forthcoming). A detailed analysis can be found in *Los movimientos sociales in Chile y la lucha democrática*, edited by G. Campero (Santiago: ILET-CLACSO, 1986).

Chapter 10

Prospects for Democracy
and Reconstructing the Political System

The first chapter of this book examined the characteristics and evolution of the Chilean political system until its rupture in 1973. Subsequent chapters discussed the changes experienced under the military regime. This final chapter will summarize the features of the political system in order to discuss perspectives on regime change—the *problématique* of the transition from dictatorship to political democracy—as well as perspectives on reconstructing the political system that go beyond the processes involved in the regime's eventual end and the transition.[1]

The Military Regime and the Political System

The military coup in 1973 afforded the opportunity for not only dismantling the existing political system but founding a new political system under a military regime.[2] The real political system since 1973 has evolved as a result of the project set up by the regime, the official political system, and the informal or extra-official system that includes surviving elements of the system described earlier in this book as well as newly developed elements that have been neither considered nor rejected by the official system.

The political system to which the military regime aspires is expressed with dazzling clarity in the Constitution of 1980, which Pinochet imposed by means of a plebiscite. The ideal context for this project is the socioeconomic

185

model of organization known as "the seven modernizations and their aims." This model seeks to create a political system with several notable features: a system in which the state is no longer the focus of collective action but has been corporatized and fragmented to the point of losing its specifically political character; the constitutionally sanctioned passage from a military type of regime to an authoritarian regime after 1988; technocratic or market mechanisms for resolving conflicts that diminish the relevance of political actors; an arena of representation that would exclude alternatives and sectors inclined toward change so that democratic mechanisms would operate only in limited spheres and on behalf of fewer social sectors; and finally, guardianship over this political system by the armed forces, which are not subordinate to it. All these features require a lengthy dictatorship or military regime in order to establish the characteristics ordained by the military coup of 1973.

The official political system partly coincides with the model officially sanctioned as the transition by the constitution, but only partly because the effects of time and the extra-official system have modified the officially proclaimed model. The state has diminished its redistributive capacity and its role as an agent of development, but it has enormously extended and intensified its capacity for coercion and control. The state has made itself impervious to popular demands and only selectively open to the demands of sectors with major capacity to exert pressure, organize, and destabilize—sectors that initially supported the regime. The regime per se combines characteristics of a personal dictatorship and a military regime, having eliminated spaces for representation before the state and directly penetrated spheres of local power that used to be spaces for representation (municipal government). Certain areas of social organization (labor, for example) are now institutionally regulated to allow for some type of corporatist collective action but to impede any kind of political linkage. As for political parties, they had no official existence until 1987, although as we have seen, they actually did exist. Since the opposition burst into the public arena with the national protests in 1983, a kind of informal recognition has been granted to some opposition organizations via the *aperturas*, but it has always been erratic, opportunistic, and reversible. The regime's 1987 promulgation of several "political laws," especially the one on political parties, sought to advance institutionalization of the authoritarian model by Pinochet's planned election in 1988. It also sought to limit opposition parties to the rules of the game by making some parties official, but restricted, while eliminating others. This approach could lead to having two party systems, an official one comprising the Right and some opposition sectors and an underground or extra-official system comprising most of the opposition.

But the actual political system is composed of the official one described and the informal or nonofficial system, whose interactions with the official system have fluctuated over the years. More precisely, there are two parallel systems with rare moments or elements of interaction. What the "political laws" have attempted is to make the two systems coincide by eliminating a significant portion of the second, a seemingly utopian undertaking. The nonofficial system has been characterized by four noteworthy features. The first is its distance from the state and the impossibility of its presenting the state with demands. The second is the presence of the Church as an alternative space for regrouping social and political actors and, for a long time, as the only actor confronting the state.

The third feature is a political party structure that could be neither eliminated nor replaced and that maintains much continuity with the party system prevailing until 1973. The major changes in the party spectrum have fallen into three categories. The first consists of the fragmentation, dissolution, and eventual reorganization of the political Right, the fragmentation and renewal of the socialist Left, a turning away from the classical Marxist-Leninist model, and the Communist party's shift toward more radical and insurrectional lines. The second category is the emergence of armed political groups that have confronted the regime militarily. The third is an increased flexibility in possible alliances among sectors of the democratic Right, Center, and Left, at least in opposing continuation of the military regime. But this situation is still dominated by functional and ideological identities that lead to exclusions and hinder precise agreements on viable formulas for ending the dictatorship. Meanwhile, two new phenomena have emerged in the relations between parties and social organizations. The first is the great difficulty in articulation that results in greater autonomy for the social organizations (although without substantially modifying the interlocking pattern noted between the two) but also in their greater isolation. The second phenomenon consists of the emergence of a kind of intermediate political "class" that is relatively independent of the political leadership and animates and activates social organizations and movements. This class, which exhibits a strong tendency toward ideological radicalization, has been formed by human rights activists, popular educators, middle-level activists in political parties, church organizations, and student groups. This sector, or "political-social fringe," has been critical in maintaining the continuity of regime opposition, although it is inclined to stake out maximalist positions relative to the main body of social organizations in which it participates.

A fourth feature of the nonofficial system is the displacement of the political system, with politics having become part of a life and death drama that has profoundly transformed the meaning of political action. Perhaps one of the most significant expressions of this feature is the dissociation of two traditionally inseparable dimensions of Chilean politics: the instrumental-national dimension, which is oriented toward institutions and toward cooperation and coordination on precise goals; and the symbolic-expressive dimension, with strong ethical and emotional content and oriented toward affirming identity, expressing a sense of belonging, defending community, and distrusting institutions and negotiations. The instrumental-national dimension remains in the hands of the political elite and organizations that cannot convoke broad mobilizations. The symbolic-expressive dimension remains in the hands of motivated and activated sectors that do not know how to transform a social force into a political force. Far away from both are the Chilean masses, who can be united politically only by a combination of these two inseparable dimensions of politics.

The real political system operating during these years has been formed by the juxtaposition of the dominant official system and the informal one, real but not official, without any institutional integration between the two. In certain periods, however, such as after the first protests, implicit interaction has taken place. It is probable that the institutionalization of the regime may yet force a convergence of the two as a result of the plebiscite in 1988. In any case, it appears that transitions from military regimes to democracy entail a time of convergence and confrontation between both systems, which has so far been lacking in Chile.

The features of the Chilean political system during the democratic period and the changes that have occurred under the military regime suggest the two large *problématique* that Chilean politics must confront in the near future: the *problématique* of the regime and its process of transition, and the *problématique* of the reconstruction of politics.

The Double Problématique of the Chilean Political System

With respect to politics, Chilean society must resolve two kinds of crises in the coming years: the crisis of the regime and the crisis of the political system as such. These *problématiques* are distinct, yet interrelated, in that the first appears to be a precondition for resolving the second and refers specifically to the change of regime or process of transition. The second is a longer and more complex process that implies rebuilding all the elements that make up a political system, which in turn fosters the stability of the new regime. Both *problématiques* are affected by other dimensions of society, of course, but here I am discussing only the political dimension.

In speaking of regime crisis, I am alluding to two phenomena. The first is the impossibility of maintaining the military regime indefinitely. Even if the regime succeeds in staying in power for a long time, it will always be questioned—that is to say, the military regime can never claim to be permanent and is thus always facing a crisis of legitimacy. The result is that the regime will always be a problem requiring resolution. The second phenomenon is the existence of contradictory projects with respect to the political regime. Most obvious is the current project of the governing core that seeks to transform the military regime into an authoritarian regime, a phase that Pinochet would like to make coincide with his staying in power as long as he lives. In contrast, rightist and capitalist sectors have proposed a project aimed at creating a restricted democracy. Unlike the authoritarian project, this one features democratic mechanisms, but they would be limited to certain social and political sectors and would exclude other sectors and alternatives entailing deeper social change. Finally, the goal of most Chileans and the political leadership is to establish a democratic regime without restrictions, in the terms understood in this study.[3] The problem facing this goal is to replace the military regime or develop a transition process from a dictatorship or military regime to a democratic regime. The most probable outcome is that the first problem will be resolved within the next year. This process might occur by means of a transition in which all the democratic institutions are established quickly, or it might occur in a gradual manner in which authoritarian elements are maintained and are slowly transformed and replaced by democratic mechanisms. These possibilities will be discussed subsequently.

The regime crisis is part of a larger crisis that touches all elements of the entire political system and their relations. Thus the regime change appears to be one dimension of rebuilding the political system, a precondition for resolving the other problems, although regime change alone cannot resolve the crisis of the whole system. As has been shown, the military dictatorship has effectively transformed and disarticulated each component of the political system, and thus ending the military regime will not be enough to repair it. The crisis here is one of politics per se, which have not only been subjugated and forbidden by the military regime but damaged by styles and practices conditioned by this regime—a reality that opposition political actors cannot escape. In the same way that the Chilean economy, society, and culture must be reconstructed over the long term, politics too must be rebuilt into a system with its own actors, institutions, and culture. I have defined the regime as the institutional dimension mediating between the state and society, nothing more and nothing less. But a political system in crisis also involves restructuring the state and defining its role in relation to collective action and the party system—as well as the relationship of these elements to society as a whole. Such an undertaking will require decades. Thus while the next few years are likely to bring resolution of the problem of the political regime, they will probably witness only the laying of the foundations of the political system as a whole: redefinition of the state in its role as a social actor and coercive institution, which implies reformulating the role of the armed forces; the strengthening of civil society; restructuring of the party system and its relations with society; and renewal of the style and forms of political action, which will involve changes in the political leadership.

Thus regime change or the replacement of the military regime involves not only a process of transition to democracy but a reconstruction of politics and the elements that make up a political system. If the first task is the precondition of the second, the second is the condition required for stability and consolidation of the first. Thus the Chilean political system in the coming decades will manifest the results of both challenges.

The Possible Transition

The first task seems to be the transition to democracy—the replacement of the military dictatorship by a democratic regime. Three questions are relevant here. What does this transition comprise? Why has Chile, unlike other countries that have experienced military dictatorships in recent decades, not yet begun its transition? What are the probabilities and scenarios for such a transition in the near future?

With respect to the first question, the ambivalence of these processes and their basic characteristics have already been discussed.[4] One need only recall that regime changes are not always produced by the overthrow or internal military defeat of those in power (in this case, the armed forces) and that such changes rarely originate from regime collapse. Once the hypothesis of military defeat or collapse from external or accidental factors has been eliminated, it becomes clear that such transitions involve a decision by the armed forces to withdraw from power for various reasons: internalization of their own failure, perception of a crisis that will threaten their institutional integrity, pressure from various sources, isolation from society, or some combination of these factors. This analysis assumes that no institutional void exists in such transitions and that the task of the opposition is to provoke a military decision to withdraw. At the same time, these transitions also result from combined processes of breakdown and isolation of the governing coalition, social and popular mobilizations directed toward political goals, negotiation between the regime and the opposition, and mediation between the regime and the opposition carried out by entities or institutions standing above both but inclined toward a democratic solution. The opposition's strategy consists of suitably combining these processes, which requires presenting a single consensual proposal or institutional solution for a military exit that allows for negotiation with the armed forces. A third point to remember is that these transitions can originate "from above" via initiatives from the regime, "from below" due to popular or opposition pressure, or from some external factor such as a war or a death, but they will probably originate from a combination of factors. Finally, it should be observed that these transitions change only the political regime, and they end when the new regime is inaugurated. Thus transitions leave pending the other social transformations associated with broadening democratization as well as aspects of political democratization and related institutional questions.

Answers to the second question, regarding the factors that have delayed the Chilean transition, can be explored on three somewhat interrelated dimensions. First, no transition project has been launched "from above," but rather, a project for going from a military regime to a permanent authoritarian regime, a process that has been personalized by Pinochet. Three factors have contributed to this lack of a transition "from above" and fostered the development of a personalized project: the combination of a personal dictatorship with a military regime, which facilitates the dictator's maneuvers during crises and hinders opposition activity; the institutionalization of this project by a constitution that reinforced Pinochet's legitimacy for the armed forces in political and institutional-hierarchical terms and provided the military with a political identity; and slow erosion of regime support, in which the capitalist sector seems to have been guided solely by its corporative interests and the political Right has been unable to consolidate loyalty to democracy. The methods of institutionalization employed have nevertheless begun to work against this project by creating dynamics of transition beginning in 1988.

A second factor delaying the transition has been the opposition's inability to trigger a transition process "from below." Setting aside the effects of the regime itself, the political opposition has faced three problems in this regard. The first has been the inability to present a single alternative formula for transition that could channel popular mobilization and allow timely negotiation with the regime. When mobilization lacks a formula or alternative institutional plan, it tends to run out of steam and become limited to activist cores that are more easily isolated. Also, the opposition is left at the mercy of the military regime's plan and must content itself with developing defensive tactics. Paradoxically, the logic of the military's own institutions forced the opposition to define a consensual response to the plebiscite in 1988. Thus the opposition will no longer be able to fall back on the myths that have existed in recent years. The second problem is that the need for a consensual formula for transition has been displaced by emphasis on forming ideological coalitions more intent on preserving political identities and positions of leadership than on ending the regime. These groupings have been characterized by mutual exclusions that only perpetuate opposition fragmentation and weaken its capacity to exert pressure and mobilize. The third problem is that the relationship between parties and the social base has been disrupted and, lacking a formal inclusive political system, bifurcation has occurred between instrumental politics and expressive or symbolic politics. This split has mainly affected the most active sectors of the young urban poor and student activists, who find among the political leadership no point of reference for channeling their aspirations to participate and mobilize. Opposition activity has consequently been hindered because it is torn among the necessities of reorganizing functionally, fighting to end the regime, and reestablishing ties with the social base.

A third factor blocking a transition concerns general problems in Chilean society that lie beyond the obstacles created by the regime or the opposition. One of these is the process of social fragmentation, the shrinking of material spaces and institutions for organizing new social actors or renewing old ones that has resulted from the social transformations undertaken by the regime in recent years. This fragmentation makes mobilizing for common goals extremely difficult in that each sector is affected by particular problems without recognizing their common origins. Yet when such commonalities are identified by political organizations, they seem too abstract to serve as the basis for a major joint mobilization. Unlike other national contexts, Chilean social transformation has not proceeded toward consolidating mass society through industrialization and state expansion, with all the implied consequences for consolidating new social forces. On the contrary, the dominant factors have been the marginalization, segmentation, and fragmentation of much of Chilean society, combined with a diminution of the role of the state as the focus for collective action. A concomitant decline in industrial production and public employment has been associated with high levels of permanent unemployment and expansion of the informal sector. These processes have not implied the rise of new social classes but rather have been phenomena of disintegration and disarticulation that have reflected the context of repression.

As observed earlier, the "backbone" of Chilean society has been disarticulated without being replaced. The historical strength of the Chilean political party structure and the consequent weakness of autonomous organizations in civil society have shown their negative sides here in the modifications in the state as referent for political action, in the base of representation, and in the ties between the base and the party structure. In effect, the party structure has remained frozen and suspended. Because no new political arena has been created, the processes of party renewal and reestablishment have become lengthy, difficult, and complex. Efforts at mobilization have found it difficult to reorganize due to a lack of mechanisms that might give them national impact. This circumstance has made any kind of activity that could lead to changes in the regime enormously difficult. Under these conditions, the classical source of political action has proven relatively incapable of destroying authoritarian capitalism, and while calls for overthrowing the regime have struck a chord with activist minorities, such invocations are only a distant echo for large social sectors. Moreover, invoking democracy as an alternative has frequently seemed to offer a political option much too removed from the agonizing daily problems confronted by the Chilean masses. This difficulty represents a relative disjuncture between the political parties' offer to supply a "democratic alternative" and the social "demand" for substantive democratization.

Certainly, when serious crises in the military regime threaten its collapse or when the regime's repressiveness intensifies, the theme of democracy acquires a fuller resonance in broad sectors and becomes a social demand. But when nothing happens, and given the disarticulation of the backbone that connected the political leadership with the rest of society, the thrusts of opposition action are reduced to limited struggles to resist repression and to create political spaces, such as the efforts to reconstruct civil society and organize genuine social forces and actors. These efforts then define the specific content of democracy. If democracy appears to be the politically significant alternative demanded when facing the repressive dimension or a regime crisis, such a response does not eliminate the need for a much more diversified political agenda in which the nature of the political regime must be projected in terms of the real social needs of the majority.

Thus in the absence of an acute regime crisis, democratization advances far more along the lines of organization, defense, and gains within society than in terms of manifestations at the level of the political regime. The result is a kind of invisible transition toward democracy that is measured not in terms of the political regime's mechanisms and time frames but in terms of democratizing society and reestablishing the opposition politically. Yet the popular mobilizations that have developed since 1983 reveal the limits of this "invisible transition": in crisis situations, in order to move toward ending the military regime, the opposition must emphasize the political dimension and convert the demand for better living conditions or social transformation into a specific demand for political democracy. This necessity implies not only intensifying mobilizations but developing an institutional formula for transition that involves a complex process of negotiation and compromise.

The second problem affecting society as a whole is the lack of external factors capable of provoking a transition and the lack of entities that could mediate between the regime and the opposition to force a negotiated transition. In this respect, the Church has played an important role in denouncing the dictatorship's violation of human rights, defending and protecting victims, and creating a free space for reorganizing collective action and social actors. But the Church has not decided to play the role of a "goal-oriented mediator" (as did the King of Spain, for example). Nor has foreign pressure, despite its active defense of human rights in many cases, succeeded in exercising this kind of influence. This outcome is partly due to the ambiguity of U.S. policy toward the Chilean military regime but partly due to the deficiencies noted in the Chilean opposition.[5] Finally, Chilean society has lacked legitimate arenas where the opposition could confront the regime and resolve the conflict in favor of democratic sectors. Again, this situation could be modified through institutional mechanisms that might in turn trigger dynamics beyond the control of the regime.

All these considerations bring us to the last question in the *problématique* of regime change: What are the possibilities for ending the military regime and establishing a democratic regime in Chile? Any answer must keep in mind that the country is facing two conflicting and alternative scenarios. One is the scenario designed by the governing core: passage from a military regime to an authoritarian regime that excludes the democratic alternative, the constitutional scenario that Pinochet tried to exploit to stay in power. The contrasting scenario favored by most of the opposition is to establish political democracy, even though the specific mechanisms for making this change have not yet been agreed upon. At this stage, the regime's scenario has little chance of being imposed, which could lead to either a transition or an attempt to go back to a dictatorship like that imposed in 1973. Such retrogression would take the form of a coup staged by the regime against itself (an *autogolpe*), which also seems unfeasible.

The role played by the opposition in the development of the transition is crucial. If the opposition does not change its mode of action, the probability of Pinochet's continuing in power will increase. In order to end the regime and establish a democratic regime, complete with transition requirements and the inclusion of all opposition sectors, the opposition will have to define the institutional scenario for confronting the regime following the plebiscite and organize its mobilizations, pressure, and eventual negotiations around this definition. If no plan is set forth in advance, the eventual result will be a belated, defensive response, under the worst possible conditions, to the scenario imposed by the regime, unless this definition should come "from outside," from an institution like the Church.

Excluding the Communist party from transition agreements will only delay such definition by depriving the opposition of a major social force for mobilization and by encouraging the more insurrectional tendencies within the Communist party, which will in turn enhance the regime's pretext for staying in power. If the thinking is that the Communist party will not be in a position to favor a democratic transition, the solution is not its exclusion, whose cost the rest of the opposition would have to pay. The better approach is to reinforce the more democratic tendencies within the Communist party and increase their room for internal maneuver in attempting to incorporate the Communist party into efforts to cooperate and coordinate, thus making the party itself pay the cost of its explicit self-exclusion.

The most probable overall outcome is that the democratic transition process triggered in Chile in 1988 will center on the struggle for change in the constitutional framework and its plan for the future. This outcome could take place in a brief period following the plebiscite. But the transition could also occur more gradually in the case of a partial transition that leaves pending such institutional adjustments as eliminating authoritarian remnants, returning to full parliamentary functions, democratizing the electoral system, subordinating the armed forces to political power, broadening ideological and political inclusiveness, and resolving problems regarding judicial consequences of violations of human rights committed by the dictatorship.

The Reconstruction of Politics

The second undertaking that Chileans will have to confront in political matters is rebuilding the political system, a goal that requires regime change as a necessary but insufficient precondition. This process involves restructuring each element of the system as well as relations among them and toward the society as a whole.[6] As has been shown, Chilean politics since 1973 has been subjugated and impaired in social significance. Thus to reconstruct politics is to restore a specific role in society, which means neither denying the relevance of politics nor considering all other activities to be politics. Rebuilding politics means restructuring political space, mechanisms, and relations with social life. Reconstruction of the political system is thus the condition needed for consolidating and stabilizing the democratic regime.

It is evident that rebuilding the political system requires a social context, an issue not discussed here. My assumption is, however, that this context will be determined by the dual tendency (interrupted in 1973) toward modernization and democratization, which is understood here as access to the benefits of modern social life and growing individual and collective participation in the decisions affecting national progress and the living conditions of Chileans. The dominant economic models, projects, and scenarios of these two processes can vary, but I am assuming that the main dynamics of society will be framed by this double dimension.

I speak of rebuilding, rather than building, because this process does not begin in a vacuum—there are elements from the past that must be recovered and others that have survived and must be developed, and because a collective memory exists that is critical of the past. All these elements must be considered in attempting to overcome the deficiencies of the political system inherited from the democratic period and to meet the challenges posed by the military experience and those that will emerge from the new historical social context in the coming decade. Four issues will have to be confronted in rebuilding the political system.

The Transformation of the State

The first challenge to be faced is redefining the state and readapting its institutions. This process entails establishing the role of the state as agent of development and as focal point for collective action. Second, the state's repressive institutions will have to be reorganized. Third, certain state institutions that are central to modernizing and democratizing tendencies will have to be transformed. Each of these three dimensions will be examined in turn.

Regarding the role of the state, it is time to abandon doctrinaire myths. In societies characterized by structural heterogeneity, when civil society's classical actors are weak, and a context of external dependency exists, the state plays a key role in forging national unity and in modernizing and democratizing society. A review of the crises experienced under military regimes or resulting from the external debt leads to the unavoidable conclusion that the state's role as agent of development and referent for collective action will not disappear, as the neoconservatives dreamed, but will increase instead. If the prevailing tendencies in public opinion are examined, the importance assigned to the state and the desire for the state to play a significant role demonstrate that this is one aspect of the Chilean mentality and culture that no market-oriented experience can eliminate.[7] Consequently, the state will have to reassume a primary role in national unity, development, and democratization, which will require reorganizing the state apparatus and restructuring its capacity for action and receptivity to social demands. But such a statement would be ingenuous if it did not take into account the crisis of the expansive state. The impossibility of simply returning to the past in this regard or ignoring this dimension of the state crisis are indicated by several major factors: the growing difficulties faced by state economic policies; the tendencies of the population toward individuation, fragmentation, self-recognition as a social force, and their participation in matters that affect them; the extreme dependency of social organizations on political power; and the irreversibility of certain modernizations imposed by the military regime. Thus while the state's roles as agent or actor of development and referent for collective action can be affirmed, any strengthening of its institutional and organizational apparatus and any increase in its efficiency and modernization must be counterbalanced. Two such counterbalancing dimensions, the strengthening of civil society and the role of the party system, will be discussed, but it is appropriate at this point to make several observations along these lines that refer directly to the state apparatus.

The key challenge is not to reduce the state's significance, a utopian dream that is not only impossible to achieve in a country like Chile but undesirable as well. The problem is how to achieve control of the state by society, or what could be called democratizing the state, without affecting the state's capacity for action and intervention. It is evident that in a country like Chile, the greatest capacity for creativity and initiative is found not among capitalists but in sectors linked in one way or another to the state. Consequently, the national interest can be calculated better within the state than anywhere else, particularly given the major initiatives that will have to be developed in such fields as scientific and technological research, education, information, and communication. If such initiatives do not come from the state, they will not emerge from anywhere else. But this approach implies that the capacity to create and found must be joined by the capacity to incorporate key social sectors in every area and gradually hand over decision-making and management responsibility to them, yet without sacrificing the link to the state.[8]

A second dimension of transforming the state is the problem of armed institutions, a difficulty that the transition will probably resolve only partially and temporarily. Here again the principle arises of social control over a state institution, and in this instance, it has three implications. The first is that the problems of national defense must become part of the public agenda and must reflect decisions reached by civil society as a whole, with technical and professional aspects delegated to specialized bodies. If this approach is taken, one of the main undertakings will be to strengthen civilian and political capacity to recognize and define problems of national defense. This approach also requires creating, inside and outside the government, centers of information and research that can counterbalance the technical and professional monopoly of the armed forces and their resultant political power. Such organizations would lead to new forms of interpenetration and cooperation between the civilian and military spheres. The second implication requires reducing the amount of economic and human resources assigned to the armed forces, along with gradually eliminating privileges and phasing out expanded military involvement in assignments and activities that lie outside its professional functions (as in military justice and productive economic functions). The third implication is constructing a model for civilian-military relationships that avoids the "cloistering" characteristic of the political system until 1973. Specific goals are to achieve interpenetration between civil society and the armed forces by eliminating the ghetto aspect of military forms of living, education, and citizen participation, and to ensure institutionally the armed forces' subordination to the political power of the state.

A third dimension of transforming the state (which also follows the same principle of expanding society's control over the state as a strong agent of development and democratization) involves reforming certain state institutions. Only two aspects will be considered here. One is revising the so-called powers of the state. In terms of the Parliament (an aspect that seems to belong to national resolution of constitutional questions during the transition period or immediately afterward), various reforms must be insisted upon: making the electoral system representative, returning all legislative and fiscal powers to the Parliament, increasing its efficiency by means of scientific and cultural resources, and society's controlling Parliament by means of mass media coverage of parliamentary activities. Regarding the judicial branch (Poder Judicial), but setting aside the issue of justice for violations of human rights perpetrated by the military regime (another issue for the transition period or soon after), profound changes will be required in the future. The years preceding the military coup and especially those under the dictatorship have demonstrated that the Chilean model of justice, despite its claims to autonomy, has suffered a conservative politicization that has rendered its independence a pure formality. There is no independent judicial system in Chile, and it will therefore be necessary to construct one. This process will involve modifying the methods of selecting and training judges and combining technical and professional functions with forms of citizen participation in the administration and control of justice. This undertaking obviously requires eliminating military justice as a rival judicial power and limiting it to purely professional issues, even here establishing necessary systems of appeal that will avoid a military ghetto mentality and aspirations to self-sufficiency.

The other problem is to decentralize the state apparatus and transfer power to local and intermediate levels where democratic participation by diverse social sectors in each area can become possible. In this sense, modifications must be made to decentralize and strengthen municipal governments set up by the military regime, which are now merely an authoritarian extension of state control, in order to ensure the effective transfer of power to levels with democratic representation and participation. This reform obviously must be accompanied by the state's preserving its capacity to regulate certain basic unifying principles (as in education) and to provide compensating resources to avoid regional and social inequalities.

This aspect of "positive discrimination" can also be extended to access to state posts and to represéntation and participation for certain social categories that have been discriminated against in the past, such as women and even unorganized poor sectors.

The Strengthening of Civil Society

The importance assigned to the state and to transforming it into an effective agent of development and democratization must be counterbalanced by a process in which civil society becomes more dense, complex, and autonomous. This view assumes that Chilean society should become capable of expressing itself through actors and entities that avoid turning the state into another arena for social conflict leading to political polarization. The state should be the main sphere for participation, while political parties are the appropriate sphere for representation.

It is evident that this process depends not only on political dimensions but largely on the structural form of economic life and the existence of educational and cultural organizations and institutions throughout the country. This aspect cannot be examined in the present context, however. In terms of the specifically political aspects, the problem of strengthening civil society has two dimensions.

The first is transferring state power to spheres where state presence is combined with societal participation, at territorial as well as functional levels, as described above. The second is constructing a system of relations between civil society and the political system, especially parties, that transcends the interlocking pattern between the political leadership and the leadership of social organizations that characterized the democratic period in Chile. The new system must also overcome the regime's having dismantled the earlier model. It is impossible to imagine a civil society in Chile that organizes social actors and resolves conflicts according to market principles, the utopia sought by the military regime and the technocratic groups implementing its policies. Yet social and cultural transformations have been produced that preclude recreating the kind of relationship between social actors and the party system that existed before the military coup. It is equally illusory to imagine a system of social actors and movements that is organized totally outside the political system or one that confronts and rejects this system. We must keep in mind the growing autonomy of social actors from the political party system, which cannot be arbitrarily regulated in the manner called for by the Constitution of 1980.[9] But paradoxically, this task in Chile will necessarily fall to political parties and to the political leadership. It is possible that if the spheres of participation and representation can be strengthened and diversified, the resulting actors and conflicts will not merely reinforce those already existing in the national political arena.

Reconstructing the Party System

The third aspect of rebuilding the Chilean political system refers to the parties themselves. Parties provide crucial means of representing and articulating interests, ideas, and aspirations and ways of bringing individuals together to cooperate and coordinate. Without parties to fill these functions, the state will either absorb society or become praetorian, or else society will fragment and disintegrate. Several points are clear: that the parties comprise neither all of society nor all of politics; that they are only one irreplaceable part of society; that the channels for representing social sectors and expressing their wishes cannot be the monopoly of the parties, which must diversify in the future; that a universal crisis is occurring within parties; and that the Chilean military regime has succeeded in partially dismantling the party system. But it is equally clear that the parties have played a key role in organizing social actors in Chile and that no other entities can replace them. Parties will continue to play a central role. The military regime has neither ended the party system, replaced it with another, nor eliminated the major parties.

All these factors make it appropriate to speak in terms of restructuring the party system rather than founding or creating it. This restructuring must confront three dimensions in the coming years.

The first step must be reorganizing a complete and inclusive party spectrum. The most probable outcome is that the tripolar scheme prevailing until 1973 will be replaced by one with four poles: a Right, a Center in which the Christian Democrats predominate among smaller social democratic groups, a renewed Socialist Left, and a classical Communist Left. Establishing this scheme, however, will raise various problems. How can a democratic political Right be formed that will break with its authoritarian and exclusionary remnants and enclaves? Such a party must be capable of representing a genuine social base despite the preeminence of authoritarian elements and the fragmentation of democratic sectors. Without a democratic Right involved in the political arena within the rules of the game, there can be no stability for Chilean democracy in the future.

A second problem faces the Christian Democrats, who must end their isolationist tendency and develop their capacity to establish alliances with the Left as a whole. A third problem is overcoming the fragmentation in the Socialist camp and unifying it around the idea of a Socialist renewal involving an autonomous leadership role among other sectors of the Left.[10] Finally, there is the problem of reconverting the Communist party to its classical line as a workers' party that struggles within the institutional political sphere. This reorientation involves separating out its most insurrectional elements in order to convert the party into a democratic minority within a Left led by the renewed, unified Socialist majority. A party spectrum organized in this manner, with elements of both continuity and renewal regarding the past, would still have to face the problem of "extra-system" political expressions, like groups on the Right nostalgic for the military regime and groups on the Left opting for the extra-institutional revolutionary solution. But this problem will have to be dealt with politically, not by military or repressive means.

As for the second dimension of restructuring, to avoid the tendencies toward polarization that characterized the 1960s and early 1970s and to respond to the challenge of deepening modernization and democratization, a broad sociopolitical majority will have to be established to confront national and international conservative obstacles while maintaining the legitimacy of the democratic regime. This necessity goes back to the problem of political alliances. A long-term Center-Right alliance seems unlikely because it would lead to restrictive policies that would threaten regime stability and legitimacy for the masses and would also split the Center. Nor does it seem realistic that the Center or the Left separately could take charge of the undertakings outlined inasmuch as neither one alone can count on the majority in attempting to accomplish such large goals. The only long-term solution possible is an alliance between the Center and the Left. But such an alliance cannot be formed if a significant, albeit minority, sector of the Left (like the Communist party) is excluded because such an approach will inevitably create problems in the Socialist camp. I am not necessarily talking about a government alliance but about a type of agreement regarding the cultural, economic, social, and political future of Chile that would allow for a variety of specific coalitions for certain periods or particular goals.

Third, the parties will have to confront problems in their institutional roles, internal organization, and relations with society. Party institutions will have to ensure their access to the media and state resources and at the same time be responsible and public in their actions. Regarding internal organization, effective democratizing will have to be assured through positions being filled by periodic elections, the participation of the so-called bases in electing representatives to public positions, and probably minimal "quotas" to ensure the participation of women. Relations with society will have to move in the directions of expanding areas of party nonintervention and enhancing the autonomy of social actors and leadership, which can only come about through the parties lessening their control but increasing their capacity to represent and express public opinion.

Renewing Political Culture and Political Leadership

The corollary to all of the above is that, given the complexity of the tasks at hand and the past significance of the political leadership in the evolution and crisis of the political system, this leadership and its cultural components will have to be renewed.

The renewal of political leadership implies, in one sense, expanding spheres of participation and representation in society in order to increase opportunities for access to leadership and hence its diversification. In another sense, renewal implies greater differentiation from other activities of society, meaning that political leadership would have effective counterweights in the intellectual world and in social organizations. Finally, renewal implies better communication with the rest of society, which entails increasing Chilean society's levels of public information and capacity for control over its political leadership, as well as more systematic access for political leaders to other social spheres, especially those generating knowledge and information.

The renewal of political culture must be directed toward the aspects of transformation noted throughout this chapter. Basically, this process entails reappraising politics as a relationship between two poles that must necessarily be strong—the state and civil society—which requires that the nexus between the two must also be strong. This process involves reappraising society and the plurality of its autonomous actors, the state as an agent of unity, development, and democratization, and politics as an activity linking both. This approach demands democratic mentalities that are more creative and less ideological, that are capable of discovering, representing, cooperating, and coming together.

Notes to Chapter 10

1. This chapter is based on my paper "Reconstrucción y democracia: la doble problemática del sistema político chileno," presented at the seminar entitled "Chile hacia el año 2000: desafíos y opciones," sponsored by the Santiago Program on the Future of Latin America of the UN Institute for Education and Research in Santiago, Oct. 1987.

2. It should be recalled that a political system is formed by the state, the regime (the institutional mediation between the state and society), the actors, and political culture. The interaction among these elements over time is generically termed *the political process*, and the contradictions within each element or among them are termed *political crises*. Both processes and crises express phenomena that occur in other spheres of society but are reproduced in the political system, which is the dimension that concerns us here.

3. See Chapter 5.

4. See Chapter 5.

5. I have dealt with this problem in more detail in *Transición hacia la democracia e influencia externa: dilemas y perspectivas*, Kellogg Institute Working Paper no. 57 (Notre Dame, Ind.: Kellogg Institute of International Studies, University of Notre Dame, 1985).

6. See note 2 of this chapter.

7. See note 6.

8. Examples of this interpenetration between society and state at the institutional level, of mutual cooperation and control, are long-standing institutions like the National Council for Research (Consejo Nacional para la Investigación) and the National Council for Television (Consejo Nacional para la Televisión) as well as various national commissions for proposing solutions to long-range problems. The various advisory bodies in state spheres providing oversight by civil society and representing various social actors are forms of social penetration and control in the state, but they do not reduce the state's significance as a historical agent of development.

9. Several articles of the constitution prevent leaders from participating in political parties.

10. See the last chapter of my book *Reconstruir la política: transición y consolidación democrática en Chile* (Santiago: Editorial Andante, 1987).

From the Military Regime to the Transition

Let us recall that the Chilean military regime that took power following the coup d'état on 11 September 1973 went from a purely repressive or reactive phase (from 1973 to 1976–77) to a kind of transforming or institutionalizing phase (from 1976–77 to 1981–82). During the latter phase, the regime sought to restructure national capitalism by reinserting it in the world economy and by building a new kind of relationship between the state and civil society, thus dislocating the traditional relationship between politics and society. This phase culminated with the political institutionalization achieved by the regime. The process crystallized in the Constitution of 1980, which ordained that the regime would go from a military regime to an authoritarian regime starting in 1989, by means of a 1988 plebiscite in which the Armed Forces would propose one candidate for approval or rejection by the citizenry.[2] In 1983, however, the crisis in the transforming project forced the regime to try to ensure the conditions for fulfilling the constitutional timetable, thus raising as a central issue the problem of regime survival while managing the crisis by means that included limited liberalizations, maintaining the repressive scheme, partially restructuring the economic crisis, and promulgating laws to implement the plan set forth in the Constitution of 1980. The goals were to create by 1988 the most favorable circumstances for the regime's passage from a military to an authoritarian regime and to make this step coincide with Pinochet's maintaining his political leadership.

The political opposition to the Pinochet regime spent these years in a process of apprenticeship, which involved going from levels of resistance and dissidence under the protection of the Catholic Church as an alternative space or actor to the level of being a subject-actor of opposition.[3] This learning process consisted of overcoming obstacles arising as much from the opposition's traits as an inherited opposition as from the nature of the structural and institutional transformations imposed by the military regime. These obstacles included three major difficulties: lack of any consensual strategy for ending the military regime that could have taken into account the particular characteristics of this kind of transition; fragmentation of the political organizations that sought resolution in terms of ideological and functional issues rather than by specific means of struggle for ending the regime; and disarticulation between the political sphere and the social sphere. This process of apprenticeship became particularly significant following the regime crisis in 1982, especially with the cycle of popular mobilizations that began in 1983. These mobilizations partially restructured the relationship between politics and society, forced modifications within the regime, and allowed the opposition to burst into the public arena, but they were incapable nevertheless of triggering a process of transition. Little by little, the opposition began to recognize that going from a military regime to a democratic regime (which I have called a political transition in the strict sense) requires complex interrelations among the disintegration of the regime, popular mobilizations channeled into a formula or institutional proposal for transition, negotiations between those in power and the opposition, space for institutional checks on both sides, and mediation by actors or institutions that can facilitate negotiations and institutional checks. This entire learning process took time, which allowed the regime to impose its own time limits and its plebiscite mechanism.

In February 1988, this learning process culminated when the entire opposition agreed to confront the military regime in the plebiscite by voting "no" and by creating the Party Agreement to Vote "No" (Concertación por el NO). All the Chilean parties joined this accord except for the Communist party. Some months later, the Communist party also called for voting "no" in the plebiscite, although it did not join the coalition. This situation left the insurrectionary factions completely isolated but channeled the entire struggle politically and institutionally against the dictatorship. An additional means was devised for transforming the self-perpetuating mechanism designed by the regime into an opportunity for transition: various opposition parties registered legally, some by maintaining their identity (the Christian Democrats, the Radical party, the Humanist party, Social Democracy, and regime parties) and others by creating an "instrumental" party—the Party for Democracy (Partido por la Democracia) for purposes of challenging the plebiscite and the transition (Socialist parties, rightist parties, independent parties, and others). By registering, the opposition parties sought to assure control of the electoral system, given that only legal parties could participate in such control. Meanwhile, the opposition made a series of demands to assure government recognition of the victory of the "No" Campaign: lifting of the various states of emergency, registration of a certain minimum number of voters, promulgation of a law that would permit television campaigning by those opposing Pinochet, an end to exile, the presence of international observers, and control of an opposition system of vote counting. All these demands were gradually met.

Thus the plebiscite called by the regime for changing from a military regime into an authoritarian regime in 1988 and for keeping Pinochet in power was transformed into the space for institutional confrontation between the regime and the opposition, a space with alternatives that could set off a process of transition. For the first time, space existed around the question of succession or maintenance of the regime. Moreover, the entire opposition seemed unified for the first time around a single tactic for confronting the regime: voting "no" in the plebiscite. For the first time also, it was possible to disassociate Pinochet's dual legitimacy in the eyes of his supporters by separating hierarchical-military legitimacy from the political-constitutional variety.

My hypothesis throughout this book has been that all likely scenarios were leading to a transition. These scenarios would obviously differ as to the quality of the transition and the time required, which in turn would affect the processes of consolidation. If Pinochet had not been the candidate proposed by the armed forces (which seemed improbable), this scenario would still have required a candidate in order to accomplish the transition. If Pinochet had won without the opposition questioning the legality of his victory, which seemed highly unlikely, we would have witnessed a Brazilian-style transition, cumbersome and frustrating but inevitable because the institutional procedures called for in the Constitution of 1980 had created functional problems of legitimacy that would have forced gradual concessions. If Pinochet had tried to ignore the victory of the "No" vote and had attempted another coup d'état, he would have dragged the armed forces into an adventure that would have violated their own institutional procedures and thus risked internal division (not a viable scheme in that Pinochet could not count on the same national and international conditions that were prevailing in 1973). In such a case, the country would soon have had to face the problem of the new regime's legitimacy, which would have forced negotiations with the opposition forces that had won in the plebiscite. Obviously, the scenario most favorable for unleashing a process of transition was recognition of the victory of the "No" vote by the regime, which also seemed highly likely, albeit problematic.

In actuality, the triumph of the "No" vote in the plebiscite on 5 October by a solid electoral margin and its recognition by the regime began a process of transition that will lead to a fundamentally democratic regime.[4]

Two scenarios seem likely following the plebiscite. The less favorable one is that Pinochet and the armed forces, as they have stated before and after the plebiscite, will follow strictly the constitutional framework established in 1980, will reject any kind of negotiation or implicit or explicit accord with the opposition to modify the constitution, and will impose it. In this case, the opposition would be forced to present a united front in the presidential and parliamentary elections scheduled for late 1989, which would undoubtedly involve increasing enormously the electoral margin achieved by the opposition in the plebiscite. Such an outcome would give the opposition presidential and parliamentary power to undertake the difficult task of changing the institutional framework, supported in these circumstances by a Right left unprotected by the military regime and reduced to a tiny minority. But only an overwhelming triumph by a united opposition could create sufficient pressure to force the supporters of the military regime, from civilian sectors to the armed forces,[5] to accept the institutional and constitutional transformations called for by the opposition.

The second scenario, which is more favorable to a transition, is the one the opposition has been proposing before and after the plebiscite. Modification of the constitutional mechanisms could occur for the foregoing reasons or due to other causes: because of internal dissension in the armed forces, because of erosion in their civil support, because of pressure from the opposition and other actors, or for all these reasons combined. This scenario consists of changing the most flagrantly authoritarian portions of the Constitution of 1980 in order to permit presidential and parliamentary elections within a basically democratic framework. Several aspects must be changed: the requirement of a partly appointed Senate, a rigid mechanism for constitutional reform that gives the constitution a stamp of immutability, and a system of exclusions and political-ideological proscriptions. These institutional changes can be accomplished by accords or explicit negotiations among the government, the armed forces, and the opposition (which seems unlikely) or by an implicit accord in which the armed forces effect the changes proposed by the opposition without any kind of negotiation (which seems more probable). In any case, authoritarian regression in the direction of a military coup or something similar seems unlikely after the results of the plebiscite, above and beyond the intentions of the actors eventually involved, because it seems improbable that conditions would exist for minimal legitimacy within the armed forces and in Chilean society itself.

Thus my hypothesis is that a transition will occur within the next few years. But it will be an incomplete transition that will leave pending not only the problems of democratic consolidation concerning aspects of democratizing Chilean society but also the problems of a genuine transition, those persisting in the forms of authoritarian enclaves.

Overcoming Authoritarian Enclaves

Even after a basically democratic regime is established, remnants of the military regime will add to the normal tasks of democratic consolidation and will undoubtedly complicate its resolution. Three major authoritarian enclaves will have to be overcome. The first will be the constitutional framework imposed in 1980, which maintains the prerogatives and guardian role of the armed forces in Chilean politics, the relative weakness of parliamentary functions, the absence of democratic mechanisms at local and state levels, and possible political exclusions that will not have been resolved during the transition. The second enclave consists of actors unwilling to abide by the rules of the democratic game. On one side are the armed forces that have acquired, in addition to their political prerogatives, elevated group and institutional privileges that they will relinquish only reluctantly; above all, they will maintain their repressive organizations associated with crimes and violations of human rights. On the other side is the problematic lack of a functionally organized democratic Right.[6] Finally, an entrepreneurial sector exists that has neither participated in democratization nor broken its ties with the military regime. The third authoritarian enclave left unresolved in the transition will revolve around the issue of justice or impunity for violations of human rights. This issue will create tension between the ethical demands expressed by the victims organized in social movements and the political logic of survival of precarious democratic institutions threatened by military resistance to such demands.

Each of these authoritarian enclaves has its own formula for resolution, but the interrelationship among them will also require complex negotiations. Thus if the coalition that triumphs in the transition is maintained, it is possible that democratic legitimacy will be strong enough to require the armed forces to cede their political prerogatives in order to keep some of their group and institutional privileges and not be subjected to justice for violations of human rights. This same democratic legitimacy can require the Right and the entrepreneurial sector to play by the rules of the game and to recycle themselves as democrats, a course reinforced by historical experience and by certain tendencies that have emerged since the plebiscite. The handling of the repressive apparatuses set up under the military regime poses an internal problem within the armed forces that can only be resolved by dismantling them, which in turn increases the negotiating strength of the armed forces in other areas. The subject of violation of human rights and punishment or impunity has a great deal of emotional and symbolic power that can unleash destabilizing forces. Yet it does not seem possible to maintain democratic legitimacy or social confidence in democratic institutions without a full accounting of what happened, a process that acts as a means of catharsis or exorcism and at least symbolic reparation and justice.

All these problems in overcoming authoritarian enclaves point out the necessity of maintaining the coalition that triumphed at the time of the plebiscite and even broadening it regarding specific terms for ending the military regime and establishing a democratic government. This process nevertheless creates tension concerning the kind of coalition or alliance that should be established in order to assure democratic consolidation, and that process of self-definition in programmatic terms can introduce divisions into the transition coalition.

The other problem linking transition and consolidation is one that concerns the nature of the first democratic government. This government will have to face the sequential tasks of completing the transition, overcoming authoritarian enclaves, and consolidating the democratic regime. To the extent that we associate the concept of consolidation, in countries like Chile, with the process of reintroducing democratization throughout the society left by the military regime, it is impossible to imagine a Center-Right government. Such a government would lead in the medium term to a radicalization of the political Center (the Christian Democrats) or to its fragmentation, which could lead to a cycle resembling the 1960s and early 1970s that would culminate in another military coup. An initial democratic government directed only by the political Center would have the same effects, all of which leads to the conclusion that one precondition for carrying out a successful transition is the configuration of a coalition between the Center and the Left. This necessity in turn raises again the subject of relations between the Christian Democratic party and the Communist party and between Socialists and Communists; the presence of a renewed and solidly unified Socialist force that has been renewed and unified can play a key role in constituting this coalition. The new coalition should also maintain basic continuity with the coalition that won in the plebiscite.[7]

Toward the Consolidation of Democracy

There is no single unique factor associated with democratic stability once the transition has begun and the authoritarian enclaves have been overcome. Conversely, there are no social actors that are "essentially democratic." What can be called the "democratic subject" tends to take contradictory shape in diverse actors, who are constantly changing positions in relation to this subject.[8] If a single factor can be associated with founding and consolidating a democracy, it is the desire for democracy on the part of the various significant actors. The concept of desirability transforms the factors or structural conditions into categories of historical action. All of which leads me to postulate that there is a radical historicity of the factors of democratic consolidation, that is to say, what is worthwhile for one society or particular moment cannot necessarily be extended to others. When it is a matter of democratic restoration, as in the Chilean case, and not of democratic foundation, this historicity of the factors of consolidation points to the characteristics that made democracy possible in the past, to the causes of its crisis or collapse, to the consolidated heritage of the dictatorial regime, and therefore to a projection of all these factors toward the future.

Applying this scheme to the Chilean case, let us recall the conclusions that have been drawn throughout this book. First, the democratic regime in Chile was accompanied by a process of progressive social democratization, by a complete spectrum of political parties, by a state with a strong capacity for intervention and leadership and a system of articulation between state and civil society that favored the party system's interlocking with social organizations. In this arrangement, the political party system was strong but civil society was relatively weak and dependent on the party system. Second, the crisis in Chilean democracy was associated with the fact that the tensions between the development model and the growing process of social democratization found no actors capable of establishing a consensus for confronting them, the result being that centrifugal forces led to growing polarization and political deinstitutionalization. This outcome allowed the sectors that perceived themselves as threatened by the process of social democratization, now radicalized by the ideological climate of the era, to find an actor that possessed sufficient strength and had become independent of the political system—the armed forces. This actor could not only end the political system in power but initiate an authoritarian process of restructuring national capitalism and the form of articulation between state and society. The ensuing military regime dislocated the relation between politics and society, generated an unequal and marginalizing modernization, and profoundly fragmented Chilean society. The third conclusion has already been noted: transition to democracy will, in all probability, be incomplete and will leave authoritarian enclaves that will have to be overcome during the processes of consolidation.

Let me now recapitulate the factors or perspectives of democratic consolidation that seem relevant to the Chilean case. The first requirement concerns certain characteristics of the political system: the state's reassumption of a directive role and its capacity for action as an agent of development; the inclusiveness of the political system as a means of recreating a full political spectrum; and the constant erosion of the military's veto power, which implies increased civil knowledge about military topics and a break with the model of cloistering the armed forces that involves greater penetration by society into the armed forces. The second point is the need to strengthen civil society, which means augmenting the capacity for action of social movements, which have been too dependent on the political party system in the past. In third place is the need to resume the process of social democratization within the framework of the incomplete and inequitable modernization left by the military regime. This goal means, above all, accentuating not only redistributive aspects and some degree of equal opportunity but also those aspects of democratization associated with effective participation in decision-making at local and state levels and in the workplace. Fourth, all of these points presuppose political actors who will combine the desire for democracy with the capacity for social change by constituting a sociopolitical majority that will adopt a long-term historical perspective and avoid conservative and authoritarian retrogressions. Specifically, this goal presupposes a far-reaching historic compromise between the political forces of the Center and the Left that together represent the middle and popular classes, whose separation and antagonism lie at the root of the democratic collapse.

As can be appreciated, this set of elements is based on the perception that the determining factor in consolidating a democracy is the will of political actors not to subordinate the problem of the regime to their own historical projects. In the end, the desire for democracy is the precondition for making a stable democracy possible.

Notes

1. This postscript was written in October 1988, two weeks after the plebiscite, and is based on a revised version of my essay "La democracia en Chile: de la transición a la consolidación posible," to be published in *Pensamiento Iberoamericano*.

2. See Chapter 7, note 16.

3. On the concepts of subject and actor, see my book *Dictaduras y democratización* (Santiago: FLACSO, 1983), chap. 3.

4. The result of the plebiscite, as announced by the Minister of the Interior, was 43.04 percent voting "yes" (in favor of Pinochet) and 54.68 percent voting "no" (in favor of the opposition), with a small percentage of blank and void votes. Abstentions comprised some 3 percent, with the percentage of voters registered for the plebiscite reaching about 92 percent of the possible total. Subsequent results published by the Electoral Service (Servicio Electoral) have widened the margin of the "No" vote, which tallies with the results reached by the "No" Command (Comando del No), which maintained an independent computerized system. The final legal results should be published by the Electoral Tribunal (Tribunal Calificador de Elecciones), which will review the entire recount, but it will not involve significant variations in the already recognized results.

5. One political effect of the plebiscite and the defeat of Pinochet and the regime hard core is the possible rise, for the first time, of genuine "soft-line" sectors. Like those found in other transitions, these soft-liners would seek accommodation and space in the future democratic regime by disengaging from the military government and building bridges to the opposition. This process seems to be occurring with the National Renovation party, which during the plebiscite campaign suffered a schism with the core known as the Independent Democratic Union (Unión Democrática Independiente, or UDI), which supported Pinochet unconditionally.

6. On the Right, two political parties identified with Pinochet continue to subsist, the fascistic National Advance (Avanzada Nacional) and the Independent Democratic Union, made up of many young regime bureaucrats who split off from the National Renovation party during the plebiscite campaign. The National Renovation party, which attempted to reunite the Right as a successor to the military regime, favored voting "yes" in the plebiscite, although without identifying itself with Pinochet, which allowed the National party to try to assume representation of the entire Right after the plebiscite (during the plebiscite, this party was split between supporters of yes and no votes). Since the plebiscite, the subject has reemerged of unifying the Right for purposes of the presidential and parliamentary elections in 1989, but deep internal splits remain.

7. The parties of the Party Agreement to Vote "No" have announced their decision to propose a single candidate in the presidential election of 1989, which will undoubtedly require a parliamentary accord. At the same time, the parties have transformed themselves into the Party Agreement for Democracy (Concertación de Partidos para la Democracia) and have announced that they will maintain the coalition until democratic institutions are fully established, including the constitutional changes already mentioned. But within this coalition is found the tendency of one Center sector, dominated by the Christian Democrats, to try to draw up a future Center government. It also remains to be determined how the Party Agreement for Democracy will deal with the Communist party. The latter seems to have abandoned its most insurrectionary ideas and is seeking a space in the political sphere in order to avoid being isolated. In the Socialist camp, divisions remain among the two large factions, the Núñez and Almeyda branches of the Socialist party, and other smaller groups. Unification of these factions appears crucial for establishing ties between the political Center and the Communist party. Finally, there is the unknown quantity called the Party for Democracy (Partido por la Democracia), whose strictly instrumental character during the plebiscite is yielding to a future projection that would include the various Socialist factions with great electoral potential among the nonideological centrist and leftist sectors of young and independent voters.

8. See note 3 above.

Index